Culture and Customs of Cameroon

Cameroon

Culture and Customs
of Cameroon

∽∘∾

JOHN MUKUM MBAKU

Culture and Customs of Africa
Toyin Falola, Series Editor

GREENWOOD PRESS
Westport, Connecticut • London

Library of Congress Cataloging-in-Publication Data

Mbaku, John Mukum, 1950–
    Culture and customs of Cameroon / John Mukum Mbaku.
        p. cm. — (Culture and customs of Africa, ISSN 1530–8367)
    Includes bibliographical references and index.
    ISBN 0–313–33231–2
    1. Cameroon—Social life and customs. I. Title. II. Series.
DT569.5.M37 2005
306'.096711—dc22   2005003527

British Library Cataloguing in Publication Data is available.

Library of Congress Catalog Card Number: 2005003527
ISBN: 0–313–33231–2
ISSN: 1530–8367

First published in 2005

Greenwood Press, 88 Post Road West, Westport, CT 06881
An imprint of Greenwood Publishing Group, Inc.
www.greenwood.com

Printed in the United States of America

The paper used in this book complies with the
Permanent Paper Standard issued by the National
Information Standards Organization (Z39.48–1984).

10 9 8 7 6 5 4 3 2 1

To the memory of Cameroon's greatest and most beloved nationalist:
Ruben Um Nyobé

Contents

A photo essay follows page 119.

Series Foreword

AFRICA is a vast continent, the second largest, after Asia. It is four times the size of the United States, excluding Alaska. It is the cradle of human civilization. A diverse continent, Africa has more than 50 countries with a population of over 700 million people who speak over 1,000 languages. Ecological and cultural differences vary from one region to another. As an old continent, Africa is one of the richest in culture and customs, and its contributions to world civilization are impressive indeed.

Africans regard culture as essential to their lives and future development. Culture embodies their philosophy, worldview, behavior patterns, arts, and institutions. The books in this series intend to capture the comprehensiveness of African culture and customs, dwelling on such important aspects as religion, worldview, literature, media, art, housing, architecture, cuisine, traditional dress, gender, marriage, family, lifestyles, social customs, music, and dance.

The uses and definitions of "culture" vary, reflecting its prestigious association with civilization and social status, its restriction to attitude and behavior in globalization, and the debates surrounding issues of tradition, modernity, and postmodernity. The participating authors have chosen a comprehensive meaning of culture while not ignoring the alternative uses of the term.

Each volume in the series focuses on a single country, and the format is uniform. The first chapter presents a historical overview, in addition to information on geography, economy, and politics. Each volume then proceeds to examine the various aspects of culture and customs. The series highlights the mechanisms for the transmission of tradition and culture across generations:

the significance of orality, traditions, kinship rites, and family property distribution; the rise of print culture; and the impact of educational institutions. The series also explores the intersection between local, regional, national, and global bases for identity and social relations. While the volumes are organized nationally, they pay attention to ethnicity and language groups and the links between Africa and the wider world.

The books in the series capture the elements of continuity and change in culture and customs. Custom is not represented as static or as a museum artifact, but as a dynamic phenomenon. Furthermore, the authors recognize the current challenges to traditional wisdom, which include gender relations; the negotiation of local identities in relation to the state; the significance of struggles for power at national and local levels and their impact on cultural traditions and community-based forms of authority; and the tensions between agrarian and industrial/manufacturing/oil-based economic modes of production.

Africa is a continent of great changes, instigated mainly by Africans but also through influences from other continents. The rise of youth culture, the penetration of the global media, and the challenges to generational stability are some of the components of modern changes explored in the series. The ways in which traditional (non-Western and nonimitative) African cultural forms continue to survive and thrive, that is, how they have taken advantage of the market system to enhance their influence and reproductions also receive attention.

Through the books in this series, readers can see their own cultures in a different perspective, understand the habits of Africans, and educate themselves about the customs and cultures of other countries and people. The hope is that the readers will come to respect the cultures of others and see them not as inferior or superior to theirs, but merely as different. Africa has always been important to Europe and the United States, essentially as a source of labor, raw materials, and markets. Blacks are in Europe and the Americas as part of the African diaspora, a migration that took place primarily due to the slave trade. Recent African migrants increasingly swell their number and visibility. It is important to understand the history of the diaspora and the newer migrants, as well as the roots of the culture and customs of the places from where they come. It is equally important to understand others in order to be able to interact successfully in a world that keeps shrinking. The accessible nature of the books in this series will contribute to this understanding and enhance the quality of human interaction in a new millennium.

Toyin Falola
Frances Higginbothom Nalle Centennial Professor in History
The University of Texas at Austin

Preface

CAMEROON is one of the most ethnically and geographically diverse countries in Africa. It is rich in customs and traditions, both indigenous and modern. The main focus of this book is to examine Cameroon's culture and customs, with special emphasis placed on those aspects that have come to define what is the modern Cameroon nation, its peoples, the unique societies that they inhabit and their institutions, and various lifestyles that define the new generation.

Cameroon's greatly diverse culture traces its origins to the country's various ethnic groups and languages, as well as the influence of European colonialism, Christianity, Islam, and other external factors, including globalization. Many indigenous institutions have been affected greatly by contact with various external influences. This book captures the broad diversity of Cameroon culture and gives readers a bird's-eye view of the salient points of the country's cultural practices. Each major aspect of the country's culture and customs presented is then illustrated with examples taken from selected ethnic groups. To make the book more accessible to readers who do not have prior knowledge of Cameroon, I have limited the examples presented to just a few ethnic groups. However, at the same time, I have made it clear that there is great diversity in the country and, hence, one must expect a wide range of both people and ideas. Also, I have opted not to use special characters, which are utilized by various traditional languages, in an effort to make the book more accessible to a broad range of readers. There are specialized books on the various groups in the country and some of them are listed in the bibliography for interested readers.

Acknowledgments

I WAS INVITED BY Professor Toyin Falola, of the University of Texas at Austin and Series Editor of Culture and Customs in Africa, to write this book. I accepted the invitation and I am grateful to Professor Falola and Greenwood Press for the opportunity to learn more about the country of my birth and share that knowledge with many readers. My editor, Wendi Schnaufer, has been very easy to work with and was very helpful in bringing the book to publication. I express my heartfelt thanks to her for her generosity and excellent editorial work.

I would like to thank the various Cameroonians with whom I discussed different aspects of this work. I especially would like to mention Prince Lawrence Mbah, Professor Joseph Takougang, Professor Nantang Jua, Professor Nicodemus Fru Awasom, Professor Charles Manga Fombad, and Professor Tatah Mentan. I learned a lot from discussions with these fellow Cameroonians and hope that they find the final product informative and interesting.

I thank my family (my wife, Theresa, my son, Fotoh Thomas Mukum, and my daughter, Vivianne Elizabeth Api) for their patience, kindness, and willingness to accept my absence from home while I worked on the book.

My biggest debt, of course, is owed to Cameroon. An incredibly diverse country; a land of beautiful, energetic, hardworking, and exciting people; a country with an extraordinary variety of cultures and customs, it is a great joy to learn more about these cultures and customs and share that information with you, the readers. I have observed and participated in some of the events and customs that have been presented in this book. Many others, I have learned about for the first time. I invite readers to visit Cameroon and enjoy its riches.

Acronyms

ALNK   *Armée de libération nationale du Cameroun* (pre-independence liberation organization in the French Cameroons)

AN   *Action nationale* (political party that formed part of the coalition that governed La République du Cameroun shortly after it came into being in 1960)

BCEAO   *Banque centrale des états de l'Afrique de l'ouest* (central bank for the West African Monetary Union and the issuing agent for the franc CFA in West Africa)

BEAC   *Banque des états de l'Afrique centrale* (central bank for the Central African Monetary Union and the issuing agent for the FCFA in Central Africa)

BMS   Baptist Missionary Society (London-based missionary society, which sent the first Christian missionaries to Cameroon)

CC   Constitutional Council

CDC   Cameroon Development Corporation

CFA   (le Franc de la) *Coopération Financière en Afrique Centrale;* and (le Franc de la) *Communauté financière de l'Afrique*

CGT   *Confédération générale de travail* (French labor union, which was quite involved in pre-independence political activities in the French Cameroons)

CNU   Cameroon National Union (Cameroon political party of the single-party era)

CPDM	Cameroon People's Democratic Movement (Cameroon political party, successor to the CNU)
CWU	Cameroons Welfare Union
CYL	Cameroons Youth League
DC	*Démocrates camerounaise* (political party that formed part of the coalition that governed La République du Cameroun shortly after it came into being in 1960)
FCFA	franc CFA (see CFA)
FRC	Federal Republic of Cameroon
GRA	Government residential area
HIV	Human immunodeficiency virus
IFAN	*Institut Français d'Afrique Noire*
IFEX	International Freedom Exchange
IMF	International Monetary Fund
IRGM	Institute for Mining and Geological Research
JBMS	Jamaican Baptist Missionary Society (Christian outreach organization formed by freed Jamaican slaves in 1842 with the intention of sending missionaries to Africa)
KNDP	Kamerun National Democratic Party (English-speaking Cameroon political party of the pre-independence and immediate independence period)
MDR	*Mouvement pour la défense de la république* (Cameroon political party)
PI	*Paysans indépendants* (political party that formed part of the coalition that governed La République du Cameroun shortly after it came into being in 1960)
PRC	People's Republic of China
RACAM	*Rassemblement camerounais* (pre-independence political organization in French Cameroons)
RDA	*Rassemblement démocratique Africain*
SAP	Structural adjustment program
SDF	Social Democratic Front (Cameroon political party, of the post–Cold War multiparty era)
SEC	*Société des études camerounaises*
SOE	State-owned enterprise
UC	*Union Camerounaise* (political party that formed part of the coalition that governed La République du Cameroun shortly after it came into being in 1960)

UDC	*Union démocratique du Cameroun* (Cameroon political party)
UNDP	*Union nationale pour la démocratie et le progrès* (Cameroon political party)
UNESCO	United Nations Educational, Scientific and Cultural Organization
UNICAFRA	*Union camerounaise française* (pre-independence Cameroon political organization)
UPC	*Union des populations du Cameroun* (Cameroon political party)
USCC	*Union des syndicates confédérés de Cameroun* (Cameroon labor union of the pre-independence era)

Chronology

1200s	The Bornu, living west of Lake Chad, fall under the control of the Kanem empire east of the lake.
1386	Attacks from the east forced the Sefuwa dynasty of the Kanem empire to move west of Lake Chad.
1472	Portuguese seafarers arrive at the Bight of Biafra, visit the island of Fernando Po, and sail into the estuary of what is now called the Wouri River in Cameroon. Struck by the presence of large schools of prawns, they name the river Rio dos Camarões (River of Prawns).
1520	Full-scale sugar plantations are established by Portuguese on both São Tomé and Fernando Po.
Early 1600s	Portuguese lose control of the slave trade to the Dutch.
c. 1642	Dutch had captured São Tomé and threatened the Portuguese control of Fernando Po by establishing a permanent trading post at the mouth of the Rio dos Camarões.
1777	Spaniards capture the island of Fernando Po, off the Cameroon coast.

1807	Britain declares its own slave trade illegal and takes steps to abolish the trade in humans along the Gulf of Guinea.
1827	Spain grants Britain permission to occupy Fernando Po (which had been captured by the Spaniards in 1777). Britain establishes a military base there to control the shipment of slaves from the Bights of Biafra and Benin.
1844	Jamaican branch of the English Baptist Missionary Society lands 42 volunteers at Clarence (Santa Isabel on Fernando Po), where the Reverends Clark and Prince had established a small worship center two years earlier.
1845	First permanent English settlement started by Baptist missionaries near Douala on the Cameroon River.
1858	Alfred Saker, who had taken over leadership of the worship center at Clarence on the island of Fernando Po, and who had subsequently been forced by Spanish Jesuits to leave, purchases land from King William of Bimbia and founds a permanent settlement, which he names Victoria, at the foot of Mount Cameroon.
1862	English traveler, Captain R. F. Burton, with the aid of Baptist missionary, Alfred Saker, successfully climbs Mount Cameroon.
1877	Several Duala kings write to Queen Victoria, offering to surrender their territory to her, in an effort to avoid conquest by rival European powers.
1880	Several traditional rulers of the Duala speak with English naval officers about their wish to cede their territories to the British Crown and complain about the fact that they had not received a reply to their earlier request.
1881, March 8	King Bell of the Duala writes Consul Edward Hyde Hewett, British representative in the Gulf of Guinea at the time, seeking British protection.

November	Both King Bell and King Akwa submit petitions to British Prime Minister Gladstone, requesting that England annex their territories.
1882	Letter from the British Foreign Office informs Kings Bell and Akwa that their request for annexation had been referred to the Foreign Secretary, Lord Granville, for further action.
1883, April 23	Kings Bell and Akwa send an alarming letter informing the English of French activities on the Cameroon River and that the commander-in-chief of a French warship was about to take control of Malimba by treaty with the territory's ruler, King Pass-All (Mukoko).
October	The Colonial Office refers the question of the annexation of territories along the Cameroon River District to the British cabinet for a final decision.
November	Consul Edward Hyde Hewett presents the government with his plan for the annexation of the territories along the Cameroon River.
December	The German government promises to take necessary action to protect German trade in Africa. Hamburg traders are informed of the government's intention to sign treaties with indigenous rulers and place their territories under German protection.
1884, February 5	Hamburg traders advise their chamber of commerce about the terms of the treaties with indigenous rulers on the West African coast. Specifically, they recommend that treaties be concluded with Kings Bell and Akwa, as well as with King Pass-All of Malimba, all on the Cameroon River.
February 6	Lord Granville, the Foreign Secretary, writes to Lord Aberdare, Chairman of the National African Company, which controlled huge concessions in neighboring Nigeria, to inform him of the government's secret plan to annex territories in the

1884	Cameroon River District and suggests that his and other English companies trading in the area pay the cost.
April 11	Lord Granville sends a letter to the admiralty requesting that ships be placed at the disposal of Consul Hewett to help him in his work of concluding treaties with traditional rulers and setting up British authority on the West African coast.
April 19	German Chancellor Bismarck informs the English government that the German Consul-General in Tunis, Gustav Nachtigal, was being sent to the West African coast "in order to complete information now in the possession of the Foreign Office at Berlin on the state of German commerce on that coast, that he was to put himself in communication with the authorities in the English possession on the said coast." The English fail to discern from Bismarck's relatively vague letter that he intended for Nachtigal to annex the territories along the Cameroon River.
April 23	Instructions are sent to English representatives on the west coast of Africa requesting that they give Nachtigal as much aid as possible.
April 22	Bismarck assures the French of the friendly character of Nachtigal's mission.
April 24	Bismarck proclaims a German protectorate over South West Africa (now Namibia).
July 12	Letter expressing the wishes of the indigenous peoples of the Cameroon River District is signed by the German consul. Treaty is signed between German traders (the firms of C. Woerman and Jantzen & Thormählen) and indigenous kings on the Cameroon River. King Lock Priso of Hickory, however, refuses to sign the treaty because of his friendship with English traders.
July 14	German occupation of territories on the Cameroon River District becomes official with the rais-

ing of the imperial flag on the right bank of the Cameroon River and the firing of salutes in several towns.

July 15	Gustav Nachtigal, now German Commissioner in West Africa, assures English traders and missionaries along the Cameroon River that their interests will not be harmed under German rule.
July 19	The Baptist Missionary Settlement at Victoria (now Limbe) is proclaimed by Consul Hewett to be a British possession. Consul Hewett then proceeds to Douala only to find out that several territories on the Cameroon River are now a German protectorate.
October 15	Germany announces to the world that it has proclaimed a protectorate over the Cameroons.
1885, March 20	English propose a boundary line between English and German possessions in the Cameroons to run along the right bank of the Rio del Rey (at the time incorrectly thought to be a river) to its source and then directly in a straight line to a point on the Old Calabar or Cross River located at 9° 8' east longitude and marked "Rapids" on an admiralty map.
April and May	Boundary agreement is reached between the English and Germans, with the terminus of the boundary set at a point marked "Rapids" on an admiralty map.
July 3	Julius von Soden becomes the first governor of the German colony of Kamerun and rules until 1891.
December	Governor von Soden dispatches his financial deputy, Puttkamer, and the explorer Krabble, to study Mount Cameroon and establish German authority over the inhabitants of the slopes of the mountain, notably, the Bakweri. During this trip, Puttkamer raises the imperial flag at Buea, which later becomes the capital of the German Cameroons.
1886, September 9	Arrangements are made under the auspices of the German Foreign Office in Berlin for the Basler

	Mission to purchase the properties of English missionaries in Victoria. The sale marks the beginning of the surrender of Victoria by the English to the Germans. The German firms of C. Woermann and Jantzen & Thormählen start plantations on the lower slopes of Mount Cameroon.
1893	Negotiations between Germany and France over boundaries in the hinterland of the Cameroons begin in July.
1894, March 15	The treaty that gave the Cameroons its form and size until 1911 is signed.
1898, November 28	The Gesellschaft Süd-Kamerun, one of two of the most important companies engaged in the exploitation of the Cameroons (the other was the Gesellschaft Nordwest-Kamerun), is organized.
1899, July 31	The Gesellschaft Nordwest-Kamerun is organized.
1911	As compensation for the surrender of existing rights in Morocco, Germany obtains from France significant amounts of territory in the French Congo, increasing the size of Kamerun.
1914, August	World War I begins in Europe. Shortly after that, German Kamerun is attacked by Allied Expeditionary Forces.
September 26	Fall of Douala and the departure of the Germans.
1915, September 21, 24	Condominium is established, following the exchange of letters between M. Delcassé, Sir Francis Bertie, and Sir Edward Grey, to provide joint ad hoc or provisional administration of the captured territories until the enemy is completely vanquished.
1916, March 4	Agreement is reached to end the condominium and delineate the zones of influence of France and Britain as follows: (1) Territories ceded to Germany in 1911 would be returned to France to be administered as part of French Equatorial Africa. (2) The British and French zones were defined in such a way that France received four-fifths of the total remain-

ing area (to be administered under the Department of Colonies in Paris, separately from French Equatorial Africa), and the British obtained two disconnected pieces bordering the colony of Nigeria and called them British Northern Cameroons and British Southern Cameroons.

1919, May 7 — Supreme Allied Council allocates the various German colonies in Africa to their respective conquerors. The Council agrees that other conquered territories would become mandates but that the status of the Cameroons and Togo would be determined through negotiation between the French and the British.

1922, July 20 — Cameroons and Togo are officially declared League of Nations Mandates under British and French administration.

1946 — Both Mandates become UN Trust Territories, with France and Britain continuing to rule their respective areas.

1957, January 28 — The first Cameroon Legislative Assembly is seated in the UN Trust Territory of Cameroons under French administration.

February 22 — New Legislative Assembly passes the Statute of the Cameroon, in which the territory is officially designated as the State of the Cameroon.

April 4 — New Statute goes into effect, providing that, except for jurisdictions to be retained by France, residuary powers would pass to a Cameroon legislative assembly (*Assemblée législative du Cameroun*) and a Cameroon government whose head, the prime minister, would be chosen by the high commissioner, but invested by the legislative assembly. The UN Trust Territory becomes an autonomous state within the French Community.

May — André-Marie Mbida is confirmed by the *Assemblée législative du Cameroun* as prime minister of a new Cameroon government.

July 13	Ruben Um Nyobé, leader of the *Union des populations du Cameroun* (UPC, at the time the largest and most important indigenous political organization in the UN Trust Territory of Cameroons under French administration), sends a letter to Prime Minister André-Marie Mbida and the high commissioner setting out "proposals for a moral and political *détente*," in which he reiterated UPC demands for amnesty, reunification (with the British Cameroons), and independence.
1958, February 19	Ahmadou Ahidjo is appointed prime minister by the high commissioner and subsequently confirmed by the *Assemblée législative du Cameroun*.
1960, January 1	The UN Trust Territory of Cameroons under French administration gains independence and takes the name *République du Cameroun* (Republic of Cameroon).
April	First election for the new country's National Assembly (*Assemblée nationale*) is won by Ahmadou Ahidjo's party, the *Union Camerounaise* (UC).
May	National Assembly elects Ahidjo to be the country's first president.
1961, February 11	UN Trust Territory of Southern Cameroons under British administration votes in a UN-supervised plebiscite to gain independence by uniting with the independent *République du Cameroun* to form a federation (Federal Republic of Cameroon).
October 1	Birth of the Federal Republic of Cameroon.
1966, June	President Ahmadou Ahidjo calls all the three political parties in the federated state of West Cameroon and obtains their permission to dissolve them, as well as his *Union Camerounaise* (UC) party, and form a new party called the Cameroon National Union (CNU); also known as the *Union nationale Camerounaise* (UNC).

September	All political parties in the Federal Republic of Cameroon unite to form the UNC, leaving only the UPC as the effective opposition. The UPC, however, was suppressed in 1971 and only reemerged as a legal political organization in the early 1990s, when multiparty politics returned to the country.
1972, May 20	Referendum leading to the abolition of the Cameroon Federation and the subsequent establishment of a unitary state.
June 2	Cameroon federation (Federal Republic of Cameroon; *République fédérale du Cameroun*) is terminated, and a unitary state (the United Republic of Cameroon; *République unie du Cameroun*) is established. The position of vice president is abolished.
1975, April	Ahidjo is reelected president of the United Republic of Cameroon (URC); the constitution is revised, and the post of prime minister is created.
June	Paul Biya (a southern Christian) is appointed prime minister.
1980, April	Ahidjo is unanimously reelected president of the URC for a fifth five-year term of office.
1982, November 4	Ahdijo announces his resignation as president and nominates Biya as his successor.
November 6	Biya constitutionally succeeds Ahidjo as president of Cameroon.
1983, August	Biya announces that he had uncovered a plot to overthrow the government and immediately dismisses the prime minister and the minister of armed forces, both of whom are northern Muslims. Ahidjo resigns as the president of the ruling UNC.
September	Biya is elected president of the UNC.
1984, January	Biya is reelected president of the URC. Subsequently, the post of prime minister is abolished

	and the country's name changed to the Republic of Cameroon (*République du Cameroun*).
February	Ahidjo and two of his close military advisers are tried (Ahidjo *in absentia*) for their alleged complicity in the August 1983 plot to overthrow the government. They are sentenced to death; the sentences, however, are committed to life imprisonment.
April 6	Rebel elements within the presidential guard, led by Col. Saleh Ibrahim (a northerner), attempt unsuccessfully to overthrow the government of Paul Biya.
1985, March	UNC is renamed the *Rassemblement démocratique du peuple Camerounais* (RDPC)—also called the Cameroon People's Democratic Movement (CPDM).
1987, July	The National Assembly approves a new electoral code, which provides for multiple candidacy in public elections. All candidates, however, have to be approved by the CPDM.
1988, April	Biya is reelected unopposed to the presidency of the Republic of Cameroon.
1990, February	Eleven people, including the former president of the Cameroon Bar Association, Yondo Black, are arrested in connection with their alleged involvement in the formation and operation of an illegal opposition political party, the Social Democratic Front (SDF).
April	Black is sentenced to three years' imprisonment on charges of "subversion."
May 20	Demonstration organized by the SDF is violently suppressed by government security forces. Six people are killed in the North West provincial city of Bamenda for supporting the launching of the SDF.
December	The National Assembly adopts legislation officially declaring Cameroon a multiparty state.

1991	About 300 people are killed throughout Cameroon in pro-democracy demonstrations, large-scale strikes, and other actions to force institutional reforms.
1992, March	Legislative elections are conducted and contested by 32 political parties. The Social Democratic Front, the country's most important opposition party, boycotts the elections. The CPDM wins 88 of the National Assembly's 180 seats, while the *Union nationale pour la démocratie et le progrès* (UNDP) obtains 68, the UPC 18, and the *Mouvement pour la défense de la république* (MDR) 6 seats. The CPDM subsequently forms an alliance with the MDR to secure the absolute majority needed to form a government.
April	Biya forms a new 25-member cabinet; Simon Achidi Achu, an English-speaker from the North West Province, is appointed prime minister.
October	Presidential election is conducted: Fru Ndi (SDF)—35.9 percent; Paul Biya (CPDM)—39.9 percent. The SDF and several opposition parties, as well as various international observers (including the National Democratic Institute in Washington, DC), accuse Paul Biya and the CPDM of electoral fraud and other irregularities, which had negatively affected the opposition.
1993, April	Gathering in the South West provincial town of Buea, organized by the Cameroon Anglophone Movement (CAM), demands a return to federalism as a way to minimize the further marginalization of the former West Cameroon.
1994, February	Security forces kill 50 members of the Arab Choa ethnic group at the village of Karena in the northern part of Cameroon.
March	More than 1,200 Cameroon citizens from the northern part of the country take refuge in Chad to escape being caught in the continuing clashes

between government security forces and bandits in the area.

September

Informal alliance of 16 opposition movements is formed and takes the name *Front des allies pour le changement* (FAC). The FAC goes on to denounce alleged human rights abuses by the government, as well as the indefinite postponement of municipal elections. The UNDP and the UDC do not, however, join the alliance, claiming that it was dominated by the SDF.

1995, July

Members of a new Anglophone political organization, the Southern Cameroons National Council (SCNC), which was demanding that the English-speaking provinces be granted independence, stage a demonstration in Bamenda. They clash with government security forces.

August

Representatives of the SCNC and the CAM officially present their demands for the establishment of an independent, English-speaking Republic of Southern Cameroons to the United Nations in New York City and urge the international community to assist in resolving the issue and averting prolonged civil strife.

October

Special congress of the CPDM reelects Biya as leader of the party for another five years.

November

Cameroon is formally admitted to the Commonwealth (a political and economic association of former British colonies).

1996, January

Municipal elections are conducted—the CPDM wins the majority seats in 56 percent of local councils and the SDF in 27 percent, while the UNDP receives popular support in the north of the country. New constitution is adopted.

March

SDF and the UNDP launch a campaign of civil disobedience to protest the government's appointment by decree of representatives to replace the elected mayors in towns, of which the opposition had gained control through the elections of January.

April	Government imposes a total ban on all media reports of the SDF/UNDP campaign of civil disobedience.
September	Simon Achidi Achu is replaced as prime minister by Peter Mafany Musonge, the general manager of the Cameroon Development Corporation.
1997, January	Government announces the postponement of legislative elections, which had been scheduled for March.
April	Government sets May 17 as the date for the municipal elections.
May 17	Parliamentary elections are carried out.
June	Supreme Court announces the results of the parliamentary elections, dismissing opposition claims that the elections had been characterized by widespread malpractice and fraud. Officially, the CPDM captured 109 seats; SDF 43; UNDP 13; UDC 5; and the *Mouvement pour la jeunesse du Cameroun,* the UPC, and the MDR obtained one seat each.
August	More polls conducted in seven constituencies where the results had been annulled as a result of alleged irregularities. The CPDM won all the seats, effectively increasing its total seats won to 116.
September	Government sets October 12 as the date for the presidential election. Shortly after the announcement, the three main opposition parties, the SDF, the UNDP and the UDC, announced a boycott of all elections to protest the government's failure to create an independent electoral commission. Later, the *Union du peuple africain* (UPA) joined the boycott. In mid-September, Biya is elected the CPDM's presidential candidate.

October	Presidential election is conducted and Biya wins reelection by capturing 92.6 percent of the votes cast.
November 3	Biya takes the oath of office to serve a seven-year term as president, as mandated by the revised constitution of January 1996.
December	Musonge is reappointed by Biya as prime minister.
1998, July	Ten of the 43 SDF deputies resign from the party to protest alleged tribalism and authoritarianism of its leadership.
September	Allegations emerge that about 60 English-speaking Cameroonians, who were allegedly demanding the independence of the Southern Cameroons, were being detained and tortured in Yaoundé.
October	SDF expels its first national vice president, Soulaimane Mahamad, following his criticism of party chairman Ni John Fru Ndi's alleged authoritarianism.
1999, January	Fru Ndi of the SDF makes known his desire to initiate direct dialogue with President Biya. The opposition condemns the government for the alleged marginalization of the English-speaking minority in the country.
April	Fru Ndi is found guilty of defamation, fined, and given a three-year suspended sentence. He is reelected chairman of the SDF by an overwhelming majority of delegates. The party, however, declines to engage in dialogue with the government until the latter creates a independent electoral commission.
June	Trial of several Cameroonians accused of campaigning for the secession of the English-speaking provinces begins in Yaoundé.
October	Three of the English-speaking defendants are sentenced to life imprisonment, others receive lengthy sentences, and 29 are acquitted. Amnesty International criticizes the verdicts, alluding to the

alleged bias of the military court, reported torture of detainees, and other irregularities.

September   Mounchipou Seydou is dismissed from his post as minister of posts and telecommunications and is subsequently arrested on charges of embezzlement of public funds.

November   UN Human Rights Committee criticizes Cameroon for its alleged failure to protect and respect fundamental human rights.

Late 2000   Construction of the Chad/Cameroon Development Project begins. A 1,070-kilometer oil pipeline is being built from southern Chad to the Cameroonian coast to export Chad's crude oil.

2002, February   International Court of Justice at The Hague begins hearings at which Cameroon and Nigeria presented their rival claims to the oil-rich Bakassi Peninsula.

June 30   Parliamentary and municipal elections are conducted. Following a by-election on September 15, the CPDM wins 149 (out of 180) seats in the National Assembly to remain the ruling party.

September   Cameroon and Nigeria agree to respect the judgment of the International Court of Justice on the Bakassi Peninsula.

October 10   International Court of Justice (ICJ) rules in favor of Cameroon in the country's long-running dispute with neighboring Nigeria over the oil-rich Bakassi Peninsula.

November   Cameroon president Biya, and Nigerian president, Olusegun Obasanjo, meet in Paris with UN Secretary-General Kofi Annan and agree to establish a UN-led commission (the Cameroon-Nigeria Mixed Commission) to defuse tension over the ICJ's ruling.

2003, August 4   International Monetary Fund issues a press release welcoming Cameroon's effort to deal with poverty in the country as exemplified in its Poverty Reduction Strategy Paper.

December 17

International Monetary Fund approves various financial disbursements to Cameroon totaling U.S. $27.4 million.

2004, April

A federal high court judge in Nigeria, Justice Stephen Ada, of the Abuja Judicial Division, declines jurisdiction over a suit brought by residents of the Bakassi Peninsula and Southern Cameroons (plaintiffs), seeking to prevent the federal government of Nigeria, President Obasanjo, and the attorney-general of Nigeria (respondents) from handing over the peninsula to Cameroon according to a judgment delivered by the International Court of Justice in 2002.

April

Cameroon-Nigeria Mixed Commission, meeting in Yaoundé from April 7 to April 9, sets the final date for the withdrawal and transfer of authority on the Bakassi Peninsula as June 15–July 15, 2004.

1

Introduction

THE REPUBLIC OF CAMEROON lies at an important geographic and demographic crossroad. While it divides the Niger and Congo river basins, it shares the physical characteristics of both, with the cultures of both regions meeting and mingling freely in the country.[1]

Cameroon has been called "Africa in miniature." It is characterized by exceptional social and ethnic diversity. The country has more than 250 identifiable ethnic groups. Its political experiences are equally varied, having been ruled directly by Germany, Great Britain, and France and indirectly by the League of Nations and the United Nations. In addition, there have been significant migrations of people from neighboring countries into Cameroon. This picture is further complicated by large internal migrations, many of which have been occasioned by population pressures and the search for opportunities for economic advancement.

Cameroon is located on the west coast of Africa, with Nigeria to the west, Chad and the Central African Republic to the east, and Congo (Brazzaville), Gabon, and Equatorial Guinea to the south. The country is located slightly north of the equator and has an area of 183,567 square miles or 475,440 square kilometers. In 2002, Cameroon had a population of 16,184,748 with an average annual growth rate of 2.36 percent. The birth rate is 35.66 births per 1,000 population.

Cameroon is made up of over 250 ethnic groups, which form five major regional-cultural groupings: (1) western highlanders (sometimes called grass-fielders), who include the Bamiléké, Bamoun, and several smaller groups in the northwest (estimated to represent about 38 percent of the population);

(2) coastal tropical forest peoples, who include the Bassa, Duala, and many smaller groups in the southwest (12 percent); (3) southern tropical forest peoples, who include the Beti, Bulu, Fang, and Pygmies (officially called Bakas) (18 percent); (4) predominantly Islamic peoples of the northern semi-arid regions (the Sahel) and central highlands, who include the Fulani, also known as Peuhl in French (14 percent); and (5) the Kirdi, non-Islamic or recently Islamic peoples of the northern desert and central highlands (18 percent).

In July 1884, Germany established a colony called Kamerun on the Cameroon (Wouri) River but lost it to Allied Expeditionary Forces after World War I. The former German colony became a League of Nations mandate under French and British administrations and after World War II was converted to a UN Trust Territory, with France and Britain allowed to retain control of their respective territories. On January 1, 1960, French Cameroon was granted independence and took the name *République du Cameroun.* In UN-supervised plebiscites conducted in February 1961, British Southern Cameroons voted to gain independence by joining the *République du Cameroun,* and British Northern Cameroons opted for unification with the Federation of Nigeria. The union between British Southern Cameroons and the *République du Cameroun* took place on October 1, 1961, and produced a two-state federation with Ahmadou Ahidjo as its first president.

On May 20, 1972, the federation was abrogated in favor of a unitary political system. In November 1982, Ahidjo resigned the office of president and handed the apparatus of government to his prime minister, Paul Biya, as mandated by the constitution.

In the late 1980s, many Cameroonians continued to criticize the government for its unwillingness to reintroduce multiparty politics in the country. Persistence by pro-democracy groups, worsening domestic economic conditions, and pressure from the international community eventually forced Biya to legalize competitive politics on December 19, 1990.[2]

Biya was elected to a seven-year term in presidential elections held in October 2004, winning more than 70 percent of the vote. The next presidential election will be held in October 2011. In December 2004, President Biya appointed Ephraim Inoni to replace Peter Mafany Musonge as prime minister and head of government.

THE LAND

Mount Cameroon is the highest point in West Africa with an elevation of 4,095 meters (13,436 feet) and is the only great mountain in Africa that lies close to the coast. It covers 800 square miles and rises from the waters of the Gulf of Guinea, presenting an extraordinarily magnificent sight from the

Atlantic Ocean. It is located at latitude 4.203 degrees north and longitude 9.17 degrees east and is one of Africa's largest volcanoes and one of only a few mountains in the world to have a historically dated B.C. eruption—an eruption at Mount Cameroon was observed by a passing Carthaginian navigator in the fifth century B.C. Since then, the mountain has experienced several violent eruptions, including ones in 1909, 1922, 1959, 1982, and 1999. In 1984, the first seismic network was installed. Today, Mount Cameroon is one of the country's most important tourist attractions.[3]

Oku Volcanic Field

The Oku Volcanic Field is located at latitude 6.25 degrees north and longitude 10.50 degrees east along the Cameroon volcanic line. It is made of maars and basaltic cinder cones. Two of its crater lakes, Lake Nyos and Lake Monoun (located approximately 100 kilometers east-southeast of Lake Nyos), have, in the last several years, produced extraordinary catastrophic gas releases. On August 15, 1984, Lake Monoun released poisonous gas that killed 37 people. This release was attributed to an overturn of stratified lake water, possibly triggered by an earthquake and landslide. On August 21, 1986, Lake Nyos released approximately one cubic kilometer of carbon dioxide (CO_2) gas, which traveled as far as 25 kilometers (15 miles) from the lake, flattening trees and vegetation, and killing at least 1,700 people and many farm and wild animals. Most of the deaths were caused by suffocation.[4]

Flora and Fauna

Vegetation in Cameroon is extremely varied, due primarily to the extraordinary diversity in its climatic conditions. Along the Atlantic coast, the climate is equatorial (hot and humid) and enhances the growth of thick mangrove swamps. The southern high plains are drained by the Sanaga and other river systems and favor the growth of dense evergreen forests with many huge trees (e.g., acajou mahogany, limba, azobé). These plains are also home to an extremely varied fauna, which include a variety of primate species, notably chimpanzee and gorilla. Other mammals such as the bongo (an extremely rare antelope), elephant, and panther can also be found in this region. On the northern flank of the Sanaga River, the forest thins and eventually gives way to savanna. The latter contains trees, beautiful grasses and shrubs, and extends into the Adamawa (Adamaoua) massif and the volcanic ridge. Throughout the savanna, patches of forest areas alternate with relatively large pockets of cultivated areas. As a result of the fact that this area is densely settled, wild animal populations have decreased significantly, giving way to domesticated livestock, such as cattle, goats, sheep, and pigs. In the Bénoué, which lies north of the Adamawa, the savanna is still liberally adorned with trees and provides an excellent habitat for a diverse variety of wildlife. In the extreme north, reaching Lake Chad, climatic conditions become more arid. In this area, one finds dry, treeless savanna and the steppe, which are home to the large wild animals found in the Waza National Park on the banks of the Logone River.[5]

THE CLIMATE

Climate differs significantly throughout the country. It is hot and humid in the south and west, with average temperatures of 26° C (80° F). Northern Cameroon is characterized by a dry plain with Sahara winds and hot temperatures, which are quite standard from October to May. Cooler winds and rains arrive between June and September, allowing for large irrigated farms and the grazing of several varieties of animals. Most of the central, southern, and eastern parts of the country are covered by a plateau of 2,000 to 4,000 feet (600 to1,2000 meters). Here, the daily heat of the dry season is relieved at night and by occasional rainfall. From May to October, rains bring significant amounts of water to the plateau. Rich volcanic soils at the foot of Mount Cameroon make possible extensive agriculture, including an extensive network of plantations owned by the Cameroon Development Corporation.

The country's coastal areas are hot and humid all year round, with an average high temperature of 32° C (90° F). These areas support large plantations of tropical crops such as rubber, cocoa, oil palms, bananas, and timber. Logging is an important economic activity, although unregulated and excessive exploitation is threatening the region's fragile ecosystem.[6]

THE PEOPLE

Evidence from studies of linguistic patterns shows that human migrations began around the border between Cameroon and Chad and spread in various directions during the last several hundred years. Islamic religious wars waged by the Fulani in the eighteenth and nineteenth centuries added to the waves of migration. Through such migratory movements, there occurred assimilation and absorption of groups, resulting in the various ethnic nationalities that inhabit present-day Cameroon. Extensive group mixing during the last several hundred years has made it very difficult to produce an accurate classification of Cameroon's ethnic groups. In fact, some of them are known by several different names.[7]

Certain external stimuli have contributed to more interaction between Cameroon's various groups. These include colonialism, which used its instruments of coercion to impose peace on the various peoples; economic developments such as the introduction of cash crops, plantations, industrial production, and urbanization; and the achievement of indigenous rule. Loyalty to one's ethnic group has remained strong. Policies introduced by the government of Paul Biya in the mid-1980s, supposedly to protect ethnic minorities, actually increased the political and economic benefits of ethnic loyalty and made the development of a national consciousness quite difficult.[8]

Cameroon's more than 250 ethnic groups speak 24 or so languages, which belong to either the Chadic group of Afro-Asian stock or one of the many branches of the Congo-Kordofanian stock. From 1884 to 1916, German was spoken and used widely in commerce and government administration. The post-World War I partition of Kamerun into French and British zones of influence saw the demise of German and the introduction of English and French as official languages—these were retained at reunification in 1961. French, however, is the dominant language in education, government, commerce, and the media. Fulfulde is widely spoken in the northern provinces, and pidgin English remains an important lingua franca, especially among people in urban centers throughout the country.

The Fulani

The Fulani are one of several groups that inhabit the northern part of Cameroon. They are said to have originated from West Africa and spread eastward from the Senegal River Valley searching for more effective grazing lands for their cattle. By the end of the thirteenth century several small groups of Fulani herdsmen had reached the Chadian basin and begun to construct settlements. Spurred by Usuman dan Fodio's holy war (1804–1810), several bands of Fulani holy warriors swept into present-day northern Cameroon and subsequently placed several communities under their rule, as well as converted many of the local people to Islam. Today, the northern Cameroon towns of Maroua, Garoua, and Ngaoundéré are important centers of Fulani political, economic, cultural, and religious activity.

As the holy warriors swept into the northern part of Cameroon, many local people either escaped into the hills or accepted conquest and converted to Islam. Some groups accepted conquest but did not embrace the Islamic religion. These groups have often been referred to as "non-Islamized pagans." Today, about 15 percent of the Fulani in Cameroon are descended from these conquered peoples—all of them have accepted Islam and adopted Fulani customs and culture, as well as the Fulani language. While the Fulani in other parts of West Africa have remained nomadic, those in Cameroon have settled down, earning their living primarily from stock raising and farming. A small number of Cameroon's Fulani, however, remains engaged in nomadic herding and can be found in the Bamenda highlands.[9]

Arabs

The majority of Cameroon's Arabs reside in the extreme north between the settlements of Fort-Foureau and Mora, although some of them can be found as far south as Maroua. In Cameroon, these people are called Choa Arabs. Since their arrival in Cameroon, they have intermarried with indigenous peoples and absorbed their cultures, producing a uniquely Cameroonian Arab group.

The ancestors of the Choa Arabs were part of the religiously motivated migrations that began in Arabia in the seventh century A.D., after their conversion to Islam. Several groups of these Arabs arrived at the Lake Chad region around the seventeenth or eighteenth century and settled in Baguirmi (part of present-day Chad). However, they did not cross the Chari and Logone Rivers until much later. Additional migrations took place after the Germans had extended their control of the colony of Kamerun as far as Lake Chad.

Cameroon Arabs are primarily herdsmen who are quite attached to their cattle, which are their main source of food and also their principal form of investment capital. They practice Islam and usually have Koranic schools in their villages. Most Arabs do not own land; instead, they lease the land from local chieftains, although in the municipality of Bounderi, the Choa Arabs enjoy autonomous rule as well as land ownership.

Kirdi and the Northern Hill Groups

The peoples who escaped to the hills rather than submit to Fulani conquest and convert to Islam consist of more than 23 different groups and are usually referred to in Fulani as pagans or Kirdi. They consist of local people who successfully retained their traditional beliefs, cultures, and customs, or they are non-Muslims and, hence, could be enslaved.

Although these peoples hail from different backgrounds, they share one thing in common: flight of their ancestors from the conquering Fulani and subsequent escape from conversion to the Islamic religion. The resentment that these groups developed for the Fulani during the years of conquest remains quite strong today. The hill people, as they are often called, have managed to adapt very well to their environment, making their living primarily by growing a variety of crops, including especially millet, on hill slopes through terracing. The hill people speak Chadic languages of the Afro-Asian stock.[10]

The Matakam, who live around the settlement of Mokolo, are the largest of the hill ethnic groups. The region in which they live in the Mandara Hills is one of the most densely populated in the northern part of Cameroon. Within the Matakam, the basic organizational social unit is the *gay,* which consists of a man, his wife or wives, and the unmarried children. The youngest son succeeds the father and takes care of the latter in his old age. Other children are expected to marry and settle elsewhere within greater Matakam society.

Within each Matakam village there exist four groups of people. From the first group are chosen the village chiefs (sultans)—this group usually consists of people descended from those who founded the village. Matakam chiefs do not have much authority but serve primarily as an intermediary between the dead and the living and perform necessary religious and agricultural rites. A second group of villagers consists of the descendants of people who arrived at the village much later and occupy a social status that is much lower than that of members of the first group. Within the third group can be found individuals who, for several reasons, were forced to leave other villages and resettle in the Matakam village in question. Called strangers (*keda*), these individuals must secure the permission of the chief before they can settle in the village and usually are never considered full members of society. The fourth group is made up of an occupational caste—individuals who assist with births, burials, and provide necessary medicinal herbs and cures for the rest of society. These people do not intermarry with the other members of the village.

North of the Matakam, between the municipalities of Mora and Mokolo, can be found the Mandara, the only hill peoples to embrace Islam. These people are mainly cultivators who live in relatively large groups, with each village equipped with a mosque of some sort. Within the northern hills, the Mandara, whose conversion to Islam is fairly recent, serve as a link to non-Islamic peoples, many of whom come to work for the Mandara in different capacities. The Mandara have adopted traditional Muslim dress, including the carrying of leather amulets that contain Koranic verses.

Other hill peoples include the Kapsiki, who can be found near the town of Mokolo and across the border in Nigeria. The Fali live near Garoua. In recent years, many of them have given up their traditional ways and moved to the plains. The Mofou live primarily in the hills, although many of them have begun to migrate to the plains. Several other groups can be found living separately and practicing their customs and traditions within the northern hills. However, over the years, many of these groups have adopted similar cultural practices.[11]

Northern Savanna Groups

Within the savanna, one can find so-called plains Kirdi, groups who had been defeated by the Fulani but decided to remain in their homelands instead of fleeing into the hills. These groups had also refused to accept the Islamic religion. Among them are the Guidar, the Guiziga, and the Daba, all of whom speak Chadic languages and are of Afro-Asian stock. They grow millet, groundnuts (peanuts), and cotton. Cattle are kept inside homes and are used for religious sacrifices. Chiefs serve as an intermediary between this world and the ancestral one, and they perform religious rites and sacrifices.

The Guidar of the northeastern part of Bénoué are a conglomerate of several groups who had intermarried after fleeing from Fulani conquest and refusing to accept Islam. Many Guidar reside in present-day Chad. Around Méri and Maroua, one can find the Guiziga, who had been hunters and gatherers here before the Fulani conquerors arrived. Although they have been influenced significantly by the Fulani, the Guiziga have not accepted Islam. Despite the adoption of some Fulani practices, many Guiziga still adhere to the old ways, including shaving their heads, filing their teeth, and ornamenting their bodies. Other smaller groups, including the Daba, can be found in the Bénoué, Margui-Wandala, and Diamaré municipalities.

A group that suffered significantly from frequent attacks by Fulani holy warriors is the Moundang, who live around the Chad border. Although they eventually adopted Fulani political organizations and forms of dress, they were never subjected to Fulani rule. The Moundang grow several crops, including their staple millet and cotton, which is their main cash crop. In addition, they raise cattle, which are used for marriage ceremonies, religious sacrifices, and the settlement of debts. Care of Moundang cattle is performed by the pastoral Fulani who live in their communities. Recently, some Moundang have adopted Islam or Christianity. The Moundang, who are said to have come from the Mandara Hills more than 13 generations ago, speak a language that has been classified as Adamawa, a branch of the Niger-Congo of the Congo-Korodofanian stock of languages.

Another group who fiercely resisted Fulani conquest and domination is the Mboum. Despite their bravery, they were eventually driven from their homes and forced to pay tribute to the Fulani. Today, most Mboum are dispersed in several settlements in the northeast corner of Ngaoundéré and south to the areas surrounding Tibati. A few Mboum live with and work as servants among the Fulani. While the Mboum are primarily cultivators of millet, many of them also fish. Mboum, as a language, is spoken widely in the areas surrounding Tibati and Ngaoundéré.

Other groups include the Dourou, who speak an Adamawa language, live between the towns of Garoua and Ngaoundéré, and have in recent years adopted Islam and Christianity. Along the eastern border, the Baya, who speak an Adamawa language, have spread as far as the western part of Central African Republic. Many of the Ngaoundéré Fulani, who in earlier times had enslaved the Baya, understand the Baya's language and frequently interact with them.

Northern Flood Plains Peoples

Among the peoples who live in the far northeast near the Chari and Logone Rivers are the Kotoko, Mousgoum, Massa, and Toubouri. All these groups speak Chadic languages and have recorded histories that begin with Fulani conquest. Their geographic conditions helped them more effectively withstand incursions from the Fulani and several groups of slavers, much more so than their southern neighbors. The peoples of the northern flood plains are primarily fishermen and farmers. However, they also raise cattle, primarily to secure wives for their sons.

The Kotoko, who are believed to be descendants of the Sao, live on lands surrounding the Chari and Logone Rivers. The Sao are believed to have been the ones who settled and developed compact settlements in the Logone valley. These settlements were later converted by the Kotoko into brick towns. Homes of nobility are located in the northern section of each town, while lower-class families and foreigners reside in the southern part of town. In the middle is the home of the sultan.

Through the years, the Kotoko have also become skilled boat builders and fishermen and have farmed only to secure food for themselves. Traditionally, the Kotoko did not engage in cattle raising, instead leaving that trade to Arab herders. However, in recent years, there has been more diversification in occupations, especially among men, many of whom have taken up cattle raising as well as cloth dyeing. The women are renowned for their pottery-making skills.

The Kotoko have converted to Islam. However, the practice of Islam is combined with other traditional worship practices that include the belief in spirits that live in water and sacred trees and rocks. The Kotoko speak a Chadic language that has many dialects.

Living south of the Kotoko are the Mousgoum, many of whom have since converted to Islam and have adopted Fulani dress and other practices, including their housing structures. Since independence, the Mousgoum have increased their migration northward toward Fort-Foureau. A significant number of Mousgoum live across the river in Chad, where they are called Moupoui.[12]

South of the Mousgoum are the Massa, a densely settled people who maintain their geographic and administrative center at Yagoua. Massa actually refers to several groups of peoples who speak the same Chadic language and share common customs as well as worship the god Olona. These peoples are also called *Banana*, which means "being in a state of fellowship."[13]

Also very densely settled and living south of the Massa are the Toubouri (Toupouri, Tupuri). Recently, they have been spreading northward, and quite a significant number of Toubouri live in Chad. The Toubouri are skilled farmers and also raise cattle. Their ruler is called *ouankoulou* and serves primarily in a religious capacity. The Toubouri men engage in a rite called *gourouna,* which was borrowed from the Mousgoum. Men participating in the *gourouna* temporarily give up their professions or pursuits and drink relatively large amounts of milk. At the same time, they sing, dance, and engage in mock fights publicly over several months. The main purpose of the rite is to reveal to the public that participants belong to families rich enough to afford the sacrifice of the participant's labor services.

Groups of the Western Highlands

The Western Highlands cut across both the English- and French-speaking regions of the country. Although this area has seen significant external influence and conflict, it remains relatively homogeneous culturally. Most of the groups who live in the western highlands have developed centralized chiefdoms headed by very powerful politicoreligious rulers. Most of them live in rural areas, where they earn their living primarily through agriculture. The peoples of the western grasslands speak Sudanic languages, which are a subcategory of the Benue-Congo family of languages of the Congo-Kordofanian stock.[14]

The largest western grasslands ethnic group is the Bamiléké, who migrated from lands now occupied by the Tikar in response to incursions from the Fulani in the seventeeth century. Southward migrations of the Bamiléké led to settlement south of the Bambouto Mountains and east of the Noun River. During the process of migration, some groups split away from well-established chiefdoms and formed their own chiefdoms. However, throughout, the Bamiléké have remained conscious of a common culture and today are quite united despite the fact that their settlements can be found in both the English- and French-speaking parts of the country.

Many Bamiléké are farmers, and some of them keep livestock. Chiefs maintain herds of livestock from which animals are selected for slaughter to celebrate important occasions. Although several Fulani cattle herders travel through the highlands during the year and in the Noun River valley during the dry season to provide food for their cattle, the Bamiléké rarely associate with them.

Because of a relatively high birth rate and one of the highest population densities in the country and an inheritance system that allows only a single male heir, younger male children are forced to migrate to other parts of the country to search for opportunities to make a living. Large-scale emigration among the Bamiléké began in the 1930s, and, by the early- to mid-1970s, more than 100,000 Bamiléké lived outside the area of their parents' birth.

The Bamiléké are one of the earliest groups to accept and adapt to the cash economy and are among some of the most important entrepreneurs in the country's urban areas today. They are also in the professions. In Douala, the country's most important commercial and economic center, Bamiléké hold approximately 70 percent of the professional jobs and 30 percent of the jobs in the civil service. In addition, they make up 60 percent of the traders, 80 percent of the artisans, and 40 percent of the laborers. Since Paul Biya came to power in 1982, however, employment patterns in the civil service have changed significantly, and the regime's nepotism has negatively affected the fortunes of the highly competitive Bamiléké. Today, the civil services are dominated by members of Biya's Beti ethnic group.

The Tikar are the most numerous of the several ethnic groups that inhabit the Bamenda plateau. Among the Tikar, the differences between dialects spoken within each village are so significant that they almost qualify as independent languages.

Oral narratives of the Tikar indicate that they originated from the northeast part of the territory between Tibati and Ngaoundéré. Since sometime in the early eighteenth century, small bands of Tikar began to migrate southward in search of new lands for agriculture and other economic activities. Such migrations increased after the arrival of Fulani religious warriors in the nineteenth century. Not all groups of Tikar, however, migrated. The Ngambe fought against a variety of sieges led by the Fulani chief of Tibati until the arrival of German colonialists, who subsequently recognized the rights of the Ngambe to their lands.

The people of the Bamoun kingdom are of both Tikar and Bamiléké ancestry. According to oral narratives and some written records, the Bamoun's Tikar ancestors came to the present location of the Bamoun in the early 1700s and conquered the Bamiléké and integrated the latter into Tikar society, producing present-day Bamoun. The Bamoun people, who speak a Bamiléké dialect, have been united under a single dynastic ruler for several generations and have successfully withstood Fulani conquest and retained their culture and traditions. One of the most important of the Bamoun rulers is Sultan Njoya-

Arouna, who came to power in 1888 and subsequently produced a written script for his people's language. Among his other achievements were the construction of schools and a printing shop and the creation of a religion based on traditional beliefs, Islam, and Christianity.

The Bamoun are typically more urban than their other highland neighbors. Most live in the city of Foumban, where the sultan's palace is located, and they rarely migrate out of their traditional territory, preferring instead to live within their kingdom, which is separated from the Bamiléké on the southwest by the Noun River.

Other ethnic groups found in the western highlands include the Widekum, who are said to have come originally from the Congo basin, settling in the southwestern corner of the Bamenda Plateau; the Banen and the Bafia, two distinct and independent groups on the southern outskirts of Bamoun territory; and the Bali, who came from farther north of the Tikar after confrontations with Fulani warriors in the latter part of the nineteenth century. After their arrival at the Bamenda Plateau, they took refuge among the Widekum, who they later attacked and conquered. Relations between the Widekum and Bali have remained strained ever since.

Southern Forest Peoples

Several ethnic groups live in the southern Cameroon forests, below the sixth parallel. However, these disparate groups are united by Christian churches, which have maintained missions in this area since before official German colonization in 1884. As a result of missionary activity in the area, the people maintain a relatively high literacy rate by African standards. Since kinship is the basis of most sociopolitical relations in this region of Cameroon, traditional chiefs have never had much authority.

The most numerous of the southern forest peoples is the Pahouin (or Pangwe), whose territory includes the bulk of the lands south of the Sanaga River. They also can be found in Equatorial Guinea and Gabon. Usually, the name Pahouin is used to refer to an agglomeration of several ethnic groups who have been referred to by outsiders as Fang-Beti. Because the latter refers to only two of the component groups found in the area, the people have usually rejected the term, instead preferring to be called Pahouin.

According to oral and written narratives, the Pahouin migrated from the savanna region to the northeast in response to southward expansion by the Fulani and pressure from other groups such as the Baboute and Mboum, who themselves were fleeing from the Fulani. Most of these migrants were either assimilated by or integrated into local groups—a process that continues to the present day.

Within the Pahouin, one can identify three important divisions—Beti, Boulou, and Fang. Each of these three groups is subdivided into several smaller groups. Beti refers to the Eton and Ewondo in the area around Yaoundé, as well as several smaller groups that live in the northeastern part of Pahouin country. The Eton arrived at their present location northeast of the city of Yaoundé searching for salt in the Sanaga River valley and were stopped in their southward migration by the Bassa, a group that is not part of the Pahouin. Within Eton society, three social strata are recognized: the Eton-Beti (families of chiefs); the Eton-Beloua (commoners); and the Beloua-Eton (descendants of slaves).

A little over one-third of the Pahouin are Boulou (Bulu), who live to the east and south of the Beti. During the last half century, the Boulou have been expanding rapidly and have, in some places, been absorbing the Fang; today they completely occupy the lands between their homelands and the Ntem River.

The Fang of Cameroon include the main group of Fang and several assimilated groups such as the Ntum and Mvae. Most Fang live in Equatorial Guinea and Gabon.

Several generations ago, the Pahouin were hunters and gatherers. Nowadays, most of them are engaged in agriculture, growing corn, cassava, and cocoa, which is their main cash crop. Cocoa was introduced in the areas around Yaoundé after World War I. The Pahouin are said not to be interested in entrepreneurial and commercial activities. However, since the coming to power of Paul Biya, the number of Pahouin engaged in commercial activities has increased significantly.

The Baboute are a small group of people who live to the north of the Pahouin and have been known by the names Wute, Bafute, Bute, and Mfute. Over the years, their population has been decimated by military encounters with the Fulani, German colonialists, and internal struggles. Today, most of them live in small villages between Yoko and Mankim.

West of the Pahouin, between the towns of Eséka and Edéa, live the Bassa, a very resilient group of people who made significant contributions to the struggle against colonialism in Cameroon and were the first southern peoples to wage war against the French for the independence of the colony. They migrated from the northeast to their present location.

The Duala, Wouri, Bakweri (Kpe), Pongo, Bodiman, and Bamboko were among the first Cameroonians to encounter European culture and institutions. They were also among the first to accept Christianity and send their children to schools operated by missionary groups. During German colonization, most indigenous intellectuals were speakers of Duala.

The Duala are found almost exclusively on both banks of the Wouri River. Before the arrival of the Germans, the Duala were divided into small kingdoms that amassed enormous wealth by monopolizing the trade on the estuary. Today, four of the kingdoms that were in existence during German occupation (Bell, Akwa, Dido, and Bonaberi) still exist. Within the city of Douala, where most of the Duala reside, they are outnumbered by Cameroonians from other groups.

The Baloundou-Mbo live on the border between Cameroon and Nigeria and are engaged primarily in fishing and gathering within the forests that surround their homes. Not much is known about these peoples except that they consist of several groups, each with its own dialect.

Cameroon's first inhabitants are thought to be Pygmies, according to oral narratives of the Bantu-speaking peoples who later settled the area. Three different groups of Pygmies can be found in the forest areas of Cameroon: the Babinga, the Bibaya, and the Beye'ele (or Bejieli). Pygmies usually live in small settlements or in small hunting and gathering bands and enjoy very highly structured symbiotic relationships with nearby cultivators. The cultivators provide Pygmy communities with salt, hunting instruments, cloth, and foods such as bananas and peanuts. In exchange the Pygmies supply the farmers with meat, animal skins, ivory, and medicinal plants. Cameroon's Pygmies have adopted the languages of the surrounding communities, live extremely simple lives, and maintain social structures that are based on the monogamous family, with the wife enjoying equality with her husband.

Foreign Groups

Other African and non-African groups make up about 13 percent of the population of Cameroon. Most of the African groups in Cameroon consist of Hausa, Igbos, and Yoruba from Nigeria; Ewe from Ghana; and several groups of refugees from neighboring countries, especially Chad. Cameroon is also home to many immigrants from several French-speaking countries in Africa. Non-African groups include Europeans, North Americans, Asians, and Middle Easterners. Among the Europeans and North Americans are significant populations of French and smaller groups of Americans, Canadians, Germans, and Britons. Greeks, Cypriots, Syrians, and Lebanese are engaged in many commercial activities.

LANGUAGES

The official languages of Cameroon are French and English, which are associated with the formal school system, the economic sector, and government administration. The electronic and print media use both languages and have contributed to their widespread use. At reunification in 1961, the federal government made a concerted effort to encourage the study of both French and English, especially by those entering the public services. However, most public workers remain fluent primarily in French and not English. English-speakers continue to have problems securing effective access to public services, including lectures at the national universities, all of which except for one (University of Buea, which became operational in the early 1990s), are located in the former French territory.

The people who live in the North West and South West provinces speak standard English, "pidgin" English, and their traditional languages. In the northern provinces, either French or Fulfulde (the language of the Fulani), is widely spoken. In other parts of the country, French and local languages such as Duala, Ewondo, and pidgin are spoken.

EDUCATION

Cameroonians take education very seriously, although, traditionally, boys have been favored over girls in the decision to send children to school. Since reunification in 1961, Cameroon has recorded one of the highest rates of school attendance in Africa. The provision of educational infrastructure in the country, however, differs by region. Education is provided by missionary societies, private entrepreneurs, and the government. Attendance in public schools is almost free of charge. The government subsidizes private schools and provides scholarships to a few outstanding students to attend these schools, most of which are owned by churches and other charitable agencies.

The central government provides nursery schools free of charge for children aged four and five. The service is available either separately or as part of a primary school. Very few children attend nursery schools. Since the early 1990s, however, enrollments in these schools have been increasing, with demand rising faster in the urban centers. Nursery schools usually open at 8:00 A.M. and close at midday. Although attendance at public nursery schools is free of charge, private nursery schools charge very high fees.

Primary school begins at the age of six and lasts for six years for children in French-speaking Cameroon and for seven years in English-speaking Cameroon. Secondary school education begins at the age of 12 or 13 and lasts for an additional seven years: in French-speaking Cameroon, secondary school is divided into cycles of four years and three years, whereas in English-speaking Cameroon, it is divided into cycles of five years and two years. School enrollment is higher in the southern part of the country than in the north. Muslim children attend Koranic schools in the evening and memorize passages from the Qur'an (Koran), the holy book of Islam.

The average rate of adult illiteracy in Cameroon is 30.7 percent (men 22.8 percent; women 38.4 percent). The central government in Yaoundé spends about 10 percent of its budget on education and maintains several schools throughout the country.

The first modern educational institutions were established in Cameroon by missionary societies. In the early years, missionary societies directed their educational efforts primarily toward evangelism. During the colonial period, Europeans used the educational system to train interpreters and individuals who could assist them in governing the territory and exploiting its resources for the benefit of the metropolitan economies. Hence, the curriculum did not reflect local needs and concerns. As they struggled for independence, nationalists argued that the postindependence curriculum would be restructured to reflect local needs, aspirations, and interests. This was never done, and instruction in many schools in Cameroon today continues to emphasize the study of the European experience.

All of Cameroon's primary schools are coeducational. The academic program is organized by subjects, which are distributed over five hours for each day, Monday through Friday. The primary school year lasts 35 weeks. Since the economic crisis of the mid-1980s, most schools have continued to suffer from a severe lack of funds for personnel and equipment. As a consequence, failure and drop-out rates have remained high. Instruction is in English in the two English-speaking provinces and in French in the eight French-speaking provinces. Hence, language is a problem for students because neither French nor English is the mother tongue of students. In recent years, educators have asked the government to allow them to begin instruction in local languages at the primary level. The program, however, is still in its experimental stages and, as yet, covers only a few of the many languages in the country.

Cameroon students complete their primary school education by taking an exit examination called the "first-school leaving certificate examination." Graduates of primary schools who want to enter secondary school must then take a competitive entrance examination. Students who are too old or unable to enter secondary school may enter two-year training courses at artisan training centers and home economics centers located throughout the country.

Although there has been a tremendous increase in secondary school education since the 1960s, only a little over 30 percent of primary school graduates proceed to the secondary school level. Attendance by girls in secondary schools in Cameroon has increased greatly during the last few decades. The academic program in secondary schools is about five and a half hours and is divided into three terms, which last a total of 35 weeks per year. The secondary school system is dominated by the French and British models, with the grammar type of general education remaining dominant. All secondary school students must take an exit examination called the General Certificate of Education (English) and the *baccalauréat* (French). Since reunification in 1961, the central government has tried to harmonize both educational systems but has faced opposition from English-speakers who fear erosion of their identity.

One of the most important innovations in secondary school education in Cameroon was the introduction of the bilingual secondary school in the early 1960s. In these schools, students receive instruction in both French and English. Secondary schools in Cameroon have been able to keep abreast of changes and developments in subject matter introduced in the United Kingdom and France through textbooks supplied by publishers in both countries and also through sending faculty to study abroad. The country has not yet succeeded in switching to books authored by local scholars and written specifically with Cameroonian students in mind.

The country's most important university is the *Université de Yaoundé,* which came into existence in 1962. Since then, the government has added several other universities. Students attending universities in Cameroon are charged a nominal fee of 50,000 francs CFA per year. Successful candidates from the country's grammar secondary schools can enter any of the faculties of the public universities. Studies are expected to last from three to seven years and prepare students to earn degrees in the faculties and professional diplomas in the professional higher educational institutions. However, language problems often prevent many students from completing their programs on schedule. Students must follow lectures in either French or English, depending on the competence of the lecturer in either language. Few students are fluent in both languages. In addition, poor and inadequate facilities continue to plague these institutions, resulting in failure rates that are approaching 80 percent for English-speaking students in some of these universities.

The government's monopoly on higher education was broken in 1990, when the Roman Catholic Church of Cameroon opened a university institute in Yaoundé, which has since evolved into a full-fledged university called the *Université catholique de l'Afrique centrale.* It currently has three faculties: theology, social sciences, and management and philosophy.

Governmental and nongovernmental organizations alike also provide preschool, special, vocational, technical, and business education. Notable in the area of special education are schools for lepers, most of which are run in hospitals by missionary societies, and schools for the blind where students study the basic elements of Braille, handicraft production, and gardening. The government runs a psychiatric hospital in Yaoundé, with facilities provided for the training of the disabled. Within the hospital is located a primary school program for educating physically and mentally handicapped children of school age. Finally, several institutions in the country educate and train young delinquents referred by the judiciary system. In these centers, the inmates are trained for jobs in industry or provided facilities to earn their primary school leaving certificates.

Many Cameroonians pursue a higher education overseas. Today, large numbers of Cameroon students can be found in Nigeria, South Africa, the United States, Britain, France, and Canada. During the Cold War, the Soviet Union and the People's Republic of China attracted a considerable number of Cameroon students, especially from the English-speaking part of the country.

CITIES

Not all of Cameroon's population groups dwell in villages. The Duala and a few other groups, most of whom were the first to encounter European colonization, established elaborate city settlements a long time ago. Coastal cities such as Douala, Tiko, Limbe, and Kribi developed in response to trade, both internal and external and with Europeans. Many of these cities once depended on trade in palm oil and several other crops for their survival. In recent years, Limbe and Douala have benefited significantly from trade in petroleum.

Northern cities are among the oldest settlements in Cameroon. Many of them, such as Maroua and Garoua, benefited significantly from the trans-Sahara trade and continue to grow today as a result of such trade.

In the early years of German colonization, Buea, located on the slopes of Mount Cameroon, was the nation's capital. The Germans later founded a new capital at Yaoundé, which is today the national capital, the second largest city in the country, and a major commercial and transportation center. Douala, the country's largest city, with a population of over 1.2 million people, is located on the Gulf of Guinea. It is the main financial, economic, commercial, and business center for Cameroon and most of central Africa, with shipping and manufacturing as well as financial services (insurance and banking) among its most important activities. The port of Douala is the conduit for most of the export trade that originates in central Africa and the import trade that comes into the region. Other important cities in Cameroon include Maroua, Garoua, Baffousam, Bamenda, Nkongsamba, and Kumba.

ECONOMY

About two-thirds of Cameroonians live in rural areas, usually in villages or very small towns, and are engaged primarily in agriculture. In 1970, 85 percent of Cameroon's labor force worked in agriculture; by 1990, that percentage had fallen to 70. The services sector, at a little over 20 percent, is the second largest employer of labor in Cameroon.[15] Most of the food crops are produced by women, while most men produce cash crops for export (cocoa, coffee, palm kernel, banana). Since petroleum became an important export commodity in the mid-1980s, the rate of urbanization has increased as many rural inhabitants have abandoned their farms in search of opportunities for economic advancement in the urban areas. Cameroonians who migrate to the urban areas, however, still maintain strong economic and social ties with their rural homelands.

The gross national product (measured at average 1998–2000 prices) in 2000 was U.S. $8.5 billion or $570 per capita. Per capita income declined in real terms during the 1988–2000 period at an average annual rate of 2.5 percent. In 1980, real gross domestic product (GDP), measured at average 1995 prices, was U.S. $6.3 billion, but by 2000, it had risen to $10 million. Between 1975 and 1984, real GDP was growing at an average annual rate of 8.5 percent, and during the 1985–1989 period, that growth rate had declined to –0.1 percent. Since then, there has been some recovery, due primarily to improved performance in the petroleum subsector. During the 1998–1999 fiscal year, real GDP grew by 4.4 percent and by 4.2 percent during 1999–2000.[16]

Agriculture remains Cameroon's most important economic sector, accounting for 43.5 percent of the GDP in 1999. The most important cash crops are cocoa beans, coffee, and cotton. Roots, tubers, and various grains make up the most important food crops. These include cassava, maize (corn), and sorghum. The country, however, is not self-sufficient in grains and must import large amounts each year to meet local needs.[17]

Cameroon's industrial sector, which includes mining, manufacturing, construction, and power, employed nearly 9 percent of the country's labor force in 1990 and in 1999 generated 18.6 percent of its GDP. During the period 1990 to 1999, industry's contribution to the GDP declined at an average annual rate of 1.8 percent. Since then, industrial production has improved significantly, and in fiscal year 1998–1999, industry's contribution to the GDP rose by as much as 5 percent.[18]

Since the early 1980s, the mining subsector, primarily petroleum, has been a major contributor to the gross domestic product. Although it employed only 0.05 percent of the country's labor resources in 1985, it nevertheless contributed significantly to government revenue. Cameroon also has significant reserves of natural gas, bauxite, iron ore, uranium, and tin. These resources remain largely undeveloped.

In recent years, manufacturing has accounted for about 10 percent of the gross domestic product and has employed 7 percent of the country's working population. Most of the subsector's activities involve the processing of domestically produced commodities and imported raw materials. Manufacturing's contribution to the GDP increased by an average annual rate of 1 percent in the 1990 to 1999 period. Since then, manufacturing has improved significantly, seeing an increase of 6.7 percent in 1998–1999.[19]

In 1999, services contributed 37.8 percent of the gross domestic product. The services sector has not performed well during most of the 1990s and continues to struggle today.

Trade is an important and integral part of the Cameroon economy. Domestically, cattle, beans, peanuts, and several grains, move from the north to the south; kolanuts, cassava, yams, and plantains from the south to the north; and corn, several varieties of grassfields yams, chickens, and other food stuffs move from the western highlands to other parts of the country.

Cameroon's most important import sources are France, Nigeria, Germany, and the United States. The country's export trade is carried out primarily with Italy, France, Spain, and the Netherlands. In recent years, Cameroon's principal exports have been petroleum and petroleum products, timber and timber products, cocoa beans, and coffee.

Cameroon's transport system does not appear adequate to meet the requirement of moving goods and people. Since reunification in 1961, improving the road, rail, port, and air infrastructure has been an important goal for the government. By the mid-1980s, Cameroon had about 62,000 kilometers of road, only 2,500 kilometers of which were paved.[20] Most roads in Cameroon are unpaved and suffer significantly during the rainy season, making it very difficult for farmers to transport their produce to markets in the urban areas. Railways connect the city of Douala to Kumba, Yaoundé, and Ngaoundéré.

Until recently, Cameroon has been served well, both internally and externally, by air links. The country's national airline, Cameroon Airlines, has had a lot of management and financial problems, which the government has tried to resolve by privatization. Privatization does not appear to have resolved the company's problems, and its future remains quite uncertain. Several carriers, however, continue to provide transport services for Cameroonians traveling abroad. International airports can be found at Douala, Yaoundé, Garoua, and Baffoussam.

The government dominates telephone, radio, television, and telegraph services. Television, first broadcast in 1985, now reaches most of the country, although only a small percentage of the people can afford TV sets. Although telephone service has increased significantly since the mid-1980s, most Cameroonians still do not have access to this critical service. In 1987, Cameroon opened a second satellite communication station and significantly improved its international telephone service. The Internet and cell phones have revolutionized communication in Cameroon as evidenced by the proliferation of

Internet cafés throughout the country. Cell phones have also become a common sight in the country, even among rural inhabitants.

Generally, economic growth and development have not been as rapid as many Cameroonians had expected at reunification in 1961. Particularly vexing has been the treatment of the English-speaking region by the Francophone–dominated central government. English-speakers' frustration at their treatment by the central government came to a head in the mid-1990s, when several of the region's intellectuals and public opinion leaders began to agitate for secession and the formation of a sovereign Southern Cameroons nation.

Many Cameroonians, however, remain optimistic and believe that the solution to their economic problems lies in the democratization of the country's political system and the introduction of a market-centered economic system. Hence, many of them have been working very hard at the grassroots level to improve governance and public accountability through the deepening and institutionalization of democracy.

GOVERNMENT

In 1990, Cameroon reintroduced multiparty politics—a system that had been abandoned in 1966, when then-President Ahidjo convinced leaders of Cameroon's various political parties to dissolve their organizations and form a single party called the Cameroon National Union. Since then, Cameroon has held two flawed presidential elections, both of which have been won by Paul Biya.

From 1961 to 1972, Cameroon was a two-state federation. However, following the referendum of May 20, 1972, the federation was dissolved and a unitary state created. On January 18, 1996, a new constitution was adopted, creating a unitary, decentralized, and multiparty state with a semi-presidential regime. The 1996 constitution allows for separate executive, legislative, and judicial branches of government.

The president of the Republic of Cameroon is the head of state and is elected by universal adult suffrage to serve a term of seven years for a maximum of two terms. He is considered a symbol of unity and is given responsibility for determining national policy, safeguarding the constitution, overseeing the smooth operation of the state, and making certain that Cameroon adheres to or complies with all international treaties and conventions. The head of government is the prime minister, who is appointed by the president and is charged with carrying out the national policy as defined by the president. The president also appoints his own cabinet.

In Cameroon, legislative power is held by the Parliament, which consists of the National Assembly and the Senate. Parliament enacts laws and monitors the activities of the government. The National Assembly consists of 180 members, elected by direct and secret universal suffrage to serve a term of five years. In December 1995, a constitutional amendment provided for the establishment of an upper house to be known as the Senate; however, this has not yet been achieved. In National Assembly elections held on June 30 and September 15, 2002, the ruling Cameroon People's Democratic Movement (CPDM) won 149 seats, the Social Democratic Party (SDF) 22, the *Union démocratique du Cameroun* (UDC) 5, the *Union des populations du Cameroun* (UPC) 3, and the *Union nationale pour la démocratie et le progrès* (UNDP) 1.

Justice in Cameroon is administered by a judiciary system headed by the Supreme Court. Although the constitution provides for the independence of the judiciary, the executive—through power of appointment—has significant influence on the judiciary system. In addition to the regular judiciary, the country's constitution has allowed the establishment of a Constitutional Council (CC), which rules on the constitutionality of laws and oversees the operation of the country's institutions. Since the CC has not yet been established, the Supreme Court is expected to carry out its duties. In addition, there is a Parliamentary Court of Justice, which is charged with the authority to judge the president and the prime minister and other members of government to whom power has been delegated for any behaviors considered injurious to the state and the security of the people.

History

The first known foreign visitors to the Cameroon coast were Carthaginians, captivated by an erupting Mount Cameroon in the fifth century B.C. Centuries later, the Portuguese arrived to exploit the enormous environmental resources along the Gulf of Guinea. As plantation agriculture proved viable in the New World, the demand for slaves increased, inviting many Europeans to the Cameroon and Guinea coasts, which were developing into important areas for the collection of slaves for shipment to the Americas. As the demand for slaves slowed, many of the slavers began to turn to the exploitation of environmental resources. During the slave trade, the Europeans secured slaves primarily through indigenous middlemen, preferring to stay away from the interior of the continent. The post–slave trade exploitation of Africa's environmental resources required the establishment of permanent settlements, which could anchor each European country's involvement in the region.[21]

In 1472, Portuguese seafarers, sponsored by Fernando Gomez, a rich Lisbon merchant, arrived at the Bight of Biafra, visited the island of Fernando Po, and then sailed into the estuary of what is today the Wouri River. Struck by the presence of large schools of edible prawns, they named the river Rio dos Camarões (River of Prawns). What is now Cameroon appeared as

Camarões on the first Portuguese maps of the region. The explorers named the magnificent mountain Mount Ambozes, a name that Mount Cameroon retained for almost two centuries. The Portuguese, however, did not establish any permanent settlement in the area.

Demand for slaves to work on the plantations of the New World had a significant impact on trade along the West African coast. By the mid-1550s, slaves had become the most important export commodity from the Guinea and Cameroon coasts, and the Portuguese were the most important suppliers of slaves to the New World. Fernando Po and São Tomé grew into important collection points from which slaves obtained from indigenous middlemen could be processed and shipped to the New World. By the beginning of the seventeenth century, however, other European countries, notably the Netherlands, had become involved in the purchase of slaves along the Cameroon coast for shipment to the New World.

In 1807, Britain, the dominant European power on the Gulf of Guinea, declared its slave trade illegal and began to police the region to stop the practice. In 1827, Spain granted permission to Britain to occupy Fernando Po and use the island as a base to prevent the shipping of slaves from the Bights of Biafra and Benin. In 1842, Reverends Clark and Prince of the English Baptist Missionary Society established a small worship center at Clarence (Santa Isabel on Fernando Po), and two years later they founded a church and school at Bimbia, one of several trading posts along the Cameroon River. Alfred Saker, who had assumed leadership of the worship center at Clarence, was forced by Spanish Jesuits to leave. He subsequently purchased land from King William of Bimbia and founded a permanent settlement, which he named Victoria, at the foot of Mount Cameroon.

Despite the fact that the Cameroon mainland had been explored by several Englishmen and several native kings had offered to sign treaties with them to seek English protection, Britain remained uninterested in annexation and focused mostly on wiping out the slave trade. The British consul in the region did sign a treaty with two native kings along the Cameroon River in 1842, specifically to encourage trade in ivory and palm oil and to discourage the slave trade. The slave trade continued, albeit clandestinely, finally ceasing only when the Duala middlemen found legitimate trade in ivory and palm oil to be more profitable. Douala eventually emerged as the most important trading center on the Cameroon River.

The German Colony of Kamerun

In July 1884, Gustav Nachtigal, then German Commissioner for West Africa, signed agreements with several indigenous chiefs on the Cameroon

River and founded a colony named Kamerun along the Gulf of Biafra. German colonial authorities eventually undertook additional explorations inland and extended the size of Kamerun as far as Lake Chad.

Like other European countries, Germany sought to secure raw materials for its industries and markets for the sale of excess domestic output. In the early years, trade by German entrepreneurs and African middlemen appeared to fulfill these objectives. However, as competition from other European countries increased, it became necessary to establish permanent settlements to protect German trading interests and ensure a more reliable supply of raw materials to the metropolitan economy.[22]

Shortly after its political authority was established and its claim to the territories was recognized by other European countries, Germany made arrangements to restructure the economy of Kamerun to serve its needs for trade and plantations. The Reichstag (parliament) was at the time unwilling to provide the costly administration that would be needed to bring these enormous resources under control, and private German capital did not wish to assume the risks of investing in plantations in Kamerun. Colonial authorities adopted a strategy that was widely employed by other European countries—they decided to award monopoly rights to German companies to exploit and "develop" the resources of the new colony. Hence, in 1899, exclusive rights to exploit the resources of large chunks of the colony were awarded to two private German companies: the Gesellschaft Süd-Kamerun and Gesellschaft Nordwest Kamerun. In addition to undertaking physical exploitation and development of the resources, each company was expected to provide the necessary institutions for the maintenance of law and order in its respective concession. The first plantatations in Kamerun, however, were established by the trading firms C. Woermann and Jantzen & Thormählen.[23]

German plantation agriculture in Kamerun began around the rich and fertile soil of Mount Cameroon, and, by 1914, close to 264,000 acres of land were under cultivation in agricultural estates. Within each plantation area, a railway system was constructed with a link to the port city of Douala. Plantation agriculture increased the demand for labor and deprived indigenous groups of most fertile farmland. The inability of indigenous groups to make a living from farming forced many of them to seek work on German plantations.

By January 1, 1913, there were 58 plantations and 195 planters (all of them non-African) in Kamerun, producing commodities such as palm oil, palm kernels, cocoa, rubber, tobacco, and bananas for export to Germany. Indigenous labor on the plantations numbered 17,827.[24]

For German officials and planters in Kamerun, land and labor were the two most important issues. Earlier, on June 15, 1896, the German government, by imperial decree, had declared all unoccupied land in Kamerun crown land and thus property of the German empire. The decree required that specific stipulations be made to protect indigenous groups. Administration of these rules under Governor Puttkamer, however, did not protect indigenous rights to land, as planters continued to expropriate such properties, forcing many indigenous inhabitants into government-created reservations that were often too small to meet even their subsistence needs. The forced resettlement policy was paving the way for the inception of wage labor, because conditions on the resettlement lands were such that the indigenous peoples could no longer make a living through the traditional ways of hunting, farming, and gathering.[25]

Most likely out of its own need for land, the Basler Mission, which had taken over the work of the English Baptist Missionary Society, sent representatives to Germany to seek relief for itself and the various displaced indigenous groups. The colonial government was directed to effect changes in land policies and, in 1902, a land commission was created to determine the needs of indigenous groups and establish boundaries between property belonging to Germans and that belonging to the various ethnic groups. By gubernatorial decree of October 1903, a missionary from the Basler Mission was made a permanent member of the land commission. Other land commissions were started throughout Kamerun to deal with similar issues. However, the land commissions failed to provide a final solution to the land problem.[26]

Labor was needed to perform a variety of tasks on the plantations, perform domestic work in the homes of planters and other Germans, carry wares to and from the trading stations in the interior, and construct roads into the interior of the colony. On the 120-mile trade route between Yaoundé and Kribi, for example, an estimated 80,000 porters (men, women, and children) were carrying goods for Germans and other Europeans by 1913. In addition, about 18,000 indigenous peoples were working as laborers on plantations. Wages varied from six to nine marks per month, hardly enough to meet the subsistence needs of the laborer, let alone those of his family.[27]

The sparse population of the Cameroon River district and the fact that many of the local people preferred to work for themselves rather than for white planters created a severe labor shortage. To make wage labor attractive to local groups, the government on July 1, 1903, imposed a head tax of three marks per year (to be paid in cash only) on all adult men and unmarried women. Married men with more than one wife had to pay a tax of two marks for each additional wife. Initially, the tax was only for the municipality of Douala, but on October 20, 1908, the tax measure was made applicable to all of Kamerun and was doubled. In 1913 the tax was further increased to ten marks. Those who were unable to pay the tax were required to perform public service or "tax work" of 30 days on public works. Several exemptions were made, but these were primarily to enhance the German administration of the colony. Although the tax was imposed to alleviate the labor problem, it did provide significant income to the colonial administration. In fact, by 1914, indigenous inhabitants of the colony were paying 2.8 million marks in taxes; public work performed in lieu of taxes was estimated at 150,000 marks.[28]

One of the most important and pronounced effects of colonization was the introduction of the exchange economy and the subsequent development of urban centers along the coastal areas of the colony. Emerging within each one of these urban centers was a new class of Africans with a value system based on labor skills, money, education, and other assorted nontraditional attributes, many of which were characteristic of the European value system. As this new socioeconomic class grew larger, traditional social and economic structures continued to disintegrate. Many of these "Europeanized" Africans asserted their economic independence from the traditional groups and were able to rid themselves of the need to be dependent on "ancient hierarchies of status and birth."[29] For coastal groups like the Duala, such a disassociation accelerated and completed the disintegration of their ancient political system. A similar fate awaited other ethnic groups in areas where the new exchange economy was producing urban centers.

Despite its apparent cruelty, the German administration of Kamerun succeeded in providing the colony with an impressive infrastructure. By 1914, harbors had been developed at Douala, Kribi, Campo, and Tiko-Victoria. Well over 400 kilometers of railroads had been constructed and made functional. The colony had three railroads, the oldest of which was the narrow-gauge light railway belonging to the Victoria Plantation Company. The line connected the plantation with its harbor at Victoria. The other two were the Northern Railway, which ran from Bonaberi (across the river from Douala) to Nkongsamba, and the Midland Railway, which started from the city of Douala and ran through Edea to the Nyong.

In addition to railroads, the Germans also constructed bridges, roads, paths, and a series of very impressive public and private houses. Many of these structures are still used. Except for the petroleum extraction and refining activities that began in the late 1970s, the German plantations at the base of Mount Cameroon are still the most important contributor to the economy of the English-speaking part of Cameroon.

The Partition of Kamerun: The British-French Condominium, 1914–1916

World War I began in Europe in August 1914, and by February 1916 Kamerun had been captured by Allied Expeditionary Forces. It took 18 months to defeat the Germans, and when it was finally over, the German force, along with Governor Ebermaier, was interned at Rio Muni.

Douala was captured by Allied forces on September 14, 1914. A condominium was established following the exchange of correspondence between France's M. Delcassé and Britain's Sir Edward Grey and Sir Francis Bertie (September 21 and 24, 1915). The decision was made to administer the city jointly until the enemy was defeated and the peace secured. As soon as German resistance had ceased and victory was imminent, Britain and France made arrangements to divide the territory and allow each nation to administer its part using its own methods and without interference from the other.

On March 14, 1916, an agreement was signed terminating the condominium. Kamerun was subsequently partitioned into French and British zones of influence and turned into League of Nations Mandates under French and British administration.[30]

The League of Nations Mandates (1922–1939)

The French Mandate

Economic developments in the French mandate must be viewed within the framework of political developments in the colony. The first factor in this framework was a web of institutions designed by France to enhance its ability to govern the colony and deal effectively with problems arising from such rule. The reaction of indigenous groups to French rule formed the second factor, and the final factor was the influence of German planters in the mandates, many of whom had returned after the war to reclaim their plantations.

France based its colonial policy in Africa, at least initially, on assimilation. French colonial authorities had intended to develop the colonies and metropolitan France "into a single, integrated political and economic unit."[31] Some colonial officers believed that the cultural gap between France and inhabitants of the colonies made implementation of the policy unworkable. It was decided to introduce another policy called *association,* which would allow France to rule each colony through a native elite, comprised of Africans who had been trained in French language, culture, and administrative procedures. Elites were given privileged positions in the colonial bureaucracy and served as a vital link between the government and the African peoples. In many rural areas, these Gallicized Africans served as minor colonial officers, representing French authority in the villages. As a result, they had considerable political and economic power.[32]

The French reinstituted forced labor and used it extensively in the building of the Douala-Yaoundé railroad and in other construction projects. The

German labor tax was abolished and in its place a head tax was introduced, which, unlike the German labor tax, applied to everyone, including women and children.[33]

The Labor Code for Overseas Territories of 1952 officially ended forced labor in the Cameroons.[34] The modification of policy toward one of moderation in French Cameroons may be attributed to the work of the missionaries, who, although they were teaching only the officially sanctioned course work, did give the indigenous peoples values that provided the impetus for challenging the status quo. The French believed that they needed native support in their struggle against Germany, given that Germans were already mounting a massive war of words to get not only their plantations back but also their colonies.[35]

The British Mandate (1922–1939)

Following the establishment of Allied control over Kamerun, property belonging to Germans was seized and placed in the hands of the custodian of enemy property for safe keeping until the war was over. The properties were publicly sold in 1924. French, British, and Cameroonian entrepreneurs purchased German holdings in French Cameroons, and, as such, German citizens did not return to French Cameroons after the war to reclaim their properties.

Properties in British Cameroons were not immediately sold. An auction in 1922 failed to elicit a fair market price for the properties. On November 24 and 25, 1924, a new auction took place in London and most of the properties were purchased by a London agent representing former German owners. Soon, the original owners were back to the British Cameroons to manage their properties.[36]

The return of German plantations to their original owners brought Germans back into their former colony—primarily into the British Cameroons, and by 1925, just one year after the sale, Germans constituted the largest European group in the British mandate; by 1938, there were three times as many German nationals as there were Britons in British Cameroons.[37]

The German propaganda machine in the Cameroons was so effective that the French felt compelled to launch their own campaign to diffuse what appeared to be growing sympathy within the colony toward the German cause. On April 15, 1938, a meeting of Frenchmen, Americans, and Europeans from countries other than Germany, called by the French, took place in Douala. Participants intended to show their support for France and the fact that they, too, like the French, were opposed to a return of the colonies to Germany.[38]

The British Cameroons were neglected during the mandate period. Little or no activity took place in the plantations during and after World War I.

The stagnation that characterized the economy in British Cameroons at this time was due primarily to the neglect of the plantations, the global depression, which produced a slump in the prices of primary commodities, and the fact that the British government was unwilling to finance capital expenditures in the colony or enhance the ability of private British capital to do so. Following the sale of the plantations back to German nationals in London in 1923 to 1924, trade with Britain fell substantially in favor of trade with Germany. In 1931, of a total export bill of 155,432 marks, Britain accounted for only 6,341 marks of that value. Germany received 109,603 marks' worth of exports from the Cameroons. In 1937, the trade situation had not changed significantly. That year, Germany provided 47.57 percent of the imports of the British Cameroons and received 79.75 percent of the colony's exports. The figures for Britain were 11.9 percent of the colony's imports and 6.9 percent of its exports. Most of the economic prosperity enjoyed by the British Cameroons during this period was made possible by German activity, especially in the management of the plantations and also in the expansion of the infrastructure.[39]

The Trusteeship Period

French Cameroons

When World War II began in 1939, the League of Nations ceased to exist and the mandates became the responsibilities of Britain and France. It was not until 1947, when the United Nations (UN) was formed, that the mandates were transferred to the new organization's care.

Acceptance of the trusteeship system by France and Britain implied that they were willing to adhere to the UN Charter's Article 76, which required that development in the territories be geared toward national autonomy and eventual self-rule. For France, this represented somewhat of a departure from its traditionally more expansionist colonial policy.[40] Thanks to reforms in the colonial policy made possible by the French constitution of 1946, African agitation, and developments at the UN, political activities in French Cameroons evolved rapidly after World War II, resulting in independence on January 1, 1960.

British Cameroons

Britain's part of the former German colony was divided into Southern Cameroons and Northern Cameroons. In May 1959, the UN General Assembly recommended that plebiscites be held in both sections to decide the question of independence. The two territories were asked to decide between joining

Nigeria or the *République du Cameroun*. On February 11, 1961, voters in Southern Cameroons chose union with the *République du Cameroun*. Those in Northern Cameroons, in plebiscites that took place February 11 and 12, 1961, opted to stay in Nigeria.[41]

The Struggle for Independence

Cameroonians had always rejected European cultural, economic, and political domination and expressed that rejection through their writings. The demands of many citizens were for a restructured system that would enhance their social and economic mobility. In addition, they wanted the modernization of their country so that the people would enjoy the same amenities that were available to the people in the metropolitan economies. The French, who had brought their assimilationist policies to Cameroon, were not receptive to the kinds of reforms that were being demanded by the colony's indigenous elites.

As gratitude for the help provided by indigenous Cameroonians to the Free French forces during World War II, the postwar colonial government, with approval from Paris, was willing to listen to nationalists. This changed attitude was reflected in the behavior of colonial administrators at their January 1944 Brazzaville Conference, during which they proposed to allow African representation in the institutional organs of the Fourth French Republic. While Africans were expected to exercise increased local autonomy, this was to be within a greater French state, because an independent existence outside the French community was not anticipated.

The first indigenous groups to play an important political role were the labor unions. In the mid-1940s, the most important labor union in the French Cameroons was the *Union des syndicats confédérés de Cameroun* (USCC), which was sponsored by France's largest labor organization, the *Confédération générale de travail* (CGT), a communist-dominated organization. After its formation, the USCC soon discovered, however, that negotiations with the colonial government were not going to be fruitful, and the state continued to favor French commercial and entrepreneurial interests. The USCC responded with several violent strikes in Douala, which were quickly crushed by the colonial gendarmes.

During the elections of 1946, metropolitan political parties made an effort to establish branches in French Cameroons. In addition, an unaffiliated local party called *Mouvement démocratique camerounais* was formed, and the *Union camerounaise française* (UNICAFRA), which had been established in 1945, made arrangements to participate in the elections. It soon became evident to these organizations that France was not interested in advancing political development in the territory. However, they disagreed on how to force change. While one group argued for political development through the existing structures coupled with cooperation with France, another group adopted a radical approach that called for autonomy outside the French union. This proposition was illegal according to the French constitution of 1946. Continued support for it led to violence, which persisted until the territory gained independence.

Disappointed with the outcome of the 1946 elections, radical Cameroonians unsuccessfully tried to convert UNICAFRA into a more effective tool for the emancipation of the country. Unable to convert the UNICAFRA, which dissolved shortly afterward, Ruben Um Nyobé and his comrades formed the *Rassemblement camerounais* (RACAM). However, it was banned almost immediately by the French for its anti-assimilationist leanings. After RACAM was proscribed, Um Nyobé and the others formed the *Union des populations du Cameroun* (UPC).

During the early years of the UPC, its leadership was dominated by Um Nyobé and other Bassa elites. However, Duala and Bamiléké elites soon joined the party and its leadership and radicalized its policies even further—a development that did not sit well with the French colonial government, and soon the French were seeking ways to either undermine the UPC or force its dissolution. In addition to transferring bureaucrats with UPC membership to remote areas where they could not easily have access to the leadership of the party, the French also made it virtually impossible for the party to use public facilities. The colonial government also provided generous support to moderate political parties and those that advocated political change within the French community and cooperation with France.

In 1951, more than 20 political parties, all of which supported evolutionary policies, as well as the UPC, competed for the French National Assembly and the 1952 elections for the Cameroon representative assembly. In these elections the vote was extended to all Cameroonians who were literate in French and Arabic—about 500,000. The results showed overwhelming support for parties supporting evolutionary policies. Afterward, the UPC, which had not performed well, decided to adopt a new platform and began calling for reunification with the British Cameroons. In 1952, Um Nyobé took the reunification issue before the UN, and, upon his return to Cameroon, the reunification issue was adopted by many political parties, including those that had supported evolutionary policies. In 1955, Félix Roland Moumié, who had recently returned from abroad and had gained control of the UPC, led the party in support of violent riots, which resulted in the deaths of many people and the destruction of much property. In July 1955, the French proscribed the party, rendering it unable to participate in political processes in the colony, including elections and representative bodies. The leadership of the party soon split into factions—Bamiléké and Duala leaders fled to the British Southern Cameroons, and, under the leadership of Moumié, they tried to affiliate with the Kamerun National Democratic Party (KNDP), and Bassa leaders under the leadership of Um Nyobé went into hiding near the municipality of Eséka. There was virtually no communication between the two factions.

Both factions engaged in violent opposition to French rule. During 1956 and 1957, most of the fighting was in Bassa country, with only minor skirmishes taking place in Bamiléké country. After the assassination of Um Nyobé in 1958 by government security officers, the major focus of the violence shifted to the Bamiléké region. However, the liberation struggle was now being directed by a new organization called *Armée de libération nationale du Kamerun* (ALNK). Between 10,000 and 80,000 people lost their lives during the campaigns, which lasted until independence in 1960.

Shortly after the 1955 elections, several political parties in the colony had severely criticized the UPC for its violence during the campaigns, especially in the Sanaga-Maritime Department of the Littoral Province. However, as time passed and also as the French became more accommodating regarding autonomy for the Cameroons, many opinion leaders began to call for reconciliation and the formation of an effective coalition between the UPC and anti-UPC groups. This period also marked the beginning of attempts by France to Cameroonize the administrative services, and, by 1956, the French colonial government was sending indigenous inhabitants to France to be trained for upper echelon jobs in the civil service.

In 1956, France enacted the *loi cadre,* which was designed to reduce the amount of time needed to develop and implement reforms to grant increased autonomy for its overseas territories. The Cameroons' representatives to the territorial assembly, chosen by the election of December 1956, formed a coalition government under the leadership of André-Marie Mbida. The coalition consisted of the *Union Camerounaise* (UC), led by Ahmadou Ahidjo; the *Démocrates Camerounaise* (DC), headed by Mbida; and *Paysans Indépendants* (PI), an agglomeration of Bamiléké interest groups led by Djoumessi Njime. The main opposition group was the *Action Nationale* (AN), which was led by Charles Asallé and Paul Soppo Priso. Except for the PI, all the political parties were formed along regional lines with membership coming from several ethnic groups.

Although Mbida's coalition lasted for a little over a year, it was quite divisive and did not further the cause of independence. For one thing, Mbida believed in going slow, ignored the reunification question, and proposed a 10-year period of social, economic, and political transformation before independence could be granted. In addition, he wanted French troops to crush the UPC rebellion, and he objected to any grant of amnesty to UPC combatants. In early 1958, Mbida's interior minister, Ahmadou Ahidjo, formed a new coalition government. Ahidjo was a Muslim from the north but was able to gain the confidence of southern leaders to form a coalition government with the PI. This north-south alliance was to prove very useful in his struggle to the top of Cameroon politics.

In December 1958, the UN General Assembly ended the French trusteeship, and France and the Cameroons agreed on a timetable for independence. On January 1, 1959, the colony was granted autonomy on all matters except foreign affairs. On January 1, 1960, the territory gained independence and took the name *République du Cameroun.*

Political developments in the two trust territories under British administration were slower and without much incident. The unification issue was complicated by the absence of agreement between the various political parties in the territory and significant political divisions within the Southern Cameroons. Originally, the UN had intended to carry out a plebiscite in February 1961 to determine the future political status of the territory, but complications arose and the decision was made to hold separate votes, one in Northern Cameroons and another in Southern Cameroons. Northern Cameroons voted to integrate with Nigeria, and Southern Cameroons opted for unification with the *République du Cameroun.*

Although Southern Cameroons leaders had consulted with Ahidjo before the Foumban Unification Conference in July 1961, no effort was made to reach agreement on the nature of the federal constitution. The Southern Cameroons delegation favored a loose federal system with a bicameral legislature and a ceremonial head of state, but it did not fight hard enough to secure it. Ahidjo wanted a centralized federal structure with most power concentrated in the executive. The constitution, which was made public in September 1961, was based on the Ahidjo model, with a strong federal executive and a unicameral legislature.

Reunification and Federation

As conditions for independence, the UN offered Southern Cameroons two options: union with Nigeria or with the *République du Cameroun,* both of which were already independent countries. It was unlikely that any of the two countries would abandon its laws and institutions and engage in the type of constitutional deliberations that would have allowed Southern Cameroonians to select rules more favorable to their values. The final constitution did not provide clear direction on the future of the union, and West Cameroonians were afraid that Ahidjo's proclivity toward political centralization would force the union into a unitary state in which West Cameroon would lose its political autonomy. Those fears were to prove prophetic as the central government eventually turned the federation into a unitary state.

Six years after reunification, many English-speakers began to openly express regret about their 1961 decision to join the *République du Cameroun*. Politically, economically, and culturally, they felt ignored, abandoned, marginalized, and, in many ways, oppressed by French-speakers. Of course, not all of West Cameroon's problems can be blamed entirely on policies of the federation. For one thing, the British left behind a very weak economy, with no viable economic infrastructure and no active industrial sector at reunification. Although the causes of West Cameroon's poverty are complex, the imposition on the state of constitutional rules that were selected without the full and effective participation of the relevant stakeholder groups contributed significantly to the political unit's marginalization.

On May 20, 1972, the federation was abolished and a unitary state established. The impact of unitarism on West Cameroon was and remains quite dramatic. Because of its relatively weak economy, West Cameroon was not able to absorb the shock caused by sudden and ill-prepared integration with the more advanced and dynamic economy of East Cameroon. Creation of the unitary state allowed the central government to direct most of its attention to national economic growth, while neglecting the needs of individual units. This neglect is today given as the reason why many groups in West Cameroon now demand secession and formation of a new sovereign nation.

Paul Biya and the Promise of Democracy

In November 1982, Paul Biya became president and promised to implement reforms to deal with corruption and the many abuses of the Ahidjo regime. During the first year of Biya's presidency, a significant level of tolerance appeared to be evolving in Cameroon, as Cameroonians suddenly found themselves able to criticize the government.[42] Many citizens, however, came to realize that the exercise of many of the new freedoms was only allowed and tolerated by the government if they directed their criticisms at the regime of former president Ahidjo.[43] Biya made no effort to repeal many of the draconian laws passed in the 1960s and 1970s to enhance the ability of the government to be repressive. Instead, he used them effectively to enhance his ability to monopolize political power. As late as 1990, Cameroonians were still being arrested for trying to start political parties.[44]

Although Biya was quite reluctant to introduce multiparty democracy in Cameroon, he was eventually forced by both internal and external pressure to legalize competitive politics in 1990. However, despite pressure from grass-roots organizations and several of the country's traditional benefactors, the government has yet to provide Cameroon with a fully functioning democratic system. Biya and the CPDM continue to monopolize politics and resource allocation in Cameroon as the country's transition to democratic governance has stalled.

The Fulani Influence

Historical narratives of Cameroon have tended to concentrate only on the coastal regions and the European influence. However, the history of the country cannot be complete without a look at the various groups (and their institutions) that invaded the country from the north and eventually contributed to its unique cultural and ethnic mix. Important among these are the Fulani who came and established emirates (states); brought with them the Islamic religion, as well as their customs and traditions; and eventually made a significant impact on the political economy of the region. In addition, the resistance of several local groups (notably the Kirdi) to Fulani conquest produced several dichotomies that continue to influence sociopolitical interaction in the region to this day.

Oral and written narratives indicate that the Chad plain was inhabited by several groups by the eighth century A.D. In that same century, pastoral Berbers and semi-Arabs came from the west and north and conquered several groups around Lake Chad. Some of the local groups were able to avoid conquest by fleeing into inaccessible mountain regions. Groups that did not flee but successfully resisted Berber domination later succumbed to Fulani conquest and the Islamic religion.

The Fulani first appeared in Hausaland (in what is now northern Nigeria) around the thirteenth century, and, by the eighteenth century, had become fully assimilated within the Hausa states and had also become Islamized. To the east, several groups that had managed to escape incorporation into the great Muslim state of Bornu had organized a relatively powerful empire in the Mandara mountains about 130 miles south of Lake Chad. In the sixteenth century, holy warriors from Bornu attacked, subdued, and Islamized several of the groups within the Mandara empire. Bornu then set up a vassal Mandara sultanate that existed until it was sacked by the Fulani in the nineteenth century.

In the latter part of the eighteenth century, an urban Fulani and devout Muslim called Usman Dan Fodio led a holy war against the Hausa states, which he believed had debased the Islamic faith. By 1810, all the Hausa states had been conquered and the Fulani subsequently emerged as the dominant ethnic group in the northern Nigeria–Lake Chad area. As word of Dan Fodio's exploits spread, many Fulani came forward to volunteer for duty as holy warriors. One such volunteer was the nobleman Adama, who was given a flag by Dan Fodio and instructed to recruit holy warriors and propagate the faith from the "Nile to the Bight of Biafra." Adama eventually made the municipality of Yola on the Benue (Bénoué) river his capital and subsequently undertook campaigns that extended the emirate as far south as the Bamoun sultanate of Foumban, including the towns of Banyo and Tibati, "southeast to Ngaoundéré; east to Rei, on a tributary of the Benué; northeast to Maroua, Mindiji, and Bogo; and north up to parts of Bornu and including much of the Mandara kingdom, whose combined forces he had defeated in 1823."[45] Adama's children later extended and consolidated the empire their father had created. However, they were not able to enjoy their successes, because invading European powers eventually forced them to recapitulate and allow their kingdoms to become part of the new colonies that were founded in the late nineteenth century.

Notes

1. Victor T. LeVine, *The Cameroon Federal Republic* (Ithaca, NY: Cornell University Press, 1971), pp. 1–3.

2. John Mukum Mbaku, "Cameroon's Stalled Transition to Democratic Governance: Lessons for Africa's New Democrats," *African and Asian Studies* 1, no. 3 (2002): pp. 125–163.

3. "Cameroon Mountain," in *Standard Encyclopedia of the World's Mountains, ed.* Anthony Huxley (New York: G. P. Putnam's Sons, 1962).

4. For more details on Lake Nyos and the Oku Volcanic Field, see W. C. Evans, G. W. Kling, M. L. Tuttle, G. Tanyileke, and L. D. White, "Gas Buildup in Lake Nyos, Cameroon: The Recharge Process and Its Consequences," *Applied Geochemistry* 8 (1993): pp. 207–221.

5. "Africa," in *World Geographical Encyclopedia, Vol. I: Africa* (New York: McGraw-Hill, 1995).

6. "Core Document Forming Part of the Reports of States Parties: Cameroon, 19/06/2000" (New York: United Nations, June 19, 2000).

7. H. D. Nelson, et al., *Area Handbook for the United Republic of Cameroon* (Washington, DC: U.S. Government Printing Office, 1974): pp. 59–60.

8. Antoine Socpa, *Démocratisation et autochtonie au Cameroun: Trajectoires Regionales Divergentes* (Leiden: Université de Leyde, 2002).

9. Nelson, et al. (1974).

10. Ibid.

11. LeVine (1964), pp. 7–14.

12. Nelson, et al. (1974).

13. Ibid., p. 68.

14. Ibid., p. 68.

15. Melvin Ember and Carol R. Ember, eds., *Countries and Their Cultures,* Vol. 1 (New York: Macmillan Reference, 2001), p. 387.

16. World Bank, *African Development Indicators, 2002* (Washington, DC: World Bank, 2002), pp. 5, 15; World Bank, *World Development Report, 2002* (Washington, DC: World Bank, 2002), p. 232.

17. "Cameroon," in *The Europa World Yearbook, 2002* (London: Europa Publications, 2002), p. 926.

18. Ibid.

19. Ibid.

20. Mark W. DeLancey, *Cameroon: Dependence and Independence* (Boulder, CO: Westview Press, 1989), pp. 138–139.

21. Information in this section comes from several sources, the most important of which are LeVine (1964); Harry R. Rudin, *Germans in the Cameroons, 1884–1914: A Case Study in Modern Imperialism* (New Haven, CT: Yale University Press, 1938); and Nelson, et al. (1974).

22. LeVine (1964), pp. 15ff.

23. Rudin (1938), p. 249.

24. Ibid., p. 249.

25. Sanford H. Bederman, *The Cameroons Development Corporation: Partner in National Growth* (Bota, West Cameroon: CDC, 1968), pp. 396–425.

26. Ibid., p. 401.

27. Rudin (1938), pp. 334–335, 224.

28. Ibid., pp. 339–344.

29. LeVine (1964), p. 49.

30. Victor T. LeVine, *The Cameroon Federal Republic* (Ithaca, NY: Cornell University Press, 1971); Richard A. Joseph, *Radical Nationalism in Cameroun* (London: Oxford University Press, 1977); Rudin (1938).

31. LeVine (1964), p. 89.

32. Ibid., pp. 90–91.

33. Ibid., pp. 106–107.

34. Ibid., pp. 118, 9–11.

35. Ibid., p. 119.

36. Bederman (1968), pp. 15–16.

37. LeVine (1964), pp. 123–126.

38. Ibid., p. 125.

39. Claude E. Welch, *Dream of Unity: Pan-Africanism and Political Unification in West Africa* (Ithaca: Cornell University Press, 1966), pp. 155–156; LeVine (1964), pp. 195–196.

40. LeVine (1964), p. 11.

41. Ibid., p. 12.

42. This section is based on Mbaku (2002).

43. *West Africa,* September 5, 1983, p. 2049.

44. Joseph Takougang, "Cameroon at the Democratic Crossroads: The Struggle for Power and Authority in an African State," *Asian and African Studies* (Haifa) 27 (1993), pp. 241–262.

45. LeVine (1964), p. 40.

2

Religion and Worldview

CHRISTIANITY IS THE MAIN RELIGION in Cameroon. More than 50 percent of Cameroonians consider themselves Christians, 25 percent adhere to traditional religious beliefs, and about 22 percent are Muslims (mostly Sunni, Muslims of the branch of Islam that adhere to the orthodox tradition and acknowledge the first four caliphs as the rightful successors of the Prophet Mohammad). Even after converting to a non-traditional religion, many Cameroonian believers still continue to practice and respect several of their traditional beliefs. This merging of religions, however, actually enhances and deepens their overall faith. Indigenous beliefs are very important in burial and marriage ceremonies, family relationships, the rearing of children, medical practice, and other social activities.

Cameroonians are free to practice the religion of their choice as long as such practices do not violate state laws. Today, religious ceremonies remain the most popular activities for most Cameroonians, even more popular than soccer, the country's most celebrated sport. It appears that as Cameroon continues to industrialize and modernize, its people have not lost their zeal for religious practices.

Throughout the world, religion has remained a very important tool for dealing with emotional problems, providing answers to questions about the meaning of life and the various challenges that one faces on a daily basis, as well as helping individuals cope with the complex world in which they live. Individuals may seek religious advice when they are faced with devastating illness, financial insecurity, death of a loved one, personal or family disaster, conflict at work, and job loss. Cameroonians also turn to religion to find answers to their myriad problems. Hence, Cameroonians pray to God or seek the help of ancestors in the case of illness, death, and insecurity; they also seek the blessing of ancestors or God when they get married, engage on a long trip, start a new job, go to war, start a new business venture, plant a new crop, want rain for their crops, or simply want peace and tranquility within the family.

Religion and worldview in Cameroon are part of the socialization process. Throughout the years, the influence of Christianity and Islam has changed the way Cameroonians view themselves and their existence. Hence, Cameroonians' worldview is affected not only by their traditional religions, but also by the new religions that were brought with colonialism and the invading Islamic holy warriors. Although Islam is concentrated in the northern part of the country, there are significant Muslim populations in the North West province and several large cities, such as Douala and Yaoundé. In addition, several Christian missions operate in the north, especially among ethnic groups that successfully resisted conversion to Islam.

WORLDVIEW

Religion plays a critical role in Cameroonians' worldview and helps explain the origins of their societies and to a certain extent, their country, the conditions they find themselves in, the future, death and the after-life. How Cameroonians view the world around them continues to change due to changes in organized religions, notably Christianity and Islam. Religion remains an essential variable in the daily lives of Cameroonians, as it is used to explain and account for the things that happen to an individual during each day. Hence, it is quite common to hear a member of a Christian household talk of "God's will" in an effort to explain the sudden and unexplainable death of a child or cries of "witchcraft" to the same incident in a household that adheres to a traditional religion. Religion also serves as important insurance against ill-health and misfortune, and hence, is supposed to guarantee well-being, prosperity, and long life. Worship and faith are considered investments in one's self and one's family.

Many Cameroonians who subscribe to a traditional worldview are strong believers in witchcraft and the supernatural. However, many converts to both Christianity and Islam may still retain, although on a selective basis, some of their traditional beliefs. Hence, their worldview would not be exclusively informed by either Christianity or Islam but by a mixture of the new religion and traditional practices. It is not uncommon for a Christian household in Cameroon to pray to God to protect their child who is about to depart for university studies abroad and at the same time, ask their ancestors to watch over her. A father whose son has fractured his leg may take the child to the nearest dispensary for treatment (i.e., take advantage of modern medicine) but later consult a diviner to determine why the incident occurred and a "witch doctor" to make sure that it never happens again.

In villages, witches are blamed for most calamities, including health problems, absence of rain (including other weather-related problems, such as floods), crop failure, an unexplainable death, and so on. In urban areas, witches are blamed for various misfortunes, including car accidents, loss of one's job, and even the contraction of certain diseases. Witches are believed to have the power to alter destinies and, hence, one must purchase "insurance" from a "witch doctor" to prevent the type of interference with one's destiny that can prove catastrophic. Witches are also capable of transforming themselves into several objects as they seek to destroy people or interfere with their destinies. In Cameroon, the owl is the most common medium used for transformation by the country's witches. Throughout virtually all communities in Cameroon, the most effective way to deal with witches and prevent them from having a negative impact on one and his family is to consult a witch doctor. Within each community, there exists a witch doctor who can provide the tools that are needed to deal with witches and minimize their impact on the individual and his family.

Since missionaries arrived in the nineteenth century and established schools and provided Cameroonians with the opportunity to be educated in ideas from other places and societies, their worldview has continued to change. In fact, at the same time that the Baptist Missionary Society was busy establishing missions and schools along the Cameroon coast, Usuman (Osman) Dan Fodio's holy warriors were introducing Islam in the northern part of the country. These foreign religions have come to have an important impact on Cameroonians' worldview.

The two most important external influences on Cameroonians worldview are Islam and Christianity. The religious penetration of Cameroon that began in the nineteenth century came to affect virtually all aspects of the country's culture and history. Unlike traditional religions, which with only few exceptions, tended to remain localized and rarely spread beyond their local borders, both Christianity and Islam spread aggressively, with their disciples often using force to gain more converts. In the case of both Christianity and Islam, those who brought these religions to Cameroon usually claimed that acceptance provided solutions to much more than spiritual problems. In fact, many Christian missions provided facilities for the improvement of community relations, education and job training, health care, and other services that improved the physical as well as the spiritual well-being of the individual. In addition, they introduced their conservative and individualistic tendencies to the new converts and significantly altered their worldview.

Many of the traditional religions in Cameroon operate belief systems that are quite receptive to the incorporation of new ideas and gods into them. Several of these traditional religions have absorbed the new knowledge brought by foreign religions, helping them to deal with the challenges brought about by the contact of their societies with foreign cultures and belief systems. This process has made their religions dynamic and more able to deal with changing societal needs. A good example of this adaptive process is the religion of the Bamoun people, which is based on Islam, Christianity, and traditional beliefs. Sultan Njoya-Arouna, the Bamoun king who is credited with having transformed his people's religious beliefs, avoided absorption and possible destruction of his kingdom's culture, customs, and religious practices by adapting traditional beliefs to the invading influences of Islam and Christianity.

When the Islamic holy warriors set out from Nigeria to secure converts in northern Cameroon, they carried with them the belief that, if it was necessary, force would be used to change societies and individuals pervaded by corruption and immorality. Hence, the holy war (*jihad*) that was quite pervasive in the nineteenth century, set out to reform pagan societies and convert the people to Islam. The Christian missions that invaded Cameroon from the coast were equally aggressive in their efforts to convert Cameroonians and also believed that it was their duty to rid the societies they operated in of corruption and immorality. Quite often, however, conflict arose over the new religious groups' concept of corruption and immorality, on one hand, and traditionally accepted practices on the other. The *jihad* was designed to resolve such a conflict and enhance the Islamization of the new societies.

Christianity and Islam were not the only religious organizations to stress probity and morality. In fact, traditional Cameroon religions require their members to be devout, honest, faithful, and spiritual. Like Islam and Christianity, traditional religions also are expected to improve one's spiritual, as well as physical health, and enhance a believer's ability to live a full, happy, and prosperous life. Many Cameroonians believe that evil and evil spirits are very strong and defeating them requires equally strong forces. Hence, in addition to the fact that religion can help heal a believer, it can also destroy the forces of evil and bad luck, and pave the way for a more balanced and spiritual existence.

Both Islamic and Christian beliefs require that the believer be community oriented ("love-thy-neighbor-as-thyself"), and help those who are less fortunate. Most of Cameroon's traditional religions also share this approach to personal behavior and interpersonal relations. The concept of the "extended family" is an important part of traditional religious practice in most of the country. Those who are blessed and showered with wealth, property, and good health are expected to share these gifts with the less fortunate. Within the traditional Cameroon household, children are expected to respect their elders; wives are required, by tradition, to respect and obey their husbands; and conflicts within the family are expected to be resolved peacefully. All members of the family must use their talents productively, contribute to family well-being, teach their children in the customs and traditions of the ethnic group, live within their means, and avoid engaging in behaviors that could embarrass the family. Many of these attributes can be found in both Islam and Christianity.

Problems brought by industrialization, modernization, and the exchange economy have undermined many of these traditional practices. Thus, highly educated Cameroonians who are employed in the modern sector and live in the urban areas are likely to try to extricate themselves from the extended family and instead accept the Western definition of family, which limits the latter to a wife, husband, and the children. The demands of modern living have contributed to many moral lapses and forced many people into such behaviors as corruption, embezzlement, theft, violence, disrespect for one's elders, child abuse, wife beating, and other activities considered unacceptable by traditional religions. Industrialization and now globalization have challenged Cameroonians' generally accepted worldview.

INDIGENOUS RELIGIONS

There are numerous indigenous religions in Cameroon. The belief systems of basically all of them profess the existence of God or some higher being and attempt to explain the origins of the universe, people, society, and the environment in which they live. While some indigenous religions profess a single god, most of them worship several spiritual beings, including ancestral spirits. Like Christianity and Islam, indigenous religions in Cameroon have many rituals, which followers are required to perform. Some of these rituals relate to or commemorate relationships between individuals, important occasions in the group's history, and other events that have a significant negative or positive impact on the welfare of the group.

While indigenous religions in Cameroon are usually localized and ethnic group specific, they share several things in common, including the belief in God, gods, and ancestors. Within many of these religions, there are also secret societies whose membership is made up exclusively of men. The latter are charged with maintaining law and order, ensuring the education of young people to take over leadership of the religion, supervising the performance of important rituals, and generally seeing to the continued perpetuation of the religion. Some indigenous religions maintain powerful witches who are capable of destroying anyone who threatens the welfare of the community.

Religion serves an important function in the life of Cameroonians. In addition to helping explain many abstract concepts, such as the origin of the universe, religion also deals with more practical and earthly issues—it provides a foundation for secular political power. In fact, many of Cameroon's traditional rulers derive their power from the group's religion. Throughout the country, religion continues to pervade all forms of social life. Religious rituals are used to celebrate a marriage, welcome the birth of a child, seek help from ancestors for several problems, including poor harvests, droughts, and external threats to the group, prepare recently deceased loved ones for their trips to meet their ancestors, and deal with other issues important to the group.

External influences, especially colonialism (including the slave trade) and globalization, have had a significant impact on the type of religions and religious practices that have emerged in Cameroon during the last century. Three traditional religions and the societies in which they are practiced will be examined here. First are the Gbaya, a fiercely independent people located both in Cameroon and the Central African Republic. Next are the Nso', a proud and passionate people, who throughout the years, have been very protective of their traditions, especially the monarchy. Finally, one of Cameroon's most famous kingdoms, the Bamoun, is discussed.

Gbaya Religion

Written and oral narratives dating back to 1840 describe Gbaya society as consisting of "many small groupings of families, scattered thinly over the savanna, that were loosely organized into territorially defined units containing several hundred people."[1] Today, the Gbaya are found primarily in the southeastern part of Cameroon, along the border and in Central African Republic.

In 1840, the Gbaya were forced to confront invading Muslim Fulani holy warriors, who had entered Cameroon from the north in response to Usuman Dan Fodio's call for a holy war to spread Islam. Although many Gbaya leaders and a few other men converted to Islam, this new religion has not seriously undermined the traditional beliefs of most Gbaya. Gbaya religion, especially of the precolonial and early colonial period, can be described as "a collection of separate rites and beliefs, including sacrifices to a man's immediate male and female ancestors, group sacrifices to a spirit specific to the locality where each Gbaya group lived, and a number of other rites oriented towards the achievement of success or good fortune in undertakings such as hunting, warfare, or relations between the sexes."[2] The Gbaya belief system included witchcraft, which was used to explain death, sickness, droughts, and other natural phenomena. A variety of rites were also critical to Gbaya religious practice and were used to prepare young men for leadership positions in society, and women for serving as wives and mothers. Within Gbaya society, however, beliefs often varied from individual to individual and from group to group, and there were no priests or full-time religious leaders to articulate and formulate religious doctrine. In addition, there were no churches or educational institutions to stabilize, standardize, and direct the propagation of religious, as well as cultural beliefs. Although certain people within Gbaya society, as a result of their age and experience, often served as diviners and leaders of religious rites, religious practice in Gbaya society did not have permanent and stable leadership.

One of the most important characteristics of the Gbaya belief system is individualism, a trait that remains to this day. Each person is expected to be responsible for his own beliefs, and as such, conversion of an individual to another religion can take place without producing significant conflict within Gbaya society and culture. It is not unusual to find within a Gbaya family members who belong to different religions, living together peacefully with each other. Hence, the Gbaya's individualism has allowed the society to absorb the shock of religious invasion without major trauma or significant social dislocation.[3]

Central and critical to the belief system of the Gbaya is the concept of *so* or *Gbaso,* which was translated by early European travelers as God. In one sense, *so* refers to the genies or spirits that inhabit the forests around Gbaya territories, and on the other, it designates God or the Great Spirit. Some students of Gbaya traditions state that in the early thought of the group, *Gbaso* may have referred to a supreme God—that is, the God of creation, but that in current Gbaya belief, this is no longer true.[4] Within Gbaya society today, oral narratives refer to *Gbaso* as a "vicious" creature who resides in the forest or plains, places that are considered inappropriate for human habitation. In Gbaya tales about powers that are capable of and do destroy life, *Gbaso* is mentioned as devouring women and children who stray into his territory, and hence, is considered an enemy.

Within several Gbaya riddles, one also finds *Gbaso* mentioned. Although *Gbaso* in the context of these riddles appears to be supernatural, it is important to note that most of these riddles are told for fun and amusement. Based on such evidence, many interpreters of Gbaya tradition now exclude *Gbaso* from the group's concept of God and instead take note of *So* or *So-e-wi,* meaning, "God-place-man," or the great God who created the universe and everything in it. The origin of this creator, however, is not known.[5] *So* (proper noun) sits alone at the top, followed in ascending order by other categories of *so* (common noun) with the *so-kao* coming first, and below them, the *so-daa.*

In Gbaya tradition, *so-kao* were the natural spirits or gods that were associated with several inexplicable phenomena or natural wonders such as huge mountains, tall trees, and large bodies of water. Among the Gbaya of Cameroon, the word *kao* means a collection of spirits or many manifestations of a single Great Spirit. The *so-daa* were the spirits of departed kin or ancestors and hence, were considered the spirits closest to humans.

As the creator and the source of all life, *So* is considered by the Gbaya to be good. However, in this world, the Gbaya argued, there were forces, such as *Gbaso,* that destroyed life. In addition, the world also contained rain and sunshine, which enhanced life. However, too much or too little of either of them produced horrible consequences. As such, God was considered to be capricious.

According to some Gbaya, God's original intention was that after birth, man would live, die, be buried, and then eventually rise again. However, man became impatient and wanted to find out if death was the end of life. A great man decided to send an emissary to God to find out about life after death. First, he sent a chameleon to seek answers. Then, unable to wait for the slow-moving chameleon to complete his task, the great man sent a toad to search for answers to life after death. The fast-moving toad was able to overtake the chameleon and arrived at God's abode only to find God quite angry. God's anger was caused first by the fact that he was being questioned about life after death, and second, by the fact that the messenger was such an ugly creature. His answer, delivered in anger, was: "Yes, it is all over. When a man dies, all that remains is to weep over him and dig the grave and that's all. Tell that to the big man!"[6] The toad took the message back to the great man and the chameleon eventually returned with the same message: There is no life after death.

Misfortune in a man's life was often attributed to some behavior that had injured some ancestor. Hence, it was necessary for the man to undertake expiation to calm the spirit of the injured ancestor and thus, assure that no more misfortune would befall him. Among the Gbaya, many people often undertook regular rituals of propitiation as insurance against misfortune. After the death of a man, his son would plan rituals to be carried out at regular intervals to appease the departed's soul. The dead man's eldest son was usually chosen to lead the performance of the rituals and ensure that no misfortune befalls relatives left behind. Families engaged in such rituals to appease ancestral spirits and minimize misfortunes to members. Each village prayed to the spirit of the land to intervene and protect it from such catastrophes as floods, droughts, and other dangerous natural phenomena, and bless it with bumper crops, victory against their enemies, good hunts, and peace.

Gbaya religious practice acknowledges and accepts creation, as well as the fact that God created man and the world in which he leaves. It also speaks clearly of a destiny for man: man will die and move on to another world, which is an extension of this one and where his ancestors, who had preceded him in death, now live. In this world, *So* (God) is an explicit and critical part. Although the Gbaya accepted death, they still considered it a sad end to man's physical existence; it took away loved ones, important community leaders, skilled providers, wives and mothers, and often children before they grew up to be contributing members of society. Death, then, was something to be feared and in many cases, abhorred.

Although God was considered quite distant, he was not an inactive being, but one who remained quite involved in human affairs. Unfortunately, man could not approach him as easily as he did his brother or neighbor. As a consequence, mediation was critical. Departed fathers served as mediators. In addition, the *so-kao* who lived in this world but who also belonged to the other world where *so* lived, were also mediators between each village and God.

Foreign religions (notably Christianity and Islam) have been among the Gbaya since the nineteenth century, and along with colonialism, urbanization and the exchange economy, have profoundly affected Gbaya traditional beliefs. *So-kao* and *so-daa* have diminished significantly in importance and in some communities are rarely mentioned. However, the old religions remain an important determinant of the Gbaya way of life and worldview. In fact, among Gbaya who have converted to either Islam or Christianity, one can find many influences of traditional religion. Many aspects of Gbaya traditional religion continue to influence both the Christian church and Islam as practiced in Gbaya villages and communities.

The Gbaya have always viewed religion in practical and pragmatic terms. Hence, religion was not used to seek answers to abstract phenomena but to deal with the needs of the life lived here on earth. One may interpret the Gbaya response to Christianity as another instrument for coping with existing needs. For, under the pressures imposed on the people by colonialism, the traditional religion did not appear to be able to provide adequate and effective answers or solutions. Christianity appeared to satisfy many emerging needs—it was able to, much more so than the old religion, deal with illness, and hunger. Of course, the approaches used by the missions to secure converts appeared to indicate to the Gbaya that Christianity was as pragmatic as the old religion. For one thing, Christian missions often brought along with them a message of salvation, medicine and education, which were considered by the Gbaya as practical and useful for everyday life. Access to both education and missionary-provided health care, however, were tied to the acceptance of the message. While this approach to evangelization worked in the early days to secure members for the Christian churches, it is no longer as effective today. This is because most of the things (e.g., education and medicine) that could only be obtained through acceptance of the faith can now be secured other ways. Money can now buy all these things, even for people who are not Christians or Muslims.[7]

Nso' Religion

Proud and passionate about their traditions and beliefs, the Nso' can be found in the northeast corner of Cameroon's North West Province. Recent estimates put the population of this grassfields group at more than a quarter of a million people. Its capital is Kumbo (Kimbo'), where the king's (fon) palace and the lodges of the group's male secret societies are located.[8]

Written and oral narratives show that the Nso' believe in a Supreme Being called *Nyuy* (God), as well as in *anyuy* (divinities and divinized ancestors). However, Nso' traditional religion did not have a formal written creed or places of worship where all believers could congregate and worship. Worship was carried out primarily through rituals that were celebrated at both the individual and community level. Two important rituals are associated with the powers *Nyuy* and *anyuy: cu,* which is part of the worship of *Nyuy,* and *ntanri,* used to honor ancestors and seek their intervention on issues important to individuals and the community. At the beginning of the Nso' year, the main country-wide *cu* is held, usually about the middle of March.

The country-wide *cu* mandates trips by a royal sacrificial team, which includes the fon, his sacrificial deputy (the *Taawon*) and his female counterpart (the *Yeewon*) to several sacred sites. Sometimes, participants in these trips would include previous sacrificial assistants to the fon. Also included in this important journey are individuals who officiate at royal burials (*vibay ve duy* or *ve kpu*), cadet royals who are descendants of earlier *ataawon,* the *won jemer ve fon* or the classificatory sisters' sons of the fon, who serve at royal burials and seek out witchcraft that is detrimental to the welfare of the kingdom. The *ataanto',* who are often charged with carrying and caring for the objects used in the *cu* ritual, are also part of the team. Also, the presence of the installer and the fon's most senior councilor, *Ndzeendzev,* is required. Special objects are required for the ceremony and these must be secured and taken along on the trip. These include palm wine contained in the "calabash of the country," camwood in the "bag of the country," and the "double-bell of the country."

The sequence in which the sacred sites would be visited is not fixed or determined in advance. All *cu* journeys of significant importance (those, for example, that end at the Old Palace site at *Kovvifem,* and the present Palace and its environs at Kumbo, those ending at "the house of the country and royal graveyard at *Kovvifem,* as well as at the refuge site of *Taavisa'* where there is a royal grave, and at the Palace in Kumbo")[9] end with the sacrifice of a ram. In today's ceremonies, the remains of the animal sacrificed are shared between the installer (*Ndzeendzev*) and the *vibay ve duy.* Usually, the fon does not partake of the sacrificial ram.

In each lineage tract among the Nso', the lineage head organizes and carries out the *cu.* Each compound's *taala'* visits his ritual sites (*vire ve anyuy*) and bestows gifts (e.g., kola nuts and wine) on everyone he encounters along the way. The Nso' believe that during such sojourns, one could meet a god (*Nyuy*) who is disguised as an earthling, most likely a stranger passing through the village. Showing kindness to such a stranger could produce blessings for the family in particular, and the community in general. At each ritual site, the lineage head recited prayers that were similar to those recited by the fon or his deputy during their own visits to the sacred sites.

The second main ritual called *ntanri,* was designed to honor ancestors. Within this important ceremony are included the sacrifices that family members offer to the dead at funerals, as well as the specific intervention sacrifices made during special occasions. The primary objects for this ritual include palm wine, a fowl, camwood, and palm oil. Camwood has always been used in many Nso' ceremonies, including the preparation of the bodies of the dead for burial. The sacrifice usually takes place on the threshold of the main lineage house (*faay-woo-ku'un-ne*) and on this spot, a mixture of camwood and oil is sprinkled. Propitiation of the dead at Kumbo Palace is undertaken by smearing the threshold of the *nggay* (the assembly hall of the dynastic group). This ritual is directed by a *taanto'.* In the case of a deceased fon, the sacrifice is performed by the *Taawon* and in the fon's grave-hut. The actual ritual involves offering invocations while a fowl is killed and its beak torn apart. Those participating in the ritual, including the audience, watch the movements of the fowl very closely, until it is completely dead. The bird's behavior during the ceremony is interpreted carefully as it indicates whether the sacrifice has been accepted by the dead. If the beak tears easily and the dying bird hops toward the sacrificer, this is an indication that the ceremony has pleased the ancestor and is accepted.

At Nso' burial ceremonies for important dignitaries, ancestral spirits are called upon to bless the people and bestow on them economic prosperity, as well as peace, good health, and lots of children. This same invocation is usually repeated when palm wine is poured at the door of the lineage house (*faay-woo-ku'un-ne*). The wine for this ceremony is carried in a special vessel called the pot of the dead (*kiikpu*). In such wine pouring rituals, the one carrying out the ceremony seeks ancestors' blessings and the bestowal on him, his family, and the larger community of good health, good harvest, and many children.

Attendance at the *anyuy* (rituals to honor ancestors) is dominated by younger members of the patrilineage. Those officiating at the *anyuy* are expected to spread the news of the *ntanri* as widely as possible among the members of the lineage. It is believed that a successful ceremony is one that is well publicized. After the ritual is completed, the individual officiating takes for himself, the most prestigious parts of the fowl—the neck and the entrails. The rest of the participants are given a piece of the bird each, no matter how small it is.

Within Nso' tradition, three forms of sacrifice used to honor ancestors are very important. First is the *saay anyuy,* which is performed following the death of any individual who, while alive, had had "baptismal pots" set up in their compounds. The pots are used during ceremonies marking the final naming of twins or other special children, as well as for their medication. Second, is the *ntanri-menwer,* a ritual used to honor the remotest ancestor that can be identified or traced, to, as described by Banadzem,[10] "mollify him or her when some offence or neglect was presumed, and which still needed to be resolved and forgiven." Finally, is the *sov-kidiv* (which literally means "piercing the calabash," with piercing used in the metaphorical sense to imply uncovering the truth). The *sov-kidiv,* whose performance required the same sacrificial objects as for a normal *ntanri,* was usually called for when it was determined that there still existed an unresolved breach between an ancestor and his descendants. To determine the failure or success of the ceremony, a small calabash was filled with palm wine and heated until the liquid boiled. Then a straw was inserted into the container containing the boiling wine and if the central vortex kept the straw in an upright position, then it was concluded that the ritual had been accepted.

The worldview of the Nso' was influenced significantly by a series of beliefs. First, is the belief in *sem,* a psychic power that is said to be possessed by some people within Nso' society. The power can be used for good or evil. For example, in the hands of opportunistic, greedy, and unethical individuals, the power can be misused. Such *sem* is associated with human witches. The fon was said to possess *sem* of the highest order (royal *sem*) and which was used for good. Within Nso' society, the fon was not the only one endowed with *sem vifon.* There were others who possessed the latter and were involved in the performance of good deeds as diviners and healers, usually to cancel the evil deeds of witches, who were using their *sem* to damage the welfare of the community.

Legend has it that *sem* was acquired through the uterine line and could be modified or reinforced. For example, "children stolen by God" (*nyuy shon wan*) usually returned with their psychic powers reinforced and now possessing royal *sem* and other powers. To make sure that these children did not grow up to misuse their powers, they had to be nurtured and trained properly so that they could develop into healers or medicine men who were capable of counteracting the evil unleashed on society by witches.

The second is belief in curative techniques called *shiv* or medicine. Distinction is made between natural or human-made objects that have intrinsic power to heal or have that power placed in them during their production, and curative plants. Several of these objects can be placed in packets or in the shells of snails and buried, or placed in such objects as bags and horns and hung from doorways in order to protect one's property from thieves. The power within these objects is supposed to inflict illness, misfortune, and other bad things on trespassers or those attempting to damage or illegally seize one's property. Liquid or powdered medicine could also be applied to cuts to make the individual's flesh unpleasant to cannibal witches and hence, prevent the latter from consuming the individual. The most important *shiv* was the barrier medicine, which was prepared in the fon's palace and placed at the entrance to houses and at road junctions throughout all of Nso' country "to avert the overflight of hostile *sem* which caused blighted crops, bareness and wasting diseases."[11] The other category of Nso' curative techniques used herbal remedies and massage to deal with such things as fractures, rashes, burns, asthma, hemorrhoids, and other common illnesses. In some instances, these traditional remedies have been more successful in dealing with several types of illnesses, especially psychiatric problems, than modern Western medicine.

Third, is the belief that the earth is endowed with very special powers. It is perceived as being both an animate and inanimate object, which is more powerful than other animate objects. Many Nso' considered the earth capable of resolving all problems. For one thing, it is where ancestors dwell and from there could intervene on behalf of their descendants. Hence, the earth was said to intervene and render justice when human institutions were incapable of doing so, as well as severely punish those who had sought its help for evil or opportunistic purposes. The earth could bestow godly gifts on individuals and communities, and it also provided those things (e.g., water, food crops, animals) that were used to sustain human life.

Finally, is the belief in kingship. The kingship and its attributes were considered sacred. It was forbidden for ordinary people to touch the fon or his things (notably his stool, staff, and calabash). These things, like the earth, were said to possess powers that were capable of rendering judgment. For example, oaths could be taken on these things and if the oath-taker lied or made false testimony, he or she could be punished severely.

The introduction of Christianity and Islam has had an important impact on Nso' religious practices. Three of the most important Christian churches working in Nso' country today are the Roman Catholic Church, the Presbyterian Church, and the Cameroon Baptist Church. Although these religious groups remain competitive in their efforts to secure members, they also cooperate in several projects designed to enhance the welfare of the communities in which they operate. For example, in recent years, all three Christian denominations have been jointly involved in the translation of the New Testament into the Lam Nso' language.

Contact by the Nso' with world religions was first made with Islam. Research has still not revealed the real date when the first contact was made. However, in the 1880s, Hausa kola nut traders were in regular contact with the Nso' and there were occasional Fulani grazers who passed through the territory on their way to German posts. After British occupation in 1916, larger numbers of Fulani herdsmen arrived, leading to disputes between them and local farmers over grazing lands. Unlike Muslims in other parts of West Africa who were aggressive, condescending to non-believers, and often violent in their evangelization efforts, the Muslims of Nso' (all of them Sunni) have, throughout the years, been accommodating and as a result, have been able to convert influential members of the community. These Muslims have been able to exercise a significant level of influence because of their honesty (especially in their commercial dealings), integrity, and the success of their medical practices. In the 1960s, when relations with their Bamoun neighbors and the Tikar of Bankim improved, then Nso' ruler, Fon Sem II (Mbinkar Mbinlo) implemented public policies that favored the Muslims. For example, he provided them with land near the palace for a mosque and adopted some Islamic practices. However, he died a Christian, although at the time of his death, he still had his 100 wives. Despite the fact that Islam was quite close ideologically to Nso' traditional religion, both citizens and their leaders came to believe that Christianity offered more prospects for the social and economic development of the society and more effective tools to deal with the challenges imposed by external forces, including colonialism. Perhaps more important was the fact that the Nso' thought that Christianity offered more attractive ethical values.

The Roman Catholic Church arrived in Cameroon (Kamerun) in 1890 and its leaders were directed by German colonial authorities to seek out those areas in which there were no Protestant missions. In addition, the church was prohibited by colonial authorities from undertaking conversion missions to the Muslim-dominated northern part of the colony. The Basel Mission, which had taken over from the English Baptist Missionary Society after German annexation in 1884, was already firmly established in several areas throughout the colony, including Bali, Fumban (Fouban), and Bagam. The Presbyterian Church took over the activities of the Basel Mission after independence. The new Catholic mission to Nso' came from the German Province of the *Sacerdotes Cordis Jesu* (Sittard Fathers) and arrived during the last days of 1912 and acquired land at Shisong. They impressed the fon by promising to build a school to educate young boys. In fact, the fon sent several young royals and retainers to be educated at the school. Religious sisters later joined the Sittard Fathers and established a school where girls could be educated, primarily in home economics. However, the work of this religious order was terminated by World War I. After the war and with Nso' now part of the British Southern Cameroons, the Vatican replaced the French Fathers (who had taken over control of the mission after the defeat of Germany) with "Mill Hill Fathers."

While the notions of the *sem* and *shiv* are still alive, they have been modernized, no longer carry their previous social and spiritual significance, and are eventually fading away. In fact, many of the names associated with the old rituals have been replaced with names that are compatible with Christian meanings such as *Kinyuy, Berinyuy,* and *Suinyuy.* The most important influence of Nso' tradition and culture on the Christian church is the use of religious Lam Nso' (language) in church services. The Catholic mass, for example, is called *cu* and the priest is described as *ngaa-cu,* a throw-back to traditional religious rites. Christianity continues to remain relevant to the Nso' as they struggle to find their place within a modern Cameroon nation.

Bamoun Religion

In late 1915, the British army reached Foumban, the capital of the Kingdom of Bamoun (Bamum) in what had been the German colony of Kamerun. German Christian missionaries, like other Germans in the colony, were forced to leave. When Christian missionaries of the German Basel Mission arrived in the area at the beginning of the twentieth century, the King's entourage (counselors of the kingdom, the great officers of the Palace, and servants) had joined the King in his practice of Islamic rituals. However, when the King decided to listen to the new Christian missionaries, several subjects decided to do likewise. The King and several parents sent their children to the new Mission school even though they continued to practice Islamic rituals. In addition, the King's subjects continued to engage in their traditional religious observances.[12]

After the German Christian missionaries departed in 1915, the incoming British administration advised the King to return to the practice of Islam, which he did for a while.[13] However, in 1916, the King introduced a new religion of salvation, which he believed would more effectively serve the needs of his people. The foundation of the new religion lay in the King's understanding of Islam and Christianity. The text was composed in a form of writing (the *a ka u ku mfe mfe* alphabet), which the King himself had composed at the end of the nineteenth century. The text of the new doctrine of salvation was named *nuet nkuete* (*Pursue to Attain*). The King believed that through concerted effort, his subjects "would accept the religious foundations of the religions of salvation, Christianity and Islam, whose similarities [King] Njoya had been struck by, and would respect the practices which the King had borrowed from the Mâlikite rite."[14] King Njoya's decision to create a new religion can only be understood in the context of historical developments in Kamerun (Cameroon) in the nineteenth century, how those developments affected the Kingdom of Bamoun, and the challenges faced by the King.[15]

When King Njoya succeeded his father in 1885, he was too young to govern. As was the tradition of the Kingdom, the great officer of the Palace, who at the time was the *Titamfon* Gbetnkom Ndombuo, was, along with the young sovereign's mother, supposed to safeguard the regency, and retire to the country when the young sovereign became the true master of the kingdom. Such maturity was supposed to have been attained between 1892 and 1896. However, shortly after Njoya ascended the throne, the *Titamfon,* who hoped to replace the King with one of his brothers, initiated a rebellion, which eventually threw the country into civil war. The sovereign decided to seek help from the Muslim Fulbe, who had migrated from Nigeria during the great *jihads* and now occupied most of the Adamawa (Adamaoua) Plateau. Responding favorably to the King's request was the Fulbe Lamido of Banyo, who intervened between 1895 and 1897. Invoking the name of God, as required by Islamic tradition, the Lamido's army quickly defeated the enemy, captured the former *Titamfon* and subsequently burned him alive. The Fulbe's quick and impressive victory was to have a significant impact on Bamoun society. Asked by the curious Bamoun what the source of their power was, the Fulbe replied that it came from the prayer to God.

Shortly afterward, the Bamoun sovereign decided to acquire for his own people those things that had given the Fulbe their extraordinary military power: horses, writing, and knowledge of the several rites that the Fulbe had told him were responsible for their military prowess. He quickly put together a cavalry and with the help of his entourage, he devised a writing system, which was different from the Arabic used by the Fulbe teachers (or *marabouts*). He then secured a few *marabouts* from the Lamido of Banyo to instruct him in Islamic practices. The King's overall objective in undertaking all these activities was to make his kingdom as militarily powerful as the Fulbe who dominated political economy in the Adamawa Plateau. Hausa *marabouts* taught the King and his entourage how to pray and he subsequently built a mosque in front of the Palace and the kingdom's first Ramadan (Islam's holy month) fast took place before the nineteenth century was over.

When Germans arrived in Bamoun country in 1902, Njoya was forced to suspend his experiments with Islam. Christian missionaries belonging to the Basel Mission had established missions in the nearby Bali-Nyonga kingdom, where the Germans had placed their first military garrison in the grassfields region of the colony of Kamerun. Some of the missionaries from Bali-Nyonga visited Foumban, intending to proselytize and establish churches in the kingdom. The sovereign gave permission to the missionaries to establish a mission in Foumban and requested that they build a school, similar to the one that had been provided the people of Bali-Nyonga. In 1906, the Basel Mission established a presence in Foumban, and, as requested by the king, they established a school. A church replaced the mosque and the king and the Christians forged a new relationship. The king closely followed the progress of the students, came to school to learn, attended Sunday services and listened to the pastor preach, and participated in catechism classes. By this time, the script invented by the king had been polished and was used to translate hymns, extracts from the Bible, and texts used for catechism instruction.

The missionaries were eager to expand their church in Bamoun country and believed that baptism of the King would enhance their ability to secure more converts. However, given that the King had several hundred wives, and, by tradition, could not part with them, his baptism was quite a complicated issue. In addition, his counselors opposed his baptism into the Christian faith. Given the political implications of the marriages of princesses, the King did not allow any of his daughters to marry Christians. By 1910, it had become evident to the Christian missionaries that their influence in the Bamoun kingdom would be quite limited. In 1915, advancing British troops captured and deported the German missionaries and subsequently encouraged Njoya to return to Islam. He did, but only briefly, and by 1916, the King decided to develop a new religion of salvation based on Islam and to a certain extent, Christianity, but adapted to Bamoun traditional beliefs.

In the kingdom of Bamoun, the King was the supreme ruler who was assisted by a group of counselors. The latter were the keepers and guardians of tradition, although together with the King, they could change these customs and traditions. In addition to being the sovereign, the King was also the priest of the traditional religion, which was dedicated to the royal ancestors—the latter are said to have transmitted their power to the King during his coronation. Each Bamoun King told the counselors in confidence which of his sons he had chosen as his successor. At any time, the King had with him six great palace officials, three of whom were of princely ancestry, and the others of palatine origin.

The King's palace was his official residence and housed his several hundred wives, their children, and the many servants. Within the palace were also found many secret societies and the special council responsible for policy, including justice, in the kingdom. The rear of the Palace was reserved exclusively for the King and it was in this area that the shrines assigned to the various cults were kept. Among these were the house where the King met the royal wives in the evening; the house where several protective powers and objects were stored, and the "house of the country," the graveyard for the interment of Bamoun sovereigns. At the front of the palace was the residence of various secret societies on whose courtyards one could find the stones used to make libations and sacrifices.

Within Bamoun society, the rituals, sacrifices, libations, and prayers were directed at ancestors and divinities called *penyinyi*.[16] Bamoun society believed in the after-life and worship of ancestors. It was believed that dead relatives could communicate with their kinfolk through dreams. Ancestors meted out punishment for the transgression of the various laws (i.e., customs), which they had helped develop to regulate sociopolitical interaction and ensure peace.

The *penyinyi* were little gods found in nature but whose origins were unknown to the Bamoun. These gods rewarded good deeds and punished those who transgressed the laws. The Bamoun belief system also acknowledged the existence of evil spirits (the *pagüm* or the singular *nzum*), which like the *penyinyi* were found in nature. The *pagüm,* however, were capable of inhabiting the belly of a person and living there. Women (but not men) who hosted a *nzum* could transmit it to their male and female descendants. Unlike the *penyinyi,* the *pagüm* imposed only harm on individuals (e.g., illness and death). A *nzum* living within an individual's belly could act without the host's knowledge or permission.

The sacrifice was one of the most important and solemn rituals in Bamoun society and its execution was strictly regulated by custom and tradition. During the feast, which marked the end of the harvest, the King executed the necessary sacrifices on the graves of those who had ruled before him and on the skull of his father located in the "house of the country." After necessary repairs to the palace were completed, the King also made sacrifices as required by tradition. Sacrifices were also made on important occasions throughout the year.

Other sacrifices were made at the lineage level by the *nzi* according to the same calendar as used by the King. Animals used in the various sacrifices included dogs, poultry, and goats. Rams and cattle were used only in the Palace. Blood was considered to be very critical to the sacrifice since it nourished the recipients of each sacrifice. Each rite was usually accompanied by libations and prayers, in which palm-wine, sorghum or millet beers (which had properties similar to those of blood) were used. The ritual of pouring libations was not reserved for sacrifices. The great officers of the palace poured libations in the house where the sovereign met his wives and in the "house in the country" on a specified day of the Bamoun week. Secret society heads also poured libations at the altars under their supervision. At a lower level, lineage heads poured libations at the thresholds of houses and at crossroads. Finally, corn porridge was left in the open for the *penyinyi* to feed on.

Access to the palace graveyard was strictly controlled. Only the King, crown counselors, the great officers of the palace who were of palatine origin, and the twins who were guardians of the graveyard were allowed to have access to it. No one else was allowed to enter the Palace graveyard, not even the King's brothers and his sons.

Prayer was very important in Bamoun society. The term used for prayer was *nzuom,* but the latter also covered an oath—as in the installation of a new Counselor of the Kingdom. The *nzoum* was recited at various occasions, including burial of a dead person, investiture of an heir, installation of the King, swearing-in of new judges, and so on. The *nzoum* was also recited during certain occasions in personal relationships. For example, a wife accused of adultery affirmed her innocence by uttering a prayer that called on misfortune and bad luck to fall on her if she had ever seen the nakedness of a man other than her husband. Prayers to affirm one's innocence were usually invoked in the name of ancestors and the *penyinyi,* which were supposed to punish the person saying the prayers if he or she lied. Hence, individuals who had actually committed the infractions they were accused of never uttered such prayers. In addition, soldiers on their way to war prayed and individuals about to embark on an important journey also prayed.

The *nzuom* usually performed two important functions, depending on how it was offered. A *nzuom* directed to an imagined future was expected to protect the existing social order (e.g., maintain good relations between a man and his wife). If it referred to transgressions committed by the people uttering the prayer, it then served as proof of the transgression, for no one "would bring misfortune on themselves by pronouncing a *nzuom* unless they believed themselves innocent."[17]

Within the palace were several wooden carvings of animal and human figures, which were coated with several substances including clay, camwood powder, and covered with leaves or bird-feathers. These items were called "forces that prohibit." If they were kept in one's house or on the farm, they served to prevent the entry of misfortune. Various powders made of vegetable ingredients were used as medicine. One could use these medicines, for example, as protection against miscarriage or to ensure success in hunting or war.

Bamoun rituals were designed to guarantee health, prosperity, and the social order. They also served as insurance against an uncertain future—to counteract any events that might bring turmoil to or threaten the welfare of the kingdom.

The religion that King Njoya created in the twentieth century is detailed in the text that he wrote. Within these 30 chapters, he details the doctrinal foundation of the new religion, enumerates the laws of God, those things that he considers good and those that he believes are bad, and the consequences of individual behavior. Throughout the text, the influence of the teachings of the Islamic scholars is clearly evident.

To embrace Islam and show obedience to the will of God, one had to first undergo a rite of purification, which involved washing one's genitals, as well as scrubbing one's head and neck several times. That was followed by a chant of the *chahada,* after which the individual then washed his shoulders and forearms. King Njoya's text calls for 5 daily prayers, with the Friday middle of the day prayer to be said at the mosque, which he had rebuilt. The Muslim ritual calendar determined the timetable for fasting; sacrifices were to be made at a date corresponding to the *Aïd al Kebir* and the individual was required to give alms to the poor. The King's new religion does not require a pilgrimage to Mecca and the Bamoun language rather than Arabic is the language of the religion.

The King disseminated his doctrine during 1916 and 1917, at a time when he displayed a certain level of hostility toward Christianity. Christian schools were replaced by royal schools at which Bamoun script and the history of the country were taught. At the end of 1917, the King gave up his doctrinal project and returned to the practice of Islam. However, today in Bamoun country, Christian, Islamic, and traditional rituals continue to influence the people's lives and their worldview.

CHRISTIANITY

Although many reasons are advanced to explain the annexation of African territories by Europeans and the subsequent founding of colonies, four of them stand out: (1) economics—a search for raw materials to feed metropolitan industries and for markets to sell excess output; (2) political interests, which included territorial expansion; (3) the desire to spread Christianity among pagan populations; and (4) the civilizing imperative—to spread European civilization among the peoples of the world. Although Christian missions were already at work on the Cameroon coast before official German colonization took place in July 1884, after colonization these missions were able to undertake successful evangelization missions inland. Religion, of course, itself became an instrument of colonial politics as Christian missionaries collaborated with the colonialists in the development and execution of colonial policies.

Missionaries often served as interpreters and judges and provided other services that were critical to the administration of certain parts of the colony, especially in the hinterland. In exchange, the colonial government provided the Christian missionaries with several benefits, including financial resources for their work and protection against competing religions (as is illustrated by the part played by the Spanish colonial government in Fernando Po in the expulsion of the Baptist Missionary Society to make way for expansion by Spanish Jesuits). In fact, in the early years of colonialism, many of the interpreters who worked for the colonial government were trained at schools owned and operated by missionary bodies.

As Cameroon became more developed and industrialized, and new professions (e.g., modern medicine, engineering, nursing, and law) began to emerge, individuals came to recognize secular education as the most common path to them. At the time, the only place to obtain such advanced training was to go to Europe or the United States. However, to do so, individuals would have had to have completed primary and secondary education, all of which at the time could only be obtained at institutions owned and operated by missionary societies. In addition, traveling abroad for advanced training required that the prospective student mobilize an enormous amount of resources. Many students were not able to do so. So, they had to depend on financial assistance from the colonial government and from Christian churches in the metropolitan countries. In fact, for many years, scholarships offered by churches in the United Kingdom, the United States, France, and Germany have been responsible for the training of many Cameroonians. Many of these churches are the same ones that sponsor the several Christian missions in Cameroon.

Today, in Cameroon, Christianity and Islam remain very attractive because they offer many opportunities for education, mobility, networking, and new answers to personal problems, especially those brought about by foreign influences (e.g., modernization, industrialization, and urbanization).

Freed Jamaican Slaves and the Introduction of Christianity in Cameroon

The liberation of Jamaican slaves on August 1, 1838 had a significant impact on the establishment of Christian missions on the Cameroon coast. One year after emancipation, Jamaican Baptists proposed to the London-based Baptist Missionary Society (BMS) the establishment of a mission to West Africa. The BMS had been active in the anti-slavery crusade and had been quite successful in gaining converts among Jamaican slaves. The newly freed slaves wanted to start a new mission, independent of the BMS, that would participate in a unique way in the propagation of Christianity in Africa. The mission that the Jamaican Christians hoped to found was also expected to enhance the repatriation of freed slaves from the Caribbean to Africa. In the spring of 1840, BMS missionary William Knibb, and two Jamaican Baptists, Henry Beckford and Edward Barrett, formally appealed for the creation of a mission to West Africa. In agreeing to establish a new mission field in West Africa to be staffed primarily by Jamaicans, the BMS indicated that it would only support white and black missionaries that it had appointed and not freed Jamaican slaves who planned to go to Africa as settlers. In 1842, Jamaican Baptists created the Jamaican Baptist Missionary Society (JBMS).

On January 1, 1841, an advance BMS party consisting of the Reverend John Clarke, George K. Prince, a medical doctor and former slave owner, arrived at Clarence on the island of Fernando Po. Their intention was to stop at Clarence en route to the interior of Nigeria. However, given the extraordinary warm welcome accorded them by the head of the British naval squadron, as well as pleas from freed slaves for the establishment of a Christian mission on the island, the missionaries decided to stay. They subsequently established a worship center at Clarence in 1842. That year, Thomas Sturgeon arrived from England and freed both Clarke and Prince so they could return to their families and also recruit more volunteers from England and Jamaica for the new mission. Notable among the new recruits were Joseph Merrick and Alfred Saker, individuals who were to play an important part in the founding of Christian missions in Cameroon.

By 1846, the mission on the island of Fernando Po had reached its apex. However, several problems, including the susceptibility of the missionaries to endemic diseases, opposition of newly arrived Spanish Jesuits to the work of the Baptist missionaries, racial attitudes of the day—the Jamaicans had thought they were equals to the English but later found out that this was not so, and the lack of financial support from the BMS, forced the missionaries at Clarence to consider abandoning the mission and moving into the interior. By 1845, Joseph Merrick had left Clarence and entered Cameroon. A proclamation from the Spanish governor of Fernando Po on May 27, 1858 requiring that only Catholicism be practiced in public forced the Baptists to seek a place of worship in which they would not be molested.[18]

In 1845, Merrick, with permission from the indigenous rulers, notably King William of Bimbia, began missionary work, opening a station among the Isubu of Bimbia, and two others at Akwa Town and Bell Town along the Cameroon (Wouri) River estuary. Although he hoped to eventually carry his work into the interior, he concentrated his initial efforts at converting the

Isubu and the Duala. Thus, he set forth to establish schools and churches and, at the same time, learn the languages of the Isubu and Duala to improve his ability to preach among them. He subsequently went on to translate several Christian texts into both languages. Merrick's work was cut short by his death in 1849, on his way to Jamaica. Today, he is recognized as the pioneer of Christian work in Cameroon.

After Merrick's death, his work was carried on by Joseph Jackson Fuller, whose father, Alexander Fuller, was a native of Jamaica and a colleague of Merrick's. Fuller stationed himself at Douala, where he undertook several activities for the church, including teaching and supervising printing operations. In 1858, when Alfred Saker, who had taken leadership of the worship center at Clarence, transferred the mission work to Cameroon, Fuller undertook most of the negotiations with King William for purchase of land for the new settlement, which was named Victoria. He was ordained in 1858 and served in the field until 1888, and during this period successfully translated many texts into Duala. After the Germans established the colony of Kamerun in 1884, Fuller supervised the transfer of the assets of the BMS to the Basler (Basel) Mission Society. Freed Jamaican slaves and English missionaries, hence, were quite instrumental in the introduction of Christianity in Cameroon.

All of Cameroon's early missionary groups emphasized education and work. Hence, they established churches and schools and helped improve farming practices as well as provided social and medical services. Today, churches continue to make a significant contribution to education and the provision of health care in Cameroon. In fact, some of the best hospitals in the country are owned and operated by missionary societies.

Impact

Throughout its more than one hundred years in Cameroon, Christianity has brought more than salvation to Cameroonians. It has also been an important instrument for the propagation of Western culture, customs, languages, and values. Despite the fact that Christianity has been successful in gaining converts in Cameroon, church leaders remain worried because many converts, even including those who are devout, continue to preserve some aspects of their indigenous cultures. In fact, in some parts of the country, Christians have incorporated many aspects of their cultures into church rituals. Several Cameroon Christians have attempted, during the last several decades to indigenize Christianity and form a uniquely Cameroon church. However, many Christian fundamentalists bitterly oppose any attempts to turn Jesus of Nazareth into a local god. While many educated Cameroon Christians may retain some of the traditions, their worldview is shaped primarily by Christianity and Western ideas. Many of them have adopted Western dress styles, food, music, books, and even language.

Among those things that Christianity has brought to Cameroon, Western education is considered one of the most important and, today, remains its most attractive feature and the reason why thousands of Cameroonians continue to flock to it. The early missionaries expected converts to attend school, not just so they could read the Bible, but also because they expected them to study European culture, abandon their "native" ways, engage in employment of a European nature (implying abandonment of such traditional pursuits as hunting and gathering), and generally become "civilized." During the 1930s and 1940s, many Cameroonians flooded mission schools as industrialization continued to create more opportunities for salaried employment. At the same time, many of the country's educated Christians began to show an interest in political power and began to actively agitate for independence and the creation of a polity controlled and managed by the indigenous peoples. Many of these Cameroonians were to form the foundation for the nationalist movements that won the country its independence.

In many societies in Cameroon, Christianity has replaced traditional religions, so it is important that Christian churches deal with the many issues that had been the purview of traditional religions. For example, in societies where people believe that evil spirits and witchcraft negatively affect their quality of life, traditional religions have fought these forces in an effort to reduce their impact on the people. For Christianity to remain relevant to the lives of the people, it must be able to deal with these issues and provide them with an environment in which they feel safe.

In general, Christian churches have had a significant impact on the social, economic, and political development of Cameroon. First, in the 1930s and 1940s, schools run by missionary societies served as laboratories for the embryonic nationalist movement that would eventually lead the people to independence. Second, the development of most of the human capital responsible for the country's economic growth had its origins in mission schools. Third, missionary societies have been and remain important health care providers, especially in rural areas. Fourth, Christian churches have been at the forefront of the struggle to rid society of traditional practices (e.g., female genital mutilation) that are harmful to the people. Fifth, Christian churches continue to lead the war against child neglect—in fact, most of the orphanages in the country are owned and operated by Christian churches. Sixth, Christian churches, along with their Islamic brethren, have served as important checks on government excesses, regularly denouncing government officials for venality, capriciousness in the implementation of public policies, political and economic decay, immorality and wanton waste of resources that could be used to help the poor, and general failure to bring about peace and prosperity to the country. Finally, these churches have made important contributions to the peaceful coexistence of population groups in the country, and continue to do so today.

ISLAM

Islam penetrated the region that is now northern Cameroon, including the region around Lake Chad long before the holy wars led by Usuman Dan Fodio and his many followers. The religion's presence and impact were limited to a few nomadic clans, mostly Fulani cattle herders. By the end of the 16th century, many Fulani converts were now fully established throughout the Hausa states in what is now northern Nigeria and as far east as Adamawa (which now constitutes several of Cameroon's present day northern provinces). These Muslims had not yet developed into a strong and viable political community. Instead, they were scattered throughout the region, serving as administrators and clerks in the courts of the several traditional rulers that dotted the landscape. After some time, many of the traditional rulers came to view Muslims as a threat to their authority and began to systematically persecute them. At the same time that the persecution of Muslims was being carried out, social and economic conditions in the region continued to deteriorate. Muslims, most of whom were Fulani, capitalized on the deplorable conditions of the masses and initiated a revolt against the traditional rulers. Usuman Dan Fodio, with the help of many disciples, including the Fulani nobleman, Adama, successfully brought the Hausa States, Bornu and Adamawa under Fulani and Muslim control. The establishment of Islam as the dominant religion in Cameroon's northern provinces, then, began with the Fulani revolt against rulers in the Hausa States and the Bornu Empire.

In the later part of the eighteenth century, Usuman Dan Fodio started a movement to purify and cleanse the Islamic faith, which he believed had been debased and corrupted by its adherents in the Hausa States of what is now northern Nigeria. Up until this time, the Fulani had resided peacefully among the Hausa in the region stretching from northern Nigeria to Lake Chad. Dan Fodio was quite successful in recruiting followers, especially among urban Fulani. Alarmed at the bold challenge against their religious practices and way of life, Hausa rulers attempted to suppress Dan Fodio's movement. In response to the violence directed at him and his movement by the Hausa elite, Dan Fodio declared a *jihad* or holy war and from 1804 to 1810, all the Hausa States were subdued and brought under Fulani control.

The *jihad* organized and carried out by Dan Fodio marked the Fulani's trans-formation into the dominant ethnic group in this region. Fulani military success was due primarily to the fact that the holy warriors, unlike their opponents, had mounted regiments, carried firearms, and fought with a fanatic and mission-ary zeal. The groups that were able to escape Fulani conquest and subsequent conversion to Islam were those that were able to escape to the mountains and hills, which were inaccessible to the mounted holy warriors. In 1806, a Fulani nobleman called Adama, returned from Sokoto to his home in the area south-west of Bornu and spread news of Dan Fodio's holy war against pagans. Most of Adama's fellow Fulani had already accepted Islam, so Adama encouraged them to form armies and follow Dan Fodio's example and capture more followers for the faith. Dan Fodio recognized Adama's efforts and officially conferred on him the title of Lamido Fumbina, with instructions to preach the faith from "the Nile to the Bight of Biafra."[19] Supported by several volunteers, including Hausa mercenaries who hoped to engage in slaving along the way, Adama set out to bring as many unbelievers as possible into the faith.

Adama established his headquarters at Yola in present-day Nigeria and began campaigns that extended the boundaries of the emirate that he founded as far as Bamoun in present-day Cameroon. His empire also extended "southeast to Ngaoundéré; east to Rei, on a tributary of the Benué; northeast to Maroua, Mindij, and Bogo; and north up to parts of Bornu and including much of the Mandara kingdom, whose combined forces he defeated in 1823."[20]

Leadership of Adama's work was taken over by his children. Two of them, Lawal and Zubeiru were very successful in extending and expanding the empire started by their father. Zubeiru ascended the throne of Adamawa in 1890 and by that time, the Germans, who had established a colony at Douala on the Cameroon River in 1884, were pushing inland from the coast and hence, represented an important threat to the kingdom. In addition, the Brit-ish were challenging Adamawa domination from the west, and the French from the east. Despite conquest by the European powers and the subsequent introduction of their political, economic, and administrative systems, Islam remains the dominant religion in the northern part of Nigeria and Camer-oon, and including all of the Lake Chad region.

Cameroon's Muslims, like their counterparts elsewhere, all believe in five important ideals—the pillars of Islam: a belief in God (Allah), and God's messenger, the prophet Mohammad; 5 daily prayers, carried out at specific times; giving of alms to the poor and the needy; fasting; and pilgrimage to the holy city of Mecca. More radical believers include a sixth pillar—the *jihad*.

Since the nineteenth century, when Fulani holy warriors invaded northern Cameroon and subjected several groups to their rule, as well as Islam, dis-tinction has been made between free people and those who were conquered.

Among the free people were the Fulani, Hausa, Bornuans, and the Choa Arabs, from whom the Fulani had borrowed many elements of their culture and social systems. However, such distinctions were abolished during the colonial period and by Cameroon's independence constitutions, which held that all Cameroonians are free and equal. Unfortunately, remnants of the old system remain throughout the so-called Fulani territories or *lamidats*.

Each *lamidat* is headed by a *lamido,* a spiritual and temporal ruler whose power, in the old days, was limited only by Islamic law and Fulani custom. In recent years, the *lamibé* (plural of *lamido*) have been quite vocal in their opposition of the increased constraints placed on the exercise of their power by the Cameroon state and its political and economic institutions. The postindependence state, however, has accommodated the *lamibé* through allowing the latter to have personal representatives on the staff of *préfectures* in the northern provinces. For many years, northern *préfects* were always Fulani.

The *lamido* is assisted by a large council of ministers, which includes a chief minister or *imam* (Muslim prayer leader), and the judge. According to Fulani tradition, the *lamidat* was collectively owned by all Fulani, with the *lamido* serving as a trustee, whose job it was to manage the property for the benefit of the collective. Accordingly, the *lamido*'s servants were considered property of the state and included people from states that had submitted to the Fulani to avoid conquest and subsequent enslavement (Mboum, Baya, and Dourou). Although these vassal peoples were allowed to rule themselves, determination of their leadership was undertaken only with the approval of the *lamido.* Under colonial rule, the various vassal chiefs were chosen by colonial officers but with input from the *lamido.* By the end of colonialism, however, the vassals had succeeded in freeing themselves from dependency upon the *lamido,* although they remained an integral part of the *lamidat* and continued to provide the *lamido* with gifts and presents. Islam, hence, has had a significant impact on the political and social organization of most of the north of Cameroon.

Islam does not allow the enslavement of true believers. Within the religion, the *lamido* serves as both the leader of all true believers and the political head. The *imam* is left with very little religious power and plays only a minor role. In addition, the *lamido* does not permit a challenge to his leadership from Muslim brotherhoods, which have not been quite influential in northern Cameroon.

Islam, which was founded in Arabia during the seventh century by the Prophet Mohammad, is based on religious faith, which itself is the core of an "extensive body of institutions, customs, and attitudes considered by its followers to be based on divine authority."[21] It has only one holy book, called the Qur'an (Koran). However, there exists a large body of Arabic literature on Mohammad's sayings and interpretive commentaries on the Qur'an. One of the most important of these interpretations is the religious legal system referred to as *sharia,* which regulates the life of a pious Muslim.

About one-fifth of Cameroonians are Muslim, a testimony to the resilience of this religion and its ability to maintain its hold on the people. Conversion to Islam, throughout the years, has been based on *jihad* (especially during the nineteenth century), trade, and missionary work. Along the way, some converts have come to the religion because of its prestige and the opportunities it has created for economic and social mobility. This was especially true during the many years that Ahmadou Ahidjo (himself a Muslim) ruled Cameroon. Of course, Islam has proved adaptive in its ability to borrow from the cultures it conquered, making acceptance by the captive populations much easier. Perhaps more important has been the fact that the traditional religions of many ethnic groups in Cameroon, including those that were conquered by the Fulani holy warriors, have a lot in common with Islam—requirement that all people live an ethical and moral life; belief in a supreme being; and the acknowledgment of the power of dreams and charms.

Unlike many of Cameroon's traditional religions, Islam has a holy book, which followers are required to read and understand. As a consequence, education and literacy are very important requirements for participation in the religion. Hence, conversion is usually followed by efforts to educate the converts and enhance their ability to have access to the holy book. Throughout this process, many previously illiterate communities have been able to attain a significant level of literacy and improve their chances for economic and social development.

Increased cooperation with Islamic communities outside Cameroon and more participation in events in Mecca have brought more prestige to the country's Muslim community and made them more conscious of their position as members of a global Islamic community. The latter continues to have significant impact on political economy not only in the Middle East, but also in virtually all parts of the world. Hence, Cameroon's Muslims, despite the apparent fall in their political fortunes since the resignation of Ahmadou Ahidjo as president of Cameroon in 1982, may actually be more politically relevant than most opinion leaders and scholars would acknowledge.

Throughout Cameroon, Qur'anic education is an important part of life in Muslim communities. Usually, young people must attain Qur'anic schools in the evenings and devote a lot of time to memorizing passages from the Qur'an. These studies expose them not only to religious dogma, but also to history, law, and Islamic social practices. At the lowest stages or levels, students are required to memorize the first 10 chapters of the Qur'an and through this process are taught to read and write. In the second or "tablet school" stage, parents usually send their children to a teacher in their neighborhood for further instruction. The teacher does not receive a salary but is given gifts and presents by the parents of the children. Completion of this stage brings the student to the "law school" stage, where he is introduced to Arabic grammar, literature, law, and elementary sciences. At this stage, emphasis is placed on accumulation of Islamic knowledge, in-depth study of the history and practices of the prophet Mohammad. Interested and highly motivated students can proceed to more advanced schools where they can specialize in certain areas of Islamic studies. Although the system encourages literacy, its repetitive nature also constrains and stunts creativity.

While traditional Qur'anic schools remain an important part of Muslim life in Cameroon, the government has made a concerted effort to encourage Muslim parents to send their children to secular schools. Today, many Cameroon Muslims attend Western-type schools and specialize in all the modern occupations. However, these educated Muslims have not abandoned their customs and traditions—many of them are bilingual in French and Arabic or English and Arabic and their religion remains very important to them. Because of overemphasis on religious education in the past, the northern provinces have lagged behind in the area of secular education. However, in recent years, efforts have been made to provide students from these provinces scholarships to study at universities in northern Nigeria, Egypt, Saudi Arabia, and other Islamic countries. Cameroon's Muslims are benefiting from financial aid supplied by many Islamic countries, particularly those in the Middle East, as well as Nigeria.

Like Christianity, Islam has made significant positive contributions to Cameroon. In addition to the fact that it has contributed significantly to literacy in the areas in which it has missions, it has been and remains an important agent of morality and upright living. Islamic leaders continuously implore believers to live moral and ethical lives, serve their communities, and help those less fortunate than they. In fact, giving alms to the poor is one of the religion's important pillars. In addition, Islamic leaders, like their Christian counterparts, have served as a check on the excesses of civil servants and politicians, condemning them for their corrupt ways and insensitivity to the country's poor and deprived. As Cameroonians begin life in the new millennium, they view Islam and Christianity as two important assets that would enhance their ability to live together peacefully and achieve sustainable economic growth and development.

RELIGION AND POLITICS

Religion plays an important role in politics in Cameroon. Religious leaders are considered an important check on the excesses of government, and both Islam and Christianity have been responsible for the education of many of the country's present leaders. Church leaders use their sermons to admonish their followers and plead with them to keep their faith and live moral and ethical lives. In times of political upheaval, church leaders have been called upon to use their moral authority to calm the nation and restore the peace.

In the late 1950s, the largest and most important indigenous political organization in French Cameroons, and the one that was expected to take the colony to independence, was the *Union des populations du Cameroun* (UPC). Although the UPC considered itself a national organization, the religious composition of its leadership was primarily Christian. UPC leaders had made it clear to the French that they would take an independent Cameroon nation out of the French community, seek to diversify the country's trading partners in an effort to minimize dependence on France, and pursue a policy of non-alignment. The French entrepreneurial class in the colony and the Catholic church raised their concerns over what they claimed was a political party that was increasingly becoming socialist and hence, anti-Christian and anti-free enterprise. In response to pleadings from the Catholic church, French commercial interests in the colony, and France's desire to maintain a client-regime in the new country, the colonial government proscribed the UPC in 1955 and effectively prevented it from participating in preparations for independence and eventually heading the postindependence government. At independence in 1960, then, the UPC, which had spearheaded the struggle for independence, was unable to lead the country because it was still outlawed. Instead, the northern-based and Muslim-dominated *Union Camerounaise* (UC), under the leadership of Ahmadou Ahidjo, formed the country's first postindependence government. In 1961, when the *République du Cameroun* joined the UN Trust Territory of Southern Cameroons to form a federation in 1961, Ahidjo became the first president of the federal republic. Thus, French manipulation of the conditions for independence allowed the Muslim north to dominate politics in Cameroon until 1982 when Ahidjo resigned his office and handed over the government to Paul Biya.

To Ahidjo's credit, he made a concerted effort to include Christians in his government. In fact, Ahidjo was well known for his ability to include representatives of most population groups in his administration. However, since northern Muslims monopolized the most important ministries (e.g., defense) and dominated the security services during his government, southern Christians considered themselves to be in the disadvantage politically. One thing was clear, despite the apparent political domination of the country by Muslims, the south was able to use its early advantage in Western education to dominate the modern sectors of the economy. In fact, throughout the 1960s and 1970s, Cameroon's economy was dominated by southern Christians, notably the Bamiléké of the western highlands. Given the fact that the state led by Ahidjo was quite intrusive and controlled virtually all aspects of Cameroon life, few Christians took solace in the fact that they, not the Muslims, controlled significant parts of the economy. Hence, Christians continued to blame Muslim domination of political economy in the country for their inability to secure important positions in government.

In 1982, Ahidjo resigned his office and handed the government to a southern Christian, Paul Biya. Since then, Muslims have continued to argue that Biya's government has implemented policies that have marginalized their region of the country and pushed Muslims to the political periphery. Like his predecessor, however, Biya has included people of other religions, notably Muslims in his government and has made other gestures toward the north, in an effort to allay the fears of many in the north that the government is insensitive to their plight. Since the reintroduction of multipartyism, northern-based political parties have emerged to fight for the rights of Muslims and other northern groups. In addition, many Muslims serve in leadership positions in the ruling Cameroon People's Democratic Movement.

Christianity continues to extend its frontiers and adapt itself to the changing political and economic environment in Cameroon. Older and well-established churches (e.g., Catholics, Presbyterians, and Baptists) dominate and have the largest membership. However, in the 1980s, when the born-again movement came to Cameroon, many young people joined these churches, especially since they tended to have more lively services, were more appealing to young people, and offered greater opportunities for either advancement within the leadership of the church or for studies abroad, especially in the United States. Some of these newer churches have been more attractive because of their more relaxed approach to priesthood, which includes opening the institution to lay members.

Islam is also growing and although most of its growth is still restricted to the northern part of the country, it is gradually making inroads into Christian-dominated regions of the country. Among Muslims, the pilgrimage to Mecca remains quite popular and many believers continue to see the trip to the birthplace of Islam as the most important achievement of their lives on earth. Cameroon's Muslim community continues to seek opportunities to improve its political fortunes, while at the same time, seeking to improve its relationship with Muslim communities in other countries. Financial aid from Saudi Arabia, Nigeria, and several other countries with large Muslim communities, has been used to improve opportunities for religious development in Cameroon. Today, the Muslim community in Cameroon is now fully integrated into the global community of Islam.

Although Cameroon's religious groups continue to compete, often vigorously, for members and other resources, including access to political power, they continue to coexist peacefully. Members of these religions work and live together peacefully and their leaders hope that Cameroon remains a society in which such peaceful coexistence can be maintained.

NOTES

1. Philip Burham, "The Gbaya and the Sudan Mission: 1924 to the Present," in *Grafting Old Rootstock: Studies in Culture and Religion of the Chamba, Duru, Fula, and Gbaya of Cameroon,* ed. Philip A. Noss (Dallas, TX: International Museum of Cultures, 1982), p. 116.

2. Ibid., p. 117.

3. Ibid., pp. 117–118.

4. Philip Noss, "An Interpretation of Gbaya Religious Practice," in *Grafting Old Rootstock,* p. 132.

5. Ibid., p. 132.

6. Ibid., p. 136.

7. Ibid., p. 148.

8. Joseph Lukong Banadzem, "Catholicism & Nso' Traditional Beliefs," in *African Crossroads: Interaction Between History and Anthropology in Cameroon,* ed. I. Fowler and D. Zeitlyn (Providence, RI: Berghahn Books, 1996), p. 125.

9. Ibid., p. 140, fn. 4.

10. Ibid., p. 130.

11. E. M. Chilver, "Thaumaturgy in Contemporary Traditional Religion: The Case of Nso' in Mid-Century," *Journal of Religion in Africa* 20, no. 3 (1990), p. 236.

12. Claude Tardits, "Pursue To Attain: A Royal Religion," in *African Crossroads: Interaction Between History and Anthropology in Cameroon* (Providence, RI: Berghahn Books, 1996), p. 141.

13. A. Njiassé-Njoya, "Naissance et evolution de l'Islam en pays Bamum (Cameroun)" (Thèse pour le doctorat du 3me cycle, Université I, Paris, 1981).

14. W. Keller, *The History of the Presbyterian Church in West Cameroon* (Victoria: Presbook, 1969).

15. See also Claude Tardits, *Le royaume Bamoum* (Paris: Librarie 1996).

16. Tardits (1996), pp. 149–150.

17. Ibid., p. 153.

18. Keller (1969).

19. Victor T. LeVine, *The Cameroons: From Mandate to Independence* (Berkeley: University of California Press, 1964), p. 40.

20. Ibid., p. 40.

21. Harold D. Nelson, et al., *Area Handbook of the United Republic of Cameroon* (Washington, DC: U.S. Government Printing Office, 1973), pp. 83–84.

3

Literature and Media

THE DEVELOPMENT OF LITERATURE in Cameroon can best be understood through an analysis of several complex and interconnected events that began with the arrival of Europeans on what are now the coastal regions of Cameroon in the nineteenth century. First is colonialism, which significantly impacted Cameroonian societies and, to a large extent, influenced the production of indigenous literature. Second is World War I, which resulted in the loss of Kamerun to Allied Expeditionary Forces and the subsequent partition of the colony into British and French zones of influence. Third is World War II, which ended in 1945 with the formation of the United Nations and subsequent transfer of the territories to the UN trusteeship system to be administered by France and Britain. Fourth is the reaction of Cameroonians to colonial exploitation and their eventual struggle for independence and nationhood. Fifth is Christianity, which was introduced into Cameroon by the English Baptist Missionary Society in the mid-1800s. While it brought many things to Cameroon, the two most important influences of Christianity on Cameroon and the people were education and the moral ideals promoted by religious teachings. The final factor is the reaction of educated Cameroonians to the contradictions inherent in Christian teachings and the support of colonial policies by European priests and pastors. These events and their interaction with each other had a significant impact on the development of literature in Cameroon. For example, Christian missions taught many Cameroonians to read and write and imbued them with several of the moral ideals that later formed the foundation for their opposition to colonialism. In addition, the Christian missions also provided many Cameroonians with opportunities to publish their creative works—many of them were reactions to continued oppression of their people by colonialism.

Cameroonians adopted several things from the European colonialists, including languages, customs, tastes, and Christianity. Such assimilation created a new educated elite, who used the tools provided by European colonialism, including Christianity, to express a Cameroon identity and forge the vision of a new society. In addition, many of the assimilated Cameroonians were either to become directly involved in the struggle for independence or provide the impetus to those nationalists who fought for the country's independence.

The English Baptist Missionary Society (BMS) was the first European Christian mission to enter Cameroon. It established worship centers and an educational system that was later expanded by the Basel Mission, which took over from the BMS when Germany established the colony of Kamerun in 1884. Today, the Presbyterian Church continues the work of the Basel Mission. Since the BMS entered Cameroon from the coast, the ethnic groups that inhabited the coastal areas, such as the Duala and the Bakweri, were the first to interact with the Christian missionaries. The Duala, in particular, took advantage of the educational opportunities offered by the BMS, and, later, the Basel Mission, to educate their children. Thus, they were the first of Cameroon's many ethnic groups to develop a literate culture that had a significant reading audience.[1]

During German colonial rule, many Duala assimilated German culture and tried to use the colonizer's modes of thought to defend their rights. For example, Rudolph Douala Manga Bell, who became king of the Duala in 1910, read law in Europe and returned home to confront the expropriation of his people's land by the German colonial government. Having acquired a thorough understanding of the German legal system and how it operated, Douala Manga Bell strongly believed that the law was on the side of his people, especially considering the fact that expropriation of Duala land was prohibited under the terms of the 1884 treaty. His legal protests to the Reichstag in Berlin were, however, unsuccessful, and he was subsequently executed by colonial authorities in 1913 for treason.

The Germans also executed another Cameroon intellectual, Martin-Paul Samba of the Bulu, who had been educated in Berlin and had served for many years as an officer in the Imperial Army. He had returned home to work for the colonial government, helping the latter oppress the people. However, he later changed course and headed an anticolonial network that sought the ouster of the Germans.

Toward the end of the nineteenth century, Sultan Njoya of the Bamoun emerged as one of Cameroon's most important intellectuals. He transformed

Bamoun society using knowledge acquired from Christian missionaries, Islam, and an understanding of his people's traditions and customs. After studying Islamic Qur'anic texts, he developed a written script for the Bamoun language, which was later used to produce tracts on traditional medicine, his kingdom's laws and customs, and a volume that contained a new religion based on Islam, Christianity, and Bamoun traditional religious practice. Royal schools were subsequently established throughout the kingdom and instruction offered in the new script. However, after Bamoun became part of French Cameroons after World War I, colonial authorities attempted to introduce a new educational system based on the French model. In addition to the fact that French was the only accepted medium of instruction, this new model of education emphasized subjects, such as French geography and history, as well as French culture and civilization, that were not relevant to the people of the kingdom of Bamoun in particular and to Cameroonians in general. The French subsequently destroyed Sultan Njoya's printing press, closed down all the royal schools, and exiled the King to Yaoundé, where he died in isolation.

These three pioneers of Cameroon intellectualism are important because "they ultimately became shared reference points for a constituency that transcended the boundaries of their own ethnic groups. Although they were martyred by the colonialist system, their images continued to embody notions of freedom and identity long after the men themselves had died."[2]

Both the Christian missions and the colonial government were interested in educating Cameroonians because they needed people who were familiar with and could function effectively in European as well as Cameroon cultures. These assimilated Cameroonians were expected to serve the Christian missions as catechists, teachers, and pastors/priests and the colonial government as junior-level civil servants. In both cases, they would serve as a liaison or bridge between the indigenous peoples of Cameroon and the Europeans.

During German rule, the most important function that an assimilated African could perform was that of secretary-interpreter. Such a function was to be retained, although in a modified form, by both British and French colonial systems. The secretary-interpreter's primary function was to help the European bosses understand local customs and transmit the dictates of colonial authorities to the Cameroon people—the colonized. The secretary-interpreters, through their work with the Europeans and travels throughout the country, came to constitute an important literate group of Cameroonians who were able to communicate across cultures and across ethnic boundaries. Many of them mastered several local languages as well as German, French, and English and, hence, were able to continue their work after the country was partitioned into English and French zones of influence after World War I.

Given their training, experiences, and access to the literary community in Paris and other parts of France, it was only a matter of time before the secretary-interpreters emerged as the colony's first group of creative writers. Thus, by the 1920s and 1930s, several of these indigenous intellectual elites had produced monographs on several topics, with some of them published in the French colonial magazine called *La Gazette du Cameroun*. Soon, members of this group were writing creative pieces that explored several topics, including the conflict between the modernization brought by colonialism and traditional practices; Christianity and traditional religions; love; and the origin of life. One of the most important of these early creative writers was Louise-Marie Pouka, a Bassa who had been assimilated to French culture through his education at a Catholic seminary. He was the first Cameroonian to publish a volume of poetry that was internationally acknowledged.

Pouka's poems, especially those written in the 1930s, show an intellectual who deeply believed in the superiority of European culture, which he hoped would emancipate his people and help them escape their miserable living conditions. Such a view of European culture was widely held throughout colonial Africa and was the impetus for many of the colonial school systems (some of them owned and operated by Christian churches) that were established to educate Africans. Most of the European-style schools were established primarily in the southern part of both British and French Cameroons, since the colonial governments had chosen to rule the northern parts of their mandated territories through local Fulani elites, the bulk of whom preferred Qur'anic schools.

The Christian missions were the most important contributor to the production of literate Cameroonians. From the late nineteenth century to the early 1930s, most of the schools that provided educational opportunities for Cameroonians were owned and operated by Protestant missions. The Catholic Church became a major participant in the education of Cameroonians in the early 1930s with the expansion of its educational efforts among the ethnic groups around Yaoundé. Although the schools were owned and operated by the churches, the French colonial government intervened frequently to make certain that instruction was undertaken only in French and not in local languages, and that the curriculum provided for individuals educated to standards in France. The French, however, discouraged the founding of secondary schools and instead encouraged the churches to carry out all post-primary education in seminaries, where Cameroonians would be trained to serve as priests or pastors. Theodore Tsala, one of eight Cameroonians to be ordained into the Catholic priesthood in 1935, published a collection of folk material titled *Moeurs et coutumes des Ewondo (Morals and customs of the Ewondo)* and is now considered a pioneer creative writer from this region of the country.

In addition to educating Cameroonians and providing them with the skills to articulate their ideas in writing, the Christian missions also operated printing presses that helped publish some of this literature. In fact, as early as the 1850s, the English Baptist Missionary Society, under the leadership of Jamaican Joseph Jackson Fuller, who had taken over the duties of pioneering BMS missionary, Joseph Merrick, had established a print shop and bindery in Bimbia. The press would be used to print many Christian tracts written or translated into the Duala language for use in church services and evangelization work.[3] American Presbyterians, who had founded missions among the Bulu-Bassa before World War I and who were allowed to stay by provisions in the League of Nations mandate, began operating a printing press at Elat near Yaoundé around 1916. Although the press' primary interest was in publishing Bulu and Bassa translations of the Bible, a Bulu newspaper (*Kalate Mefoe* or *Book of News*) was also being published. Most of the authors of articles appearing in the newspaper were members of the church, and materials published ranged from sermons to narratives of travels by the flock. This press published the first Cameroon work of prose fiction in 1939 titled *Nnanga kôn (The White Ghost)*, which was authored by Jean-Louis Njemba Medou. The book examines life among the Bulu at the time of the arrival of the first Europeans. Many of the characters created by Njemba Medou were so popular that they eventually became a central part of Bulu folk traditions. In 1948, the press published Ondoua Engutu's *Bulu bon be Afri kari (The Journey of the Children of Afri kari)*, which examined the origins of the migrations of the Fang. Although the Presbyterian press at Elat was established primarily to serve the needs of the church in its efforts to win souls for Christ, it also contributed enormously to the creation of a reading and intellectual community among the Bulu.

Catholic publishing efforts also created a similar intellectual community among the Ewondo around Yaoundé. In the early 1930s, church authorities introduced the Ewondo newspaper, *Nleb Bkristen (The Christian Adviser)*, which went on to attain a circulation of more than 6,000 readers. One of the most important creative products of this period was the Ewondo poem called *Nkat Zamba (Judgment of God)*, which was authored by Tobi Atangana, a priest, in the mid-1930s and was adopted as part of the standard curriculum in all Catholic schools in Ewondo country. These efforts by Christian churches to develop reading communities within various ethnic groups in Cameroon would later form the foundation for the type of reading public that was needed for nation-building.

In British Cameroons, the colonial government made little effort to promote literacy in English. Until after World War II, most European activities in the mandated territories were among the German plantations, where indigenous workers from the various ethnic groups in the territory congregated, and pidgin English emerged as the *lingua franca*. Most education was provided by Christian missionary societies, with the colonial government making no attempt to standardize the curriculum or enforce the use of English as the main medium of instruction. Hence, the curriculum in the schools was determined by the churches, some villages and municipalities did not have schools, and local languages were used widely in instruction. As late as 1947, the Christian churches were responsible for educating more than 90 percent of the British Cameroons' pupils. The first secondary school in the territory was St. Joseph's College, Sasse, established by the Catholic Church in 1938. In the mid-1930s, a teacher's training institute was established in Kumba. Most of the British Cameroons' early literate elite were educated at Sasse and later at the Cameroon Protestant College (CPC), which was opened by the Basel Mission at Bali in 1949. CPC—called Basel Mission College until 1957, when governance was acquired by the Presbyterian Church and the Cameroon Baptist Convention—was the first secondary school in the grassfields region of the British Southern Cameroons. Given the paucity of opportunities for secondary school education, many parents in British Cameroons sent their children to secondary schools in Nigeria, primarily in Enugu and other major cities of eastern Nigeria. Many of the Cameroonians educated in Nigeria often found more lucrative jobs in Nigeria's urban areas and remained there instead of returning home.

The nature of the intellectual climate that emerged in Cameroon, and which was to have a significant impact on the nationalist project, was determined and shaped, to a great extent, by Christian missions. Since its beginnings in the late nineteenth century, the Christian mission's main objective has been to win souls for Christ, and, hence, educational facilities were established to enhance the achievement of that goal. Instruction at mission schools, then, included a high level of moralization, which later became an important part of the writings of many of the country's intellectuals, although the message was not usually carried through exactly in the manner in which it was proclaimed by the missionaries. Missionary moralization and emphasis on ethics provided the indigenous elites educated at these schools with a frame of reference for developing the nationalist project, which condemned colonial exploitation and demanded independence. Perhaps more important was the fact that these Christian missions produced a highly literate group of Cameroonians who were able to recognize the contradictions between colonialism's so-called civilizing mission and its policies, which were designed to make Cameroonians second-class citizens in their own country.

Before the end of World War II, French Cameroons had developed three distinct and significant literate communities: the first was among the Duala, the second among the Bulu and Bassa, and the third among the Ewondo and other Beti groups around the city of Yaoundé. The war had a significant impact on the nationalist project in Cameroon. It exposed Cameroonians, especially the literate elites, to new perspectives, and it also improved the ability of these elites to form nationalist associations that eventually developed into avenues for them to articulate their ideas about independence. Reading groups formed by French unionists, who had become involved in colonial governance when the Popular Front came to power in France, exposed literate Cameroonian elites to radical interpretations of colonialism and made them aware of the fact that, although they were from different ethnic groups, they faced similar exploitation by the colonial government and, hence, were more likely to organize across ethnic boundaries and fight their common enemy—colonial exploitation. Among those who participated in reading groups were Um Nyobé, Charles Assalé, Léopold Moumé Etia, Jacques N'Gom, and several others who were to play critical roles in the country's nationalist project.

In the immediate post–World War II period, the indigenous peoples of French Cameroons faced two distinct and conflicting forces: assimilationism, which had informed and governed French colonial policy and was reenforced by the resolutions of the Brazzaville Conference, and the white supremacist beliefs of the colony's settler community. These two forces shaped Cameroon's intellectual climate, and the responses of individual Cameroonians to these forces became the central theme in many of the pro-independence literature authored by indigenous elites.

The Cameroons Welfare Union (CWU), founded in 1939 in Victoria, was the first attempt to create an association of literate individuals across ethnic boundaries in British Cameroons. The CWU had branches in several Nigerian cities. In 1940, the Lagos (Nigeria) branch of the CWU was succeeded by the Cameroons Youth League (CYL), which later established several branches in Nigeria and in such Cameroon cities as Kumba and Bamenda. Dominated by literate Cameroonians, the CYL was formed to promote a sense of solidarity among Cameroonians, preserve their culture, and foster peaceful coexistence of the territory's many ethnic groups. Prominent members of the CYL were E.M.L. Endeley, P.M. Kale, N.N. Mbile, and John Ngu Foncha, all of whom became important political leaders in post-independence British Cameroons. During this time, illiteracy was quite high in British Cameroons and the territory had only one printing press.

In 1935, the French governor of the Cameroons founded the *Société des études camerounaises* (SEC), which, together with its journal, *Etudes Camerounaises,* served as important tools to be used to achieve France's civilizing mission in Cameroon. After World War II, the SEC became part of the *Institut Français d'Afrique Noire* (IFAN), located in Dakar, Senegal. Despite its name,

Cameroonians were not allowed to participate in the activities of the SEC and its journal. In fact, during the journal's more than 20 years of existence, it published only one full-length article authored by a Cameroonian. Studies of Cameroon that were published in *Etudes Camerounaises* reflected European interpretations and not those of the indigenous peoples. However, several Frenchmen such as Roger Lagrave, Jean-Marie Carret, and Henry de Julliot (the latter two were Catholic priests) helped create a literary culture in French Cameroons through encouraging and nurturing aspiring indigenous writers. Of special importance was the founding of the *Club du Livre Camerounais,* which was devoted to publishing books by Cameroonians. Jean-Marie Carret, who spent a significant part of his life working as a missionary among the Bassa, built many schools and encouraged the development of a literary culture among his pupils.

De Julliot was a literature teacher at the prestigious Collège Libermann in Douala for many years and founded *Frères Réunis,* the only full-service bookstore in the colony. In addition, de Julliot published a literary column on a regular basis in *La Presse du Cameroun,* delivered many public lectures on literature, and helped aspiring indigenous writers publish their creative works in Europe. These three men judged their Cameroon underlings using French standards, which did not always take into consideration the writer's worldview or African reality as perceived by the Africans themselves. Although all three men wrote about Cameroon, their works portrayed Africans as people who could not achieve their full potential without accepting French culture, as well as accepting the patronage of those in France.

After the Brazzaville Conference, assimilationism gained more currency in Cameroon through the establishment of more schools. The French government and the Christian missions (notably the Catholic Church) increased the construction of schools, including those at the secondary level. The official curriculum was revised and made the same as that in France. While many Cameroon parents supported the change because they wanted their children to receive an education that enhanced their chances to access opportunities for advanced training in France, the new curriculum emphasized the study of French literature and culture and failed to teach the pupils about their own societies. The Eurocentric approach to the education of Cameroonians, however, did not prevent the Cameroonians from trying to reconcile the two worlds. In fact, in 1957, a study group called *Rencontre de Deux Mondes* was formed at the seminary in Otélé with the expressed purpose of helping develop priests who could be effective mediators between the African and European cultures. The work of this study group appeared in *Lumina,* a review that was published during the late 1950s and early 1960s. The review was a significant contribution to the development of literature in Cameroon. Within its pages were published transcriptions of oral narratives, criticisms of and attacks on colonialism, poems that reaffirmed the dignity of black people, writings on the compatibility of traditional customs and Christian (notably Catholic) belief, and critical essays on traditional ethnic practices.

Cameroonian writers were faced with creating literature that reflected the moral idealism and intellectual rigor that they had learned at mission school (including the seminaries) and, at the same time, confronting in an effective manner cruelties imposed on the people by colonialism. Many of the colony's indigenous writers, however, chose in the 1950s to identify strongly with assimilationism—the creation of a French Union consisting of France and peoples from its former colonies, with leadership coming from Paris. Literature produced by these individuals emphasized the various benefits enjoyed by Africans through assimilation. The greatest assimilationist Cameroonian writer was Louis-Marie Pouka, whose 1943 poem *Pleurs sincères* laments the indignities imposed on French citizens during German occupation but totally ignores the cruel and violent rule of Cameroon by the French, especially the *régime de l'indigénat* and forced labor. Pouka, like many other assimilationist writers, regarded French colonialism in Cameroon and other parts of Africa as part of God's plan for the black people. During his stay in France in the 1940s and 1950s, Pouka came face to face with a civilization that was quite different from the one he had idealized in his many publications. While in France, Pouka finally discovered that he had been duped, but he refused to give up his faith in French culture. Instead, he resolved the contradiction in French rhetoric and colonial practices by referring to any abuses in the latter as aberrations in God's plan for the liberation, from backwardness and ignorance, of the Cameroon peoples.

As reflected in his many writings, Pouka was a believer in poetic justice. Eventually, as he intimated in his works, the evildoers, including cruel and exploitative colonialists, would be punished. As a consequence, it was not necessary to take any concrete action to stop colonial oppression. After Pouka returned to Cameroon in the 1950s, his experiences in France began to show up as a form of "vague uneasiness" in his poetry.[4] While in France, he had come to realize that French colonialism was not compatible with his views of equality. However, he could not abandon his commitment to either French culture or equality because both had become very critical to how he defined himself. Thus, upon his return to Cameroon, he was forced to deal with the possibility that the assimilationism that he had so much faith in was not built on a firm foundation.[5]

Pouka was not the only Cameroonian writer whose works implied that the indigenous peoples had benefited from colonialism (i.e., that colonialism had liberated and saved the people from their savagery and backwardness as well as ignorance and superstition and integrated them into the modern world). One such writer was Jospeh Owono, who in 1953 published an essay about the plight of Cameroon women. That essay was the only full-length article written by a Cameroonian to have been published in *Etudes Camerounaises.* The essay praised the French colonial system for destroying the dowry system, which he argued had enslaved Cameroon women. He later expanded and modified the essay and published it as the novel *Tante Bella,* in an effort to reach a larger audience. However, the theme remained essentially the same: colonialism's destruction of anachronistic traditional systems had advanced the welfare of Cameroon women.

The assimilationist assumption runs through most of the literature of the pre-independence period in Cameroon. *Ngonda* (Marie-Claire Matip) and *Doigts noirs* (Jacques Kuoh-Moukouri), for example, both examine the lives of Cameroonians who were saved from the pestilence of their backward traditional societies by assimilationist education and brought into the modern world, where they could participate fully and effectively in civilized pursuits. Both novels portray individuals from humble beginnings, who, through their assimilation of European values, rise to pave the way for the civilizing of their own communities.

In the British Cameroons, a few indigenous elites did identify with British culture in the same manner that Pouka, Kuoh-Moukouri, Owono, and others had identified with French culture. British colonial policy in the Cameroons was not assimilationist because the English never expected Africans to fully assimilate their culture. The center of British Cameroonian intellectualism was located in Nigeria, where many of the territory's literate elites lived. Lagos and other Nigerian cities (e.g., Enugu) were chosen because they provided better access to publication outlets, including those in Britain.

Although by 1949 Vincent Nchami had already sold several of his stories to the British Broadcasting Corporation (BBC), the territory's literate community was not very active. Bernard Fonlon, while a student at a Nigerian seminary, wrote several poems, among which were "The Fear of Future Years" and "Nightmare." As argued by one critic, Fonlon's poems "illustrate how an attachment to the good, the true, and the beautiful can sustain an individual even in a morally corrupt environment."[6] Within his poetry, however, one does not find the defensive tone that is common in assimilationist French-speaking literature.

The most significant British Cameroons writer of the pre-independence period was Sanke Maimo, who at the time was a high school teacher in Nigeria. At Ibadan in 1955 he founded the journal, *Cameroon Voice.* He subsequently produced a play titled *I Am Vindicated* and a book for children titled *Adventuring with Jaja.* The play deals with the problem of identity and concludes that Africans must adopt the European worldview in order to deal with life in a beneficial manner. In the children's book, Maimo emphasizes the concept of individualism, which is closely linked to modernization and the development of nation-states in Europe.[7] Ironically, although many literate Cameroonians were generally opposed to continued European rule, many of them in their writings also demanded the right of the people to self-determination, a direct application of Western political values to the Cameroon situation.[8]

By the end of World War II, contradictions in assimilationism had become quite clear to a significant number of individuals in the various literate communities in Cameroon, as reflected in their writings and also in increased political activism in favor of independence instead of continued existence within a French Union. One of the most important political developments of this period was the formation of the *Rassemblement Démocratique Africain* (RDA) in Bamako (Mali) by representatives of political parties based in the African territories under French rule. The RDA was expected to pursue institutional reforms within the French-ruled territories along the lines of the Brazzaville agreement. Meanwhile, in French Cameroons, the *Union des Populations du Cameroun* (UPC), which would later become the radical alternative to assimilationist political organizations, was emerging. Founded in 1948 with support from radical French labor unions, the UPC initially planned to achieve its objectives by working within the French Union. The party was allied with the RDA; however, after the latter's leadership convinced its members to sever their relationship with the French Communist party, the UPC decided not to go along. Labeled a communist sympathizer in Cameroon, the party was despised by French entrepreneurial and commercial interests, as well as the Catholic Church. At the same time the UPC was suffering increased persecution from French colonial authorities, the latter increased their campaign for the various local constituencies (which included the RDA and several groups of assimilationists) to support the French Union. The UPC eventually emerged as the sole advocate for self-determination for Cameroon and the creation of a nation based on democratic governance.

The UPC's intellectual leader was Ruben Um Nyobé, a Bassa who had been educated at various mission schools operated by the American Presbyterian Church. Armed with the ideals inculcated in him at the mission schools, his rich Bassa cultural heritage, the thorough understanding of the determinants of French colonialism provided by his participation in the Marxist reading groups, and his experiences as a magistrate's clerk, Um Nyobé set out to educate Cameroonians about the evils of colonialism, the deceit of assimilationism, and the importance of self-reliance. He outlined his ideas in various publications, pamphlets, personal communications, diaries, and speeches. In 1951, he appeared before the trusteeship committee of the UN and presented a case for Cameroon nationhood. His speech was later published as a pamphlet titled *Ce que veut le peuple Camerounais (What the Cameroon People Want)*. Despite efforts by French colonial authorities, copies of the speech were widely circulated throughout the territory. Restrictions on travel by UPC leaders and other non-assimilationist indigenous elites forced them to rely more on printed and mimeographed materials to spread their message. This approach encouraged the formation throughout the territory of many reading groups where printed materials produced by the UPC and other nationalist groups were read and discussed.

A very important publication of the era was a tract called *Religion ou colonialisme,* produced by Felix-Roland Moumié, who, at the time, was considered the most radical leader in the UPC. In it, he condemns European Christian priests for supporting colonialism, a practice he argued was not compatible with the message being propagated by the church. UPC literature was specifically addressed to a national Cameroonian audience, without reference to any specific ethnic group. Hence, it promoted two important concepts: peaceful coexistence of all of the territory's ethnic groups and the creation of a Cameroonian national identity. Most Cameroonian literature produced during the 1950s reflected these concepts.

The French colonial government proscribed the UPC in 1955 and forced it underground. Its main message—formation of a sovereign multiethnic Cameroon nation—remained relevant and continued to be reflected in most of the literature that was produced from the mid-1950s to independence in 1960. Apparently, the UPC had been quite effective in its struggle against assimilationist forces, as evidenced by the fact that, after its proscription, support for national independence and reunification with the British Cameroons continued to increase. The production of literature increased as both individuals and groups started newspapers in French and several local languages. Some of the newspapers were started by individuals interested in promoting their political careers and others by Cameroonians interested in a national debate on the future of the territory. For example, newspapers by Louis-Paul Aujoulat *(Cameroun de demain)* and Soppo Priso *(Cameroun espoir)* served primarily the interests of their owners, whereas Marcel Bebey-Eyidi's *L'Opinion au Cameroun* was launched to provide all Cameroonians with an outlet to voice their opinions about colonialism and support the struggle for independence. Given *L'Opinion's* orientation and objectives, it was frequently confiscated by the colonial government. The UPC also published a newspaper called *Cameroun mon pays.* This and several successors to it were also seized regularly by the colonial government. However, despite the many constraints placed on them by the colonial government, the production of newspapers continued.

The Christian churches played a crucial role in the development of a journalistic tradition in the country. Although the Catholic Church had initially supported the assimilationist project and opposed independence, it was to change its position, as more and more indigenous Cameroonian priests took leadership positions in the church. Sunday sermons and regular religious instruction began to reflect the position that Christianity was not incompatible with independence. Among the most influential newspapers to emerge from the journalistic surge of the 1950s was *L'Effort Camerounais*, a Catholic weekly. The first director of *L'Effort*, however, was a French priest, Pierre Fertin. He was an avowed anti-Communist, who believed in justice and human rights and "empathized with Cameroonian aspirations for freedom and the right to define a collective identity in harmony with their own cultural heritage."[9] Father Fertin's paper published many articles on the territory's history, traditional practices, as well as creative works by Cameroonians, including commentaries on developments in the colony, and editorials supporting the territory's independence struggle. In addition, a column was created to discuss, on a regular basis, liberation movements in other European colonies in Africa.

The territory's first indigenous bishops were Jean Zoa and Thomas Mongo, both of whom published newspapers. These were *Pour un nationalisme chrétien* (Zoa) and *Principes pour le pays* (Mongo). In his paper, Zoa argued that, although nationalism was a legitimate and healthy struggle for human dignity, it had to be guided by Christian principles, and he called upon Catholics to provide the moral leadership needed to lead the territory to independence. While agreeing that Cameroonians should found a nation based on sound Christian principles, he cautioned against the adoption of political and economic systems such as communism and capitalism that contradict those principles. These indigenous priests were using their newspapers to redefine the struggle for independence in Christian terms.

In the late 1940s and early 1950s, the colonial government brought many Cameroonians to France to study in an effort to secure support for a French-speaking community. However, many of these students instead developed an anti-assimilationist view and began to use the tools that they had acquired through their education to criticize and chastise French colonialism. Many of them produced a burst of literature that sought to present a more realistic view of Cameroon and challenged the stereotyped view advanced by colonialism. Among these were the poets François Sengat-Kuo, Elolongue Epanya Yondo, and Jean-Paul Nyunaï and the novelists Ferdinand Oyono, Mongo Beti, Benjamin Matip, and Jean Ikelle-Matiba. These young Cameroonian writers rejected the assimilationist rhetoric found in such works as Carret's *Kel'lam* and advocated immediate independence for the French ruled territory. They wrote with a passion about freedom and national identity and published many essays, poems, short stories, and novels. In addition, they formed reading and discussion groups at which critical issues about Cameroon were examined.

Part of the work produced by these students was published in *Présence Africaine,* a magazine that was linked to the Negritude movement and dedicated to pan-Africanism and the rehabilitation and preservation of African culture. The editor of *Présence Africaine* was Alioune Diop, whose wife was a Cameroonian. The family home became a home-away-from-home for many Cameroon students, and Diop served as a mentor to many of them. In fact, virtually all the Cameroon students who later became internationally acclaimed literary figures were mentored by Diop.

In the late 1950s, Abel Eyinga, who would later become a giant in Cameroonian scholarly circles, with the help of Beby-Eyidi, founded *La Revue Camerounaise,* which published essays on Cameroon culture, colonial exploitation, and appeals to Cameroon's literate community to use its talents and skills to fight colonialism and demand independence for the territory. Cameroon student writers also published their work in journals produced by religious groups, including *L'Etudiant Africain Protestant,* and dedicated to the struggle for independence in the African colonies.

The student community in France in the 1950s was dynamic, passionate, and highly dedicated. It went on to produce a literature of liberation that not only affected the struggle for independence in Cameroon but that in other colonies in Africa. Poems by Sengat-Kuo, Epanya Yondo, and Nyunaï challenged the assimilationist work of authors like Pouka. In doing so, these scholars paved the way for most of the literature in support of independence and nation building that was to be produced in the immediate pre- and post-independence period.

The most important prose fiction produced in the immediate pre-independence period included works by Oyono, Beti, Matip, and Ikelle-Matiba. The most important theme in these works was colonialism and its negative impact on Cameroon societies and the imperative for independence and the creation of a nation in which the various ethnic groups could live in peace.

In the late 1950s, John Ngu Foncha, leader of the British Cameroons' Kamerun National Democratic Party (KNDP), used the reunification idea to win the premiership of the territory. Shortly afterward, he traveled to French Cameroons and met with Soppo Priso, who provided him with the resources he needed to start the trust territory's first newspaper, *The Cameroon Times.* The newspaper was an important outlet for discussions on the future of the territory and significantly increased creative writing. Political figures such as S. A. George and P. M. Kale produced tracts in which they defined their view of a uniquely Cameroonian identity, characterized by multiple ethnicities and common German colonial experience. Aloys Tellen published *Kamerunian's Bedside Catechism* to set straight Catholics' views on independence. Ndeh Ntumazah, who had founded the One Kamerun Party as an offshoot of the UPC, published several pamphlets in which he attacked colonialism and called for immediate independence and reunification with the French Cameroons. In Ibadan, the student wing of the One Kamerun Party, writing in its newspaper, *The Patriot,* also called for independence and reunification. These modest efforts helped launch a print culture in the British Cameroons.

A major development in the production of Cameroon, as well as African, literature came in 1963 with the founding of the Centre de Littérature Evangélique (Editions CLE). The literature published by the new publishing house characterized the moral idealism of the period and reflected the desire by virtually all of Cameroon's writers for peaceful coexistence, harmony, and progress. The works of all these writers were influenced by their traditional experiences, as well as the moral idealism that had characterized their education at mission schools, including seminaries. In addition, this literature drew heavily on the authors' personal experiences, and, in several cases, these novels were thinly disguised accounts of the authors' lives. In the novels, the authors explored, usually in a frank and honest manner, their life experiences and sought to reveal to readers the means through which they evolved into the people they now were. In this genre, the individual uses moral idealism as the standard from which to judge his behavior and define himself. One of the most important works of this period was Bernard Nanga's *La Trahison de Marianne,* a powerful account of an assimilated Cameroon who had vested his entire identity in the belief that French culture represented the ultimate ideal. Then he moves to France, and his experiences with the country and its people, as well as other immigrants from Africa, allow him to regain his lost identity.

Other works that reflected this search for liberty and self within the context of a morally idealistic worldview include *Un enfant comme les autres* (Pabe Mongo), *L'enfant Bamiléké* (Jean Mba Lenou), and *Tout pour la gloire de mon pays* (Victor Fotso). Each novel reveals how Christian self-reliance can help an individual overcome adversity and rise to success without compromising his or her principles.

When the Protestant publishing house, Editions CLE, came into being in Cameroon in 1963, independence had already been achieved and the apparatus of government was in the hands of indigenous elites—Ahmadou Ahidjo was president of the federation, and John Ngu Foncha was his vice president. The novels published by Editions CLE at this time reflected the Christian moral values that had been instilled in their authors during their education at the mission schools. In addition, they continued to promote moral upliftment, while at the same time criticizing the government for not doing enough to improve living conditions for the country's poor. Almost without exception, the authors use the concept of poetic justice in their novels to reward the ethically sound and punish the corrupt and emotionally opportunistic. Virtually all of the Editions CLE novels of this period supported the government's policy of national unity. Among important works that depict Cameroon reality in this way are *Quand saigne le palmier* (Charly-Gabriel Mbock), *La Colline du fromager* (Daniel Etounga Manguélé), and *Bogam Woup* (Pabe Mongo).

In the 1970s and 1980s, Editions CLE novels made reconciliation their main theme—between Christianity and traditional Cameroon religions; between tradition and modernity; and between the younger generation and the older one. This theme is pervasive in novels by Mbock, Manguéle, Mongo, and Francis Bebey, as well as in Etienne Yanou's *L'Homme-dieu de Bisson* and Samuel Mvolo's *Les Fiancés du grand fleuve*. The latter two novels illustrate how a modern Cameroon identity, based on emotional honesty and respect for the individual, can be formed through the synthesizing of Christianity and traditional beliefs. These, like other CLE novels, reflect the influence of Christianity on their authors as well as on the definition of self by educated Cameroonians. The spirit of reconciliation and unity that runs through many of the novels published by CLE was in line with the Ahidjo government's cultural politics of national unity.

After the abrogation of the federation and the institution of the unitary state in 1972, a new literature, aimed primarily at young readers, emerged in English-speaking West Cameroon. Most of this literature emphasized the territory's colonial past and tended to neglect contemporary issues. These novels were used by their authors to teach moral idealism, emotional honesty, and self-reliance. Among these novels were *The Promise* (Jedida Asheri) and *The Little Gringo* (René Simo). Working hard and maintaining one's principles in the face of difficulties are themes that run through these novels, as exemplified by *The Good Foot* (Nsanda Eba). While European colonization is considered an evil and exploitative system that denigrated the people, destroyed local cultures, and committed many atrocities in the country, it also brought with it certain values that educated Cameroonians (as exemplified by Mbamu, the main character in *The Good Foot*) assimilated at school and subsequently used to liberate themselves from ignorance. As also depicted in many French-speaking Cameroon novels, self-reliance and moral idealism feature prominently in the works of such English-speaking Cameroon novelists as Kenjo Jumban and Joseph Ngongwikuo. Jumban's *The White Man of God* is one of English-speaking Cameroon's most important novels of the

1970s. In it the author relates the struggles of a young boy to come to terms with the two worldviews that exist in his Nso' society—one traditional and the other Christian. The young boy lacks the intellectual maturity to realize that he can easily reconcile both worldviews, because they are not really that different from each other. As in *The White Man of God,* Jumban's books for children (*Lukong and the Leopard* and *The White Man of Cattle*) allow readers to independently draw their own conclusions about the relevance of traditional practices and modern institutions to the contemporary situation in Africa.

Ngongwikuo's *Taboo Love* deals with the important issue of the "autonomous individual" who has the right to maximize his or her own values. Like other English-speaking novels of the period, it seeks to show that traditional and modern values can be reconciled to create a worldview that meets the needs of contemporary Cameroonians.

During the period from World War I to reunification in 1961, there was not as much literary activity in British Southern Cameroons as there was in the French Cameroons. However, by the 1970s, the English-speaking production of literature had increased significantly, and many of the themes (individualism and moral idealism) that had pervaded French-speaking literature were now being emphasized by novels written by English-speakers. Since the so-called peaceful revolution of 1972, most literature produced by both English- and French-speaking Cameroonians has emphasized individual identity, self-reliance, moral integrity, and emotional honesty.

Ferdinand Oyono and Mongo Beti are two of Cameroon's most famous writers—their works reveal strong anticolonialist sentiments. During the colonial period, Beti used his novels to incite Cameroonians into rising up against European exploitation and demanding their right to self-determination. Unlike Beti, "Oyono is a detached humanist who believes that all people live in a harsh, unfair world where artificial social distinctions often distort their perceptions of themselves and their relations with others; his attack on colonialism is based upon its refusal to respect the fact that Africans are just as human as Europeans."[10] In three novels—*Une vie de boy, Le vieux nègre et la médaille,* and *Chemin d'Europe*—Oyono deals with the dilemma faced by Africans who assimilate to the European cultural ideal as a way to define themselves. Such Africans soon encounter the many contradictions inherent in colonialism as a civilizing institution and agent of European culture on the one hand, and colonialism as an oppressive, exploitative, and violent political and economic system and agent of white supremacy on the other. In each of these novels, European colonialists, including settlers, consider themselves superior to Africans and believe that their mission is one of benevolence— they have come from Europe to rescue the black people from themselves, assimilate them to European culture, and enhance their ability to successfully enter the modern global community of civilized beings. To many Africans, these Europeans hold in their hands opportunities for education and training and the development of skills that would help them participate gainfully in the new exchange economy. At the same time, the novels portray these same Europeans as insecure beings who justify their extremely poor treatment of Africans by perpetuating the myth of their own superiority. The way they view themselves is based on the belief that Africans are inherently inferior; hence, the colonialists must work continuously to maintain the myth of white supremacy. The result is the maintenance within the colony of a governance system that denigrates and marginalizes the indigenous peoples.

In Oyono's works, Africans believe that assimilation to the French cultural ideal would shower them with significant benefits, including an enhanced status within their Cameroonian community. This struggle to European-ize themselves seems to be supported by genuine encouragement by French colonialism. In the end, however, they come to realize that such rhetoric is designed to enhance the ability of the French to exploit the indigenous peo-ples and their resources for the benefit of the French economy. Thus, they learn that colonialism is not a genuine effort to assimilate Africans and accept them as equals in European society.

Beti's literary career is usually broken up into two major periods: the last 10 years of colonial rule, during which he wrote four novels protesting colonial-ism, and the postcolonial period, in which he returned from "retirement" to protest the country's neocolonial state. Beti saw colonialism as a system set up by Europeans to oppress Africans and, through education and religion, condition them to accept their inferior status permanently. He believed that the initiative to change this state of affairs and rid African societies of these exploitative institutions must be made by the African people themselves. His writings represented his contribution to the struggle against the oppression —he sought to expose the lies behind colonial rhetoric and help Africans understand the deceit inherent in many of the images used by colonialists to support their so-called civilizing mission. Thus, in the four novels that he produced before the French Cameroons gained independence on January 1, 1960, Beti sought to demystify the false images of Africans created by the Europeans, as well as demand that the assumptions underlying colonialism be thoroughly reexamined.

During this period, Beti strongly believed that the colonial enterprise and its evils should be central to any socially and morally responsible African literature. Thus, the four novels that he produced during this period are anticolonialist and emphasize what he believed were the main constraints to the liberation of the African people from colonial exploitation: an oppressive institutional environment and a mentality (created by colonialism) that takes the existing situation as a given. For Beti, the job is to use his creative works to set the record straight—Africans must recapture their image, which has been soiled by the opportunistic colonial enterprise. In this period, Beti was addressing two main audiences: first, the Europeans, whom he wanted to acknowledge and come to terms with the hypocritical, violent, and unjust colonial enterprise; and, second, his fellow Africans, whom he hoped to wake up from their colonially induced sleep, so that they could see the reality of their oppression at the hands of the colonialist, recognize the structures (which included assimilationist dreams of an enhanced self-image) that were used to oppress them, and rise up and dismantle this institutional environment, liberate themselves, and take control of their own destiny.

In 1972, Beti, who had retired from writing novels and who had accepted a job as a high school teacher in France, returned with *Main base sur le Cameroun.* It was the first book that he had published in 14 years. His return to writing was triggered by the trials, by the Ahmadou Ahidjo government, of the Catholic bishop of Nkongsamba, Albert Ndongmo, and Ernest Ouandié, both of whom were accused of treason and of plotting to assassinate the president. Beti interpreted the Ouandié-Ndongmo trial as a failure of the postcolonial state in Cameroon and further evidence that the oppressive and exploitative state, which had been established by European colonialism, had never been reconstructed and reconstituted after independence to provide structures that could enhance peaceful coexistence and ensure social and economic justice. Instead, Ahidjo had retained most of colonialism's exploitative structures and was using them, just as the European colonialists had done, to oppress and exploit the people. Like the colonialists, Ahidjo's government in Cameroon was supported by French entrepreneurial and commercial interests —benefits of post-independence economic growth continued to flow primarily to members of the ruling class in Cameroon and the French economy. Most people continued to suffer just as they had during the colonial period. *Main basse* was Beti's attempt to explain the situation in Cameroon under Ahmadou Ahidjo and emphasize the fact that exploitation of the indigenous peoples, which had begun during the colonial period, had continued with the support of Paris. The Ahidjo government was essentially a neocolonial enterprise that produced benefits for the ruling class and its French benefactors but continued to subject the mass of indigenous peoples to untold injustices. French reaction was swift and decisive—the book was banned, all published copies were seized, and the government unsuccessfully sought to deport Beti back to Cameroon. Although a new edition of the book was successfully released in France in 1976, the book remained banned in Cameroon during Ahidjo's reign.

After *Main basse,* Beti published five novels, including a detailed account of his struggles with the government of Paul Biya (who became president of Cameroon in 1982). All these post-independence novels are designed to force a rethinking of a Cameroon identity within a truly free and independent society. Beti believes that the Cameroon people will eventually triumph and create a truly free and independent country. Mongo Beti (born Alexandre Biyidi at Akométan, Cameroon) died in Cameroon on October 7, 2001. He had returned to Cameroon in 1991 after 32 years of exile in France, during which he taught at the Lycée Corneille de Rouen, France. In addition to his novels, he also edited the highly acclaimed journal, *Peuples noir, peuples africains.*

WOMEN WRITERS

Since independence, there have been significant improvements in opportunities for the education of women. As a consequence, many young women have been able to enter professions that were previously forbidden or closed to them. Some of these educated women have used the skills acquired to protest, through novels, the poor treatment of women and to demand their right to self-determination. Delphine Zanga Tsogo is one such writer, who has used her skills to protest the poor treatment of women by both traditional and modern institutions. She was educated in Cameroon and France as a nurse. After a distinguished career in nursing, she entered public service and in 1975 was appointed Minister for Social Welfare, becoming one of the first women of her generation to attain such a high position in government. She published two novels *(Vies des femmes* and *L'Oiseau en cage)* in which she preaches a feminism that seeks to empower women and enhance their ability to forge their own identities. She argues that, in order for Africans to enjoy the fullness of their humanity, they must enfranchise the women and rid themselves of dominant attitudes and social institutions that oppress women.

Another famous Cameroon woman writer is Calixthe Beyala, who was educated in Cameroon, the Central African Republic, and France. She traveled widely throughout Africa and Europe before finally settling in France. As a child growing up in Cameroon, she was quite disturbed by the pervasiveness of poverty throughout the country. As a novelist, she advances the cause of womanhood. Her works deal with the exploitation, oppression, and marginalization of women not only in her native Cameroon but also throughout the world. She portrays men as spiritually immature, violent, domineering, exploitative, and always eager to use their physical advantages to dominate women. Since her first novel in 1987 *(C'est le soleil qui m'a brûlée),* she has published many others, including *Les honneurs perdus,* which won her the *Grand prix du roman de l'Académie française.*

In her writings, Beyala makes it clear that becoming a woman has little to do with being recognized by men as a desirable sex object. Rather, womanhood involves the development of genuine relationships within a family in which love, respect, and caring are pervasive. She argues further that passing into womanhood also involves discovering the global community of women and the fact that exploitation and marginalization of women is a universal problem. Women, as a community, must continuously seek ways to resist oppression by both traditional and modern institutions.[11]

Other female writers in Cameroon include Marie Clare Dati, Lydie Sophie Dooh Bunya, Marie Félicité Ebokea, Marie Charlotte Mbarga Kouma, Stella Irene Virginie Engama, Angele Kingue, Thérèse Kuoh-Moukoury, Marie Claire Matip, Evelyne Mpoundi Ngole, Justine Nankam, Geneviève Ngosso Kouo, Rabiatou Njoya, Yonko Nana Tabitha, Marie-Thérèse Assiga Ahanda, Philomène Isabelle Mandeng, and Monique Bessomo.

NEWSPAPERS AND MAGAZINES

Cameroon's complex colonial heritage has had a significant impact on its media laws and policies. During the colonial period, especially in the French Cameroons, media laws were designed to enhance the ability of the colonial government to administer the colony and prevent the dissemination of information that was considered injurious to the colonial enterprise. There was very little press activity in British Southern Cameroons. In the French Cameroons, there were several magazines, all of which were controlled by either the colonial government or private newspaper conglomerates in France. The only African contributions that were accepted for publication in these magazines were ethnographic descriptions, folk materials, commentaries on proverbs, and works that supported the assimilationist project. Some of these magazines included *La Gazette du Cameroun, Togo-Cameroun,* and *La Presse du Cameroun.* The latter was established in the French Cameroons in the 1950s by the Paris-based De Breteuil consortium, which earlier had purchased the territory's most important newspaper. Most of the articles published in *La Presse* were taken from the parent company's wire service. Although articles by Cameroonians were accepted for publication in *La Presse,* these had to be only those that were not critical of the colonial enterprise, including missionary activities. The newspaper favored articles by indigenous writers that promoted assimilationism and rejected any opinion pieces that were critical of French policy in the colonies. In fact, while several letters from Cameroonians criticizing the anticolonialism nationalist party, *Union des populations du Cameroun* (UPC), were regularly accepted for publication, the magazine never offered the leadership of the party the opportunity to defend itself. In

1935, then territorial governor J. Repiquet founded the *Societé des Etudes Camerounaise* along with a journal called *Etudes Camerounaises.* The latter served as an instrument of France's civilizing mission in the colony. As with all colonial enterprises, the journal was only opened to Cameroonians who believed in assimilation and supported it.

By 1916, the American Presbyterian Church had established a printing press at Elat near Yaoundé and subsequently started the publication of a Bulu newspaper called *Kalate Mefoe (Book of News).* Although it had a circulation of a little more than 3,000, its readership was limited to local members of the church. In the 1930s, the Catholic diocese of Yaoundé introduced an Ewondo newspaper called *Nleb Bkristen (The Christian Adviser)* with a circulation of more than 6,000.

Between 1955 and 1960, there was an explosion of newspaper publishing, especially in the French Cameroons. By this time, France had seen independence for the territory as inevitable. Its primary interest was to secure a post-independence government that would keep Cameroon within the French community and allow French entrepreneurs to have effective access to their investments and to the resources of the former colony. Hence, the colonial government was interested in supporting Cameroonians who had bought into the idea of closer relations between an independent Cameroon nation and France. Several newspapers sprang up to support independence and speculate on the nature of the new nation. More than 149 newspapers—in French and several local languages, were officially registered with the colonial government at this time.

The many newspapers that became operational in the French Cameroons at this time were owned by political parties, trade unions, religious groups (especially the Catholic and Protestant missions), ethnic associations, and private individuals. Louis-Paul Aujoulat, leader of the *Bloc démocratique Camerounais* (BDC) used his newspaper, *Cameroun de demain,* to promote his political views. Soppo Priso used his *Cameroun Espoir* in a similar fashion. Marcel Bebey-Eyidi, on the other hand, opened his *L'Opinion au Cameroun* to a variety of opinions, including that of UPC intellectual leader Ruben Um Nyobé, who wrote critically of the colonial project and demanded that Cameroonians rise up and destroy it. *Cameroun mon pays,* the official newspaper of the UPC, was quite popular and widely read. However, it was, like *L'Opinion,* often confiscated by the colonial government and prevented from reaching its readers. A highly restrictive and draconian 1939 press law prohibited the publication of any material considered detrimental to the colonial administration of Cameroon. Although passed earlier to minimize German propaganda, it was now being used to suppress the fight for independence.

Churches were very active in the publishing of newspapers. In fact, the territory's longest-surviving and most influential newspaper was the Catholic weekly, *L'Effort Camerounais,* which had been started in the mid-1950s by a French priest, Pierre Fertin. He was a staunch anti-communist, who believed that Catholics (whether French or African) should live a moral life. He supported his indigenous believers' desire for freedom and to "define a collective identity in harmony with their own cultural heritage."[12] Unlike other newspapers headed by Frenchmen, *L'Effort* welcomed the publication of essays by Cameroonians, including those that were critical of French colonialism and in support of independence.

Partly because of low literacy rates (and, hence, a significantly smaller reading public) and also because of the attractive opportunities offered by Nigeria's bustling metropolitan areas (Lagos, Ibadan, and Enugu), literary entrepreneurs in British Cameroons operated primarily in Nigeria. In 1955 at Ibadan, a British Cameroonian named Sankie Maimo, founded a journal called *Cameroon Voice.* The first English newspaper in the British-administered trust territory was *The Cameroon Times,* started by John Ngu Foncha in 1959. The Ibadan student wing of the One Kamerun Party, an offshoot of the UPC, maintained a newspaper called *The Patriot,* in which it attacked colonialism and promoted immediate independence and reunification with the French Cameroons. Although there was a strong press tradition in the French Cameroons before independence, the press in the British Cameroons was still in its embryonic stages when the territory achieved independence in 1961.

The 1962 Ordinance for the "Repression of Subversion" virtually killed the media in Cameroon. In addition to the 1962 law, there were other pieces of legislation that made publishing newspapers or operating other media outlets (e.g., radio and television) virtually impossible. These included the Press Law of 1966 and several laws designed to fight the UPC rebellion. The provisions of these laws were vague and granted the central government enormous powers, which were used to subvert press freedom and prevent any civil society criticism of the government. It was the extreme suppression of freedom of the press that provided Ahidjo with the wherewithal to found and sustain his highly oppressive and authoritarian state. Virtually no newspapers were published in Cameroon after reunification until the government came out with the *Cameroon Tribune* in 1974. Since the explosive riots and demonstrations that characterized the late 1980s and early 1990s and resulted in the legalization of multiparty politics in the country, there has been a relaxation of press laws with a relatively strong private press emerging in the country.[13]

The private newspapers that emerged in the early 1990s were quite effective in helping Cameroonians engage in a national discourse about political and economic issues, as well as about national identity and the issue of citizenship. Governance was, however, the most important and compelling issue examined by the people through opinion pieces, letters to the editor, "man-on-the-street" interviews, and essays authored by university professors, lawyers, retired politicians, traditional rulers, and other informed members of society. For the first time since Biya took office in 1982, Cameroonians were able to discuss the president and his policies openly. In addition, there were criticisms in the papers of the government's pomposity, venality, and other activities that were injurious to the health of the state and its inhabitants. Newspapers such as *Le Messager, Challenge Hebdo,* and the *Cameroon Post,* which were very effective in accurately articulating the demands of ordinary Cameroonians for a more transparent, accountable, and participatory governance system, were targeted by the Biya government for censorship. In fact, on January 13, 1998, Pius Njawé, editor-in-chief of *Le Messager* and *Le Messager Popoli* was convicted and sentenced to two years imprisonment and fined 500,000 francs CFA (about U.S. $1,000) by a court in Douala for supposedly spreading false news about president Paul Biya's health.[14]

Despite the enormous contributions that private newspapers have made to the transition to democratic governance that began in Cameroon in the late 1980s and culminated in the 1990 legalization of multiparty politics, the private press has lost some of its effectiveness because of several internal policies. Several newspapers have transformed themselves into instruments for the maximization of the objectives of opposition political parties and, in the process, have lost their ability to objectively analyze issues critical to the people as well as report the news accurately and without bias. Many of these papers have presented what cannot be considered objective and constructive criticism of the incumbent government. Of course, the ruling party (Cameroon People's Democratic Movement) finances a few newspapers *(Le Patriote, Le Temoin,* and *Le Temps),* which take an overt pro-government line in their reporting.[15]

Readership remains quite small for most newspapers in Cameroon. First, the majority of papers are published in English and French, and most Cameroonians are not literate in these languages. Second, most newspapers are published and distributed primarily in the major urban areas with little or no effort made to make them available to the people who live in rural areas. As well, these people, who constitute more than 70 percent of the population, have very high illiteracy rates (especially in French and English) and would not be able to read the papers. Third, most newspapers in Cameroon cover events in the urban areas and rarely venture into rural happenings. It is unlikely that rural folk would find these papers attractive. Fourth, the poor nature of Cameroon's transportation network makes nationwide distribution of newspapers virtually impossible. Finally, given the high levels of poverty and material deprivation, most people, who are struggling to meet their daily basic needs, are not likely to spend CFA 250 to buy a newspaper when they could use the money to purchase food. In fact, newspapers are financially out of reach for most wage earners in the urban sectors as well as to farmers in the rural regions of the country.

Internationally recognized organizations such as Amnesty International, International Freedom of Exchange, Media Watch, and Index on Censorship have provided detailed accounts of the physical intimidation, torture, and detention without trial of Cameroon journalists by the government.[16] According to the U.S. State Department's annual report on Human Rights Practices in Cameroon, in 1999, Cameroon, Nigeria, The Gambia, and Togo had the poorest records for the treatment of journalists and other media personnel in all of Africa. In fact, during the last several years, more than 50 journalists who have written articles criticizing the government about increasing levels of corruption in the public sector have been prosecuted under various laws. Among the charges filed against these reporters have been libel, dissemination of false news, incitement to sedition, and rebellion. Many of the reporters have been convicted and sentenced to many years in prison and their papers forced to pay heavy fines. For example, in November 1998, *Le Quotidien* was forced to suspend publication after a court fined it CFA 25 million. *Le Quotidien* joined *Galaxie* and *La Détente,* which had been forced to close earlier as a result of heavy fines imposed on them by the government. Unscrupulous, opportunistic, and corrupt state custodians (politicians and civil servants) have effectively used criminal libel suits to extort money from the private press and to persecute their political competition. In addition to these lawsuits, many journalists have been threatened, arrested, questioned, detained, and subjected to various forms of intimidation in an effort to prevent them from performing their jobs. Many of them have chosen exile as a way to avoid further stress on themselves and their families.

There is no question that Cameroon now has a strong and viable private press, effectively breaking the government's monopoly on the dissemination of information and the interpretation of events. Despite its failings and the difficulties it continues to face, the private press has successfully exposed civil service incompetence and ineptitude, public corruption and financial malfeasance, and the general failure of the postcolonial government to serve the needs of the people. Still, it is premature to say that Cameroon now has a press that is capable of effectively serving as a guardian of the country's new democracy. The overall quality of journalistic output remains poor and needs improvement.

BROADCAST MEDIA

Cameroon's broadcast media consists of radio and television. Radio is currently the broadest and most effective means of disseminating information in the country. It transcends the barriers of language and geography, and it is also much easier to own and maintain. A government interested in keeping its citizens informed of public policies would have been eager to enhance private ownership of radio and television stations. However, the Cameroon government has refused to surrender the monopoly on radio that it has enjoyed since independence.

Cameroon Radio and Television (CRTV), which is part of the Ministry of Communication, owns a network of 10 provincial, 1 national, and 2 FM radio stations (Douala and Yaoundé) and a national television station in Yaoundé. While the CRTV is described in official circles as designed to serve the public, it is controlled by the minister of communication, who is the official spokesman of the government. Until 1990, when the new media law was passed, it was illegal to operate a private radio or television station in Cameroon. The new media law's Section 36 formally abolished CRTV's monopoly on the broadcast media by providing for the establishment of private radio stations.

In 1996, an amendment to the 1990 media law provided for the licensing of private radio and television stations. However, the regulations needed to operationalize private ownership of radio and television stations have not been provided by the Biya government despite significant pressure from the public. Since the "third wave" of democratization that began in Africa in the late 1980s, there has been a significant proliferation of private, local, and commercial radio and television stations throughout Africa. In fact, in relatively poor countries such as Togo, Burkina Faso, and Mali there has been a boom in private ownership of media outlets. Yet, in Cameroon, which has a larger and much more dynamic economy than many of these other countries, there is still no formal legal instrument allowing private broadcast media outlets to operate freely.

As a result of a loophole in the 1990 law, a project funded by Canada to provide five radio stations in Kembong, Oku, Foutouni, Lolodorf, and Mouturewa was approved in 1997. Given the fact that these rural radio stations have been granted permission to operate only in thinly populated areas, they do not pose a threat to CRTV's media monopoly. The government has not intervened to stop the Catholic Church from operating an FM station *(Radio Reine)*, which rebroadcasts programs of the Vatican radio service. Three other private radio stations also operate in the country: *Radio Lumière,* which broadcasts music from a high school in Yaoundé; an FM station in Mbalmayo, which only discusses women's issues; and *Radio Soleil.* From time to time, the minister of communication has warned these unlicensed radio stations of their illegal activities. However, the government has not made any effort to shut them down. This is perhaps because the activities of these stations have not threatened CRTV's media monopoly and because the stations have not directly criticized the government.

Government Monopolization of the Broadcast Media

CRTV, which monopolizes the broadcast media in Cameroon, is supposed to function as a public-service entity, engaging in activities that enhance the national welfare and promote peaceful coexistence of population groups. However, its present set-up, management, and control do not allow for it to function as such. All CRTV workers are civil servants who have been granted special privileges by the government. All of them receive compensation packages that are much larger than those received by similarly qualified workers in other government ministries. Promotions and appointments within CRTV are dependent on political considerations (especially loyalty to the president and the ruling CPDM) and not on professional competence. As a consequence, CRTV journalists who critically analyze government policies or run stories that reflect unfavorably on the government are harassed, arrested, and detained, violently interrogated by the police, transferred to nonbroadcast positions within the corporation or to a remote part of the country, or, worse, fired.

There is some evidence that by 1994, of the 50 reporters and announcers who joined CRTV during its first three years of operation, about 27 had left the corporation disappointed, angry, and frustrated over their inability to carry out their duties professionally and honestly.[17] CRTV management is so eager to turn journalists and announcers into loyal "praise singers" for the government that it has succeeded in demoralizing most of its experienced and skilled journalists and forcing the exit of quite a large number of them. This obsession with retaining only workers who are loyal to the government has resulted in the retention of mediocre and inexperienced individuals. In fact, on occasion, the management has resorted to appointing non-journalists to present the programs or read the news on radio and television.

Within existing press laws in Cameroon, CRTV's independence is not guaranteed. Given its dependence on the government, it is highly doubtful that CRTV can operate as an effective instrument of public service. Like the colonial media outlets, CRTV exists to serve the needs of the government and not those of the Cameroon people. Its coverage of the various elections that have taken place in the country since multiparty political competition was legalized in Cameroon in 1990 confirms the belief by many observers that the CRTV serves only the interests of the president and his party and totally ignores many issues that are important to Cameroonians. During all these elections, CRTV's airwaves have been used to promote the president and the CPDM, while opposition political parties have been denied access to CRTV's services, making it very difficult for them to bring their message to the people.

To provide the country with an effective and genuine public-service facility, it is necessary to change the laws regulating the operations of CRTV. Privatization, of course, is the most appropriate way to enhance efficiency and make sure that CRTV's operations are not subject to control by opportunistic civil servants and politicians. Some people are likely to argue that public media structures (e.g., a public broadcasting service) are critical, especially in a developing country. Such a service, however, must be granted autonomy so that it can function without undue influence from the government and must do so in an environment in which it is forced to compete with private media companies. Hence, the first line of business should be either to privatize CRTV or undertake institutional reforms to allow entrepreneurs to establish radio and television stations that can compete effectively with CRTV. Within such a competitive environment, CRTV should no longer be able to dominate the dissemination of information and the analysis of events in the country.

Cameroon continues to struggle with its transition to democratic governance. So far, the media has done a relatively good job of enhancing that transition. However, in order for the media to continue to perform its job effectively and help Cameroonians deepen and institutionalize democracy, press freedom must be constitutionally guaranteed. The constitution must not only guarantee freedom of expression, but it must also prohibit the imposition, by the government, of restraints on journalism and journalists, including censorship and other state-sponsored activities detrimental to the maintenance of a healthy and viable press.

NOTES

1. Richard Bjornson, *The African Quest for Freedom and Identity: Cameroonian Writing and the National Experience* (Bloomington: Indiana University Press, 1991), p. 21.

2. Bjornson (1991), p. 22.

3. W. Keller, *The History of the Presbyterian Church in West Cameroon* (Victoria: Presbook, 1969).

4. Bjornson (1991), p. 41.

5. See, for example, Louis-Marie Pouka M'Bague, *Poèms* (Yaoundé: Lumen, 1971).

6. Bjornson (1991), p. 44.

7. Ibid., p. 45.

8. Ibid., p. 46.

9. Ibid., p. 52.

10. Nicki Hitchcott, *Women Writers in Francophone Africa* (New York: Berg, 2000), pp. 128–151.

11. Bjornson (1991), p. 71.

12. Ibid., p. 52.

13. Charles Manga Fombad, "The Mass Media and Democratization in Africa: Lessons from Cameroon," in *The Transition to Democratic Governance: The Continuing Struggle,* eds. J.M. Mbaku and J.O. Ihonvbere (Westport, CT: Praeger, 2003), pp. 221–247.

14. Lyombe Eko, "Hear All Evil, See All Evil, Rail Against All Evil: *Le Messager* and the Journalism of Resistance in Cameroon," in *The Leadership Challenge in Africa: Cameroon under Paul Biya,* eds. J.M. Mbaku and J. Takougang (Trenton, NJ: Africa World Press, 2004).

15. Fombad (2003), p. 232.

16. Ibid., p. 234.

17. See, for example, Eko, "Hear All Evil, See all Evil, Rail Against All Evil."

4

Art, Architecture, and Housing

In Cameroon, the predominant form of art is sculpture. However, Cameroonians are involved in other forms of media. Traditional art differs in both form and style from region to region. Artistic expression in the north is influenced by Fulani culture and Islamic religious practices. Here, handicrafts, which include the decoration of calabashes, pottery, and leatherwork, dominate Fulani art. Among other population groups that inhabit northern Cameroon, woodcarving is the predominant form of artistic expression.

Throughout the country's history, the people of the western highlands have been noted for their extraordinary varieties of art. Success in producing extremely high quality art objects in this region has been driven primarily by powerful kings and chieftains, who have been important patrons and benefactors. The kings provided skilled artists room at the palace to practice their craft and also provided resources for artists to train and develop their skills. However, because skilled artists often migrated from one imperial court to another, there was a significant diffusion of styles, making the determination of the origin of art objects quite difficult. The process, however, produced what is often referred to as the "grasslands art style."

In the history of Cameroon art, Sultan Njoya-Arouna of the Bamoun is considered the most important art patron. Among art objects produced during his reign (c. 1888–1933) were carved masks, drinking horns, tobacco pipes, objects cast in brass and bronze, exquisitely handwoven cotton fabrics (all of which were embroidered or dyed in indigo), and several other items, including carved and decorated calabashes, as well as stools or thrones. The most famous throne in Bamoun art history was that of Njoya-Arouna now in a German museum. Many of these carved objects were decorated with beads of various colors.

Besides King Njoya-Arouna, various Bamiléké, Nso', Bali-Nyonga, Kom, Oku, Aghem, Bafut, Mankon, Bangwa, Babanki-Tungo, and other grasslands kings also supported the arts and made significant investments in developing an art culture throughout their kingdoms. This is evident in many of the art objects found throughout the grasslands region and in museums in Western Europe and North America.

Among the Pahouin in the southern forest region of Cameroon, wood sculpture is very popular. Figures carved with wood include those of ancestors, as well as masks used for various ceremonies, including especially religious ones. In addition, drums, stools, walking sticks (staffs), and kitchen utensils were also made of wood and decorated with various figures. Because many of these sculptures were associated with various traditional rites that were found by Christian missionaries to be objectionable, most of the region's traditional art forms were banished along with the abolition and subsequent replacement with Christian practices of what missionaries termed "heathen" rites. Today, most Pahouin art consists of Christian religious art and commercial pieces produced exclusively for the tourist industry. Art objects with Christian themes decorate the various houses of worship throughout the region.

Among the Duala, traditional painting has existed for many generations. The Duala are widely known for their cattle masks, which are painted in black, white, red, and blue. They are also famous for their beautifully decorated canoe prows.

Although representations of Cameroon art in books published in the West and in Western museums are dominated by wood sculptures, the genres and forms of the country's art are multiple and diverse. Cameroon art embodies both modern and traditional styles. Today, many young Cameroonians can go to a special school to study the various art media, although the traditional method in which young artists serve as apprentices to skilled and accomplished practitioners remains quite popular. As they have done for many generations, Cameroon artists continue to produce rock paintings and engravings; various types of decorated pottery; and sculptures made of clay, stone, wood, bronze, ivory, and other locally produced materials. Modern and traditional art styles in Cameroon are reflected in the country's architecture, body adornments, and the various rites and rituals associated with religion and other practices.

Modern Cameroon art is significantly influenced by religious practices (traditional, Christian, and Islamic). Before the arrival of Islam and Christianity, art was used in traditional religious ceremonies and rituals. Such art objects included musical instruments (e.g., drums, flutes, and cymbals) used in religious ceremonies; carved doors and house posts used to decorate homes; thrones made of wood, bronze, and ivory, as well as stools for other lesser ruling elites; carved ornamental staffs carried by important officials, as well as utilitarian staffs used for support by the elderly and people with physical disabilities. Today, the religious significance of art remains quite strong. In fact, ornamentation of Christian churches with locally produced art objects has become quite a popular practice. However, such art objects invariably are based on Christian themes, with most of them decorated with biblical images.

ROYAL ART IN THE WESTERN GRASSLANDS

In Cameroon's western grasslands, kings use art to enhance royal prestige and authority. In fact, in most inter-kingdom alliances over the years, art objects (especially those carrying a royal seal or symbol) have been exchanged. Throughout the years, such exchanges have contributed significantly to the sharing of cultures across royal courts, resulting, as mentioned earlier, in the development of what is generally referred to as the "grasslands art style."[1]

The development of the royal courts of the western grasslands peaked in the nineteenth century, a period of significant inter-kingdom trade. Flourishing trade during this period made available to court artists materials that could be used to enhance and enrich their creations. Almost without exception, grasslands societies were well structured, with the king (or *fon*), who was considered a divine being, sitting at the apex. The rest of the society consisted of commoners or the mass of the people, and nobility. The nobility was made up of the descendants of the male children of the kings and commoners who had been promoted as a reward for service to the king. In these kingdoms, art and its enjoyment were limited to the sovereign; nobles could, at the king's discretion or grace, use art objects for various activities. It was understood, however, that all art in theory belonged to the king. In fact, the king retained a monopoly on all precious metals, imported beads and fabrics, as well as so-called royal animals (e.g., the elephant, leopard, crocodile, buffalo, and serpent), which could be used to produce art objects. In many of these kingdoms, only the sovereign could use these animals as symbols. Parts of these animals (e.g., ivory) in art could only be used with the king's permission.

German, French, and British colonial rule significantly damaged the authority of Cameroon's kings and destroyed some of the kingdoms. Some kings were deposed and forced into exile (e.g., King Njoya of the Bamoun was deposed by the French and forced into exile in Douala, where he eventually died), and others were killed by colonial authorities (e.g., in 1913, King Douala Manga Bell of the Duala was executed by German colonial authorities). European colonial officers and, to a certain extent, missionaries often considered these traditional rulers recalcitrant individuals who hindered their so-called civilizing mission in the country and sought ways to either discredit or get rid of them.[2]

King Njoya (c. 1870–1933) of the Bamoun became the sovereign after the death of his father, King Nsa'ngu, in battle between 1885 and 1887. However, due to his age, he was only able to assume the throne officially between 1892 and 1896. He was a brilliant, articulate, and visionary ruler who fully understood the duties and responsibilities of a sovereign. He recognized the fact that he came into power at a time when his kingdom, as well as all of the German colony of Kamerun, were going through tremendous changes, most of which were brought about by such external forces as Christianity, Islam, and European colonialism. While making every effort to protect the integrity of Bamoun traditions and culture from these external forces, he also understood the need for change and adaptation and, hence, undertook institutional reforms that enhanced the ability of his kingdom to deal effectively with the new forces and continue to prosper.

King Njoya studied both Christianity and Islam and undertook a series of reforms and innovations. Three of these stand out. First, he created a new script or writing system (based on Arabic, Western forms, and traditional divination signs), which was used to document the kingdom's precolonial history, medical knowledge, traditional religious practices, and important forms of court etiquette. Second, he established schools that taught the new script along with other subjects—notably history of the kingdom, art, and culture. Third, he introduced a new religion based on Christianity, Islam, and Bamoun traditional religious practice.

During his reign, King Njoya made many artistic innovations, borrowing freely from Islamic and Western sources. For example, he created a new dress style for his court based on Islamic and Western (particularly German) as well as traditional Bamoun styles and his own personal innovations. The king wore many of the new dress designs, including embroidered robes, turbans, and boots modeled after fashions of Islamic Hausa-Fulbe rulers to the north. Again, drawing from foreign styles and traditional practice as well as his own innovative contributions, he built a series of palaces, many of which can be seen in Bamoun country today. Although he borrowed from Islamic and Western architectural styles, he brilliantly incorporated local styles and materials. This is evident in the palace he built in 1912 under the supervision of the artistically talented Prince Ibrahim Njoya. This three-story building used many local materials, including earthen bricks, in a design influenced by German, Islamic, and traditional styles. The interior design was influenced by Fulbe-Hausa building traditions. King Njoya lived in this extraordinarily beautiful palace until he was exiled to Yaoundé by French colonial authorities in 1931.

During his short reign, King Njoya introduced building technologies, metalworking, textiles, new design motifs (several of which were modeled after animals such as spiders and frogs) that were made available to artists in the royal court, and he abolished royal monopolies on certain materials, such as ivory, as well as on subjects previously considered the purview of only royal artists.

The throne is one of the most important objets d'art in the western grasslands. Carved from a single piece of wood, it is divided into several parts and depicts humans or animals. Generally, thrones are decorated with images of human beings and animals of mythical strength and importance, such as double-headed serpents, dragons, leopards, elephants, and lions. In some kingdoms, only the king was allowed to sit on stools decorated with images of humans or animals. The images presented on a throne are not randomly placed there, but are selected and carefully placed to embody the king's power, virility, judiciousness, wealth, and lordship over his kingdom. The throne of King Nsa'ngu, which was made of wood and decorated with glass beads and cowries, was given to the German emperor Wilhelm II in 1908 in appreciation of the help provided by the Germans in securing the return of the head of King Njoya's father from their bitter enemy, the Nso'. Today, it can be found in the Museum für Völkerkunde in Berlin.[3]

In the western grasslands of Cameroon, stools are considered a very important political symbol. Carved and elaborately decorated stools are often given by sovereigns as gifts to traditional heads of local governments within the kingdom (e.g., loyal chiefs and those who have served the king well or have excelled in battle). When kings and chiefs traveled, their stools usually traveled with them to make certain the ruler sat only on an approved and empowered stool. Leopards and elephants are considered throughout the continent as important symbols of dynastic power, so images of these two animals figure very prominently in most royal art in Africa. Royal stools in the Cameroon grasslands frequently display a hybrid leopard-elephant animal.

Stools, including especially thrones, were usually empowered through elaborate ceremonies before they were ready for use by the sovereign or some other ruler, such as a chief. In the kingdom of Bamoun, after a new throne was carved, it was brought to the palace and taken to the "house of the earth (or gods)," where the empowering ceremony was conducted. First, a ram was sacrificed on the throne's surface. Second, a special sacred bag containing the royal relics was carried around its circumference. Third, special substances with extraordinary powers were rubbed into the surface of the throne. In addition to making the throne powerful, these substances were supposed to transform it into a tool that could be used only by the king. At this point, the throne was capable of destroying anyone who dared to usurp the king's power by sitting on it. In fact, no one was allowed to touch the throne or any stool that had been sat on by the sovereign except special stool carriers of the court. The stool carriers had sworn an oath of absolute fidelity and hence were trusted to faithfully carry out their duties without compromising the integrity of the royal stools.

ARTIST-KINGS

A significant portion of royal art in the palaces of many kingdoms in Cameroon was produced by a king or some other royal. Within the grasslands of Cameroon, the artist-king is a widespread phenomenon. In fact, artistic creativity was considered an important and critical part of a king's prerogative. The phenomenon of artist-king is common among the Bamoun, Kom, Bali-Nyonga, Babanki-Tungu, and Bangwa kingdoms of the grasslands.

When Jinaboh II, king of the Kom, was presented to the people in January 1976, he was surrounded by sculptures produced by the artist-king Fon Yu (1865–1912). During the ceremony, the new king drew support from the figures as he completed his transition from an ordinary citizen of the kingdom to its empowered sovereign.[4]

King Fon Yu of the Kom was considered an extraordinarily talented and skilled ruler. In addition, he was also a very gifted artist as evidenced by the works he left behind. The sculptures *(ngoyou)* on display at the enthronement of King Jinaboh II in 1976 depict a king, his principal or first wife, and the queen mother and are considered the most important sacred objects in the kingdom of Kom. These objects symbolize dynastic continuity. In fact, the figure of the ruler among these objects was sold in the 1960s, causing so much distress in the kingdom that an international effort was devoted to its return. During its absence, various problems in Kom, including poor harvests, were blamed on the "sacrilege" committed against the state by selling it. Its return in 1974 was accompanied by elaborate celebratory ceremonies and is said to have returned peace, stability, and prosperity to the kingdom.[5]

King Yu also produced other figures, including that of a queen (carrying a planting stick, which symbolizes the importance of women of the grasslands in farming and agricultural production) that now stands in the Museum für Völkerkunde in Berlin. Each of the figures carved by the king stands on a stool decorated with royal symbols, including the buffalo. No one is allowed to sit on these stools. However, each figure and its stool depict the importance of seating among the grasslands peoples. In the kingdom of Kom, after the death of a king, all his sons and those of earlier kings were brought to the palace, and from among them kingmakers would choose a successor to the deceased ruler. After the choice was made, the kingmakers would rub empowering medicines on the king-to-be and sit him on a royal stool. Throughout the grasslands, throne figures are used to depict both the power of the individual ruler and the importance of the office of the king.

REGIONAL ART

For cultural and artistic purposes, Cameroon can be divided into four areas: the forest zone, the grasslands of the southwest, the western region bordering Nigeria, and the north. The grasslands, as mentioned, has an extraordinarily rich artistic culture that has, over the years, been encouraged and sustained by its many kings and chiefs. Divided into various independent kingdoms and chiefdoms, it has attracted interest among Western European scholars, entrepreneurs, and travelers because of its rich artistic heritage.[6] Most of that interest has been concentrated in the Bamiléké, Bamoun, Tikar, and a few others such as the Nso', Bali-Nyonga, Bangwa, and Kom—kingdoms that have had very strong and influential sovereigns with significant support for the arts.

The production of art objects in the grasslands area of Cameroon has traditionally been associated with ceremonies at the sovereign's palace and various rites designed to enhance the welfare of the people (e.g., ceremonies to honor ancestral spirits and seek their favorable intervention in earthly challenges such as droughts and wars). Certain art objects (e.g., large carved figures of animals and humans; thrones, including special stools; and other prestige objects such as staffs) are reserved for the sovereign, who uses them to assert his authority. The mask, which is one of the most important grasslands art objects, is generally worn during important ceremonies (e.g., an annual festival to thank the ancestors for a good harvest; burial ceremonies for important leaders; and rites to seek favorable ancestral intervention in an upcoming military encounter).

Throughout the years, each grasslands kingdom has developed its own unique artistic style. However, as mentioned, frequent migration of artists (quite often in search of more generous patrons) has resulted in a significant diffusion of styles. Still, it is possible to trace the origin of many of the masks found in the region. For example, as described by one scholar, "Bangwa figures ... display an encrusted patina and filed teeth typical of the fashion of this kingdom. Northern Grasslands kingdom masks and figures have a deeply grooved coiffure ... and Bamum masks are often covered by a sheet of metal."[7] In fact, one usually finds that similar types of masks are produced within the various kingdoms. During the burial ceremony for an important dignitary, the lead dancer (most likely a man) wears a mask decorated with royal paraphernalia (e.g., cowrie shells and beads). Such a mask would be a "man's" mask and may be followed by masks representing a woman and various animals. A woman's mask is usually designed to embody the kingdom's view of femininity. Within the various grasslands kingdoms, one can find several types of male masks, each displaying various coiffures. For example, among the Bamoun, a popular male mask is carved with an open-worked coiffure decorated with spider motifs and used during ceremonies held at the palace of the sovereign.[8]

Among the Bamiléké kingdoms, two zoomorphic masks are prominent. First is the elephant mask that is constructed of cloth decorated with beads and used exclusively in Kuosi ceremonies, which bring together royals and members of the warrior class. Second is the "helmet" mask carved in the image of a buffalo head and believed to belong exclusively to the sovereign. Also among the Bamiléké one frequently finds several forms of headdress carved out of wood. Carved headdresses are also found among the Tikar and other groups within the grasslands area of Cameroon.

Statues, most of which represent ancestors, can be found among the Bamoun and other kingdoms in the western grasslands region of Cameroon. These are usually life size and incorporated into a throne to form part of the backrest. Some of these statues, including those representing the king's wives and various palace attendants, are usually stored in secret or forbidden areas and brought out for display during special occasions, including the visits of important foreign dignitaries, and during special ceremonies honoring the sovereign.

Within the grasslands area, figures decorated with beads are quite popular and represent the most well-known sculptures of the region. In fact, Bamiléké and Bamoun sculptures carved of wood, covered with cloth, and decorated with multicolored beads have gained international acclaim. Statues from the kingdom of Bangwa, including that of a dancing queen, have also gained international fame. Smaller figures, which are used in healing and anti-witchcraft ceremonies, can be found throughout the region. A popular figurine is a pregnant woman with rounded features. Other popular carved items include stools, tables decorated with beads of various colors, bracelets (those carved of ivory are considered especially precious and are often worn exclusively by princesses; bracelets are also made from beads and cowries), large bowls, carved horns (most of which were used for royal feasts), bronze pipes, and coiffures of red feathers and reserved for special ceremonies. Various musical instruments are also produced by artists. These include anthropomorphic and zoomorphic drums and metal gongs, which are used in various dances and especially in ceremonies honoring the sovereign.[9]

The people who live in what is referred to as the forest zone or coastal areas of Cameroon were the first to have contact with Europeans who came as missionaries and invading colonialists in the nineteenth century. There is significant mixing among the various ethnic groups that reside in this region and, as a consequence, the art objects produced by the various groups are stylistically similar. The Duala, the people found around the Cameroon (Wouri) River, are distinguished producers of zoomorphic masks, stools for kings (chiefs), and decorative canoe prows. In the pre-colonial period, Duala artists produced extraordinarily beautiful objects with ivory. In recent years, however, a significant number of Duala artists (as well those of other groups in the region) have been producing primarily for the tourist trade. Although many of these pieces still reflect the Duala's rich artistic heritage, some are mass produced, and some critics believe that today's artists are not as dedicated to the craft as their ancestors.

Along the Nigerian border live various groups, including the Kaka, the Mbembe, the Todkom, the Mfumbe, the Banyang, and the Anyang. The social and cultural practices of these peoples have been affected significantly by their neighbors—the grasslands peoples to the east and various Nigerian groups to the west. The Kaka are expert wood carvers who produce masks and figures. Many of their figures are characterized by open and screaming mouths. Speculation is that these objects were used during burial ceremonies or funerals, as well as during various initiations.[10]

In addition to being expert traders, the Mbembe are also renowned for their carved art. Especially noteworthy are large basalt columns used to decorate the graves of the group's nobility. Another famous Mbembe art object is the carved large slit drum sporting the figure of a chief holding a prisoner's head at the end.[11] Among the Mbembe, such drums are used as communication tools to summon men in an emergency.

Artistic traditions among the Todkom and Mfumbe reflect an amalgamation of Cameroon and Nigerian artistic traditions. Within these groups are autonomous village communities that carve masks and figures used in various ceremonies. Many of the figures carved in these villages exhibit extremely distorted features characteristic of the Tikar people of the grasslands region of Cameroon and the various groups of the Cross River region of Nigeria.

Cameroon's northern region is home to many ethnic groups with various artistic traditions. Among these are the Mambila and the Namji in the west, the Wute and Vere in the south, the Fulani in the east, and the Kirdi in the north.

The Mambila are well known for masks that have a heart-shaped face and red and white pigments. Figures produced by Mambila artists appear with bent legs and an enlarged head outlined in wooded pegs and are thought to embody the group's ancestors. These objects are used for various ceremonies. For example, during the dances celebrating the end of the planting season, a man wearing a helmet mask usually leads the dancers, followed by a contingent of assistants, each wearing secondary masks representing various animals.

The Namji people of Cameroon have gained a reputation in the West for wooden dolls that exhibit geometric features and are decorated with multicolored necklaces.

Among the Wute and Vere peoples, most artistic effort is devoted to the production of baskets and necklaces. The latter are made of metal and are quite rare.

Because the Fulani are primarily nomadic peoples, they have not produced many works of art. However, they carve bowls and many utilitarian objects.

Among the Kirdi, artistic output is limited to objects produced with leather, metal pieces (including special iron garments used by women in special ceremonies), and small terracotta figures. These figures are believed to be stylistically related to those belonging to the Sao civilization, which dominated the north of Cameroon, Chad, and Nigeria from the twelfth to the nineteenth centuries.[12]

HOUSING AND ARCHITECTURE

Architectural styles in Cameroon, like those in other countries, have been influenced significantly by such factors as climate, available building materials, social use of space, and patterns of living. Shelter forms in Cameroon range from temporary structures common among the Pygmies (Bakas) of the southern tropical forests and the nomads of the northern semi-arid regions to modern high-rise buildings in urban centers.[13]

The nomadic cattle-herders of the far north of Cameroon build relatively light shelters that can easily be dismantled and carried along as they migrate from one grazing place to another. These houses are usually beehive-shaped or semispherical. First, a series of light, flexible, wooden poles are set up in the form of a semisphere. Second, the structure is covered with leaves, mats, or the stalks of millet plants. At night, the door to each house is covered with a mat or netting produced by sewing together strips of cloth. Interior furnishings consist primarily of a large wooden frame bed, a mortar used to grind millet (the food staple), calabashes (which serve several functions), various types of basins, and a few tools. As the dry season approaches and grazing conditions deteriorate, nomads dismantle their abodes, collect their belongings, and take their livestock to new grazing areas where they can set up house again.

Fulani of the northern semi-arid regions and central highlands who have settled in permanent towns and villages live in two distinct types of houses: round mud houses with cone-shaped thatched roofs and rectangular houses constructed of sun-dried brick, usually with flat roofs. Usually, houses belonging to members of a family are built together around a single courtyard and are enclosed by a fence or mud wall. Such a grouping of houses is referred to as a *saré*. The main entrance to the *saré* is through an attached building in which a guard sleeps. The house of the head of the family is in the courtyard, as well as houses for all his wives. Each wife has her own house in which she resides with her daughters and young sons. The older unmarried sons must be lodged in the attached building that serves as an entrance to the compound. The kitchen, storage space for food, and quarters for servants and older members of the family are located in separate buildings. Behind each house are ditches that are screened off by mats and serve as toilets. The water supply is held in large earthen pots in front of the houses.[14]

Inside each Fulani house, the floor is stamped earth and the house is decorated with simple and mostly utilitarian items, including beds made of thin wooden sticks and covered with mats, weapons hung from the ceiling, a copy of the Koran (Qur'an), or alternatively wooden tablets containing verses of the Koran. It is common to see in a Fulani man's house a trunk near the bed where personal items and clothing are stored. In a woman's house, one finds an iron pot (usually imported) in which jewelry and other personal items are stored. Alternatively, women may place their personal items in nets that are hung from the ceiling. Armchairs and stools are found primarily in the homes of chiefs and other nobles.

Among other inhabitants of the Adamaoua Plateau (e.g., the Baboute, the Mboum, the Dourou, and the Baya), housing styles are similar to those of the Fulani. However, houses are usually roomier, round or rectangular, with pyramidal or conical roofs made of straw. The inside of the house is partitioned into two rooms—one for sleeping and the other for storage or food preparation. Among these groups, one finds compounds similar to the Fulani *saré*—here, members of a family build houses around a courtyard and secure them with a mat fence. In the larger villages, several of these compounds are grouped together around a large open square.

Inside each house, one can find Fulani-style beds for the men and mats for women and children. There rarely is any furniture, except for a few stools. Most of these people are farmers engaged in the production of groundnuts (peanuts) and millet. During the harvest season, farmers must work in fields far away from home, often for long periods of time. Hence, they construct temporary housing using tree branches and leaves. These structures, which are located close to the fields or farms, are usually dismantled or abandoned after the harvest is completed and the crops secured.

In the northern hills, one can find a group of relatively small houses perched on top of steep rock faces. The houses are constructed of dry stone walls and straw roofs. They are located close to each other. Houses for women and the grown children, as well as storage areas for grain and animals, are usually interconnected with the entire complex and accessed only through the house of the family head. Unlike the Fulani *saré*, compounds of the northern hills people do not have interior courts. Each woman is provided with a silo of her own in which she stores the food to feed her family. Family heads also maintain silos in which they store grain for various purposes, including subsidizing the stocks of wives and also as insurance against unexpected changes in economic conditions.

Along the border with Chad live the Moundang, who maintain fortress-like compounds of square houses and granaries constructed of mud and having high rounded roofs. The houses are arranged in a circle. Each compound is surrounded by a low, circular mud wall, with entrance gained through a single gate flanked by two towers. Within the compound, the house of the family head is located between the stable and the storehouses and faces the gate. The woman's house consists of three main sections: a kitchen, a bedroom (with a mud bed built into the wall), and a storeroom. Illumination of the interior of the house is through one or two round windows—a calabash or gourd is used to cover the hole in case of rain.[15]

The Bamiléké of the western highlands are one of Cameroon's largest ethnic groups. Their houses are usually larger than those of the northern peoples. However, like the northerners, Bamiléké architecture effectively utilizes local materials to build houses that serve residents' needs well. The typical village house in Bamiléké country is 12 to 15 feet square and is made of large sun-dried bricks with a pyramidal thatched roof. In recent years, corrugated iron sheets have become a popular roofing material. Each house is usually red, yellow, gray, or white. Doors on houses are about five feet high and about five feet wide, with the eaves and side decorated with art. Ceilings usually project beyond the wall and are supported by wooden columns. These overhangs provide shaded areas for family gatherings and sports and social activities for children. Bamiléké compounds consist of about 10 to 20 houses and are surrounded by farms and/or gardens where crops are grown.

A typical Bamiléké house consists of a single room with a granary sandwiched between the roof and the ceiling. The granary is accessed through a hole in the ceiling using a ladder. In houses occupied by women, pots and pans and other cooking utensils are stored on bamboo shelves. Food is prepared in the middle of the house on a clay hearth (about eight inches high) designed to support a cooking pot. Other furnishings include a bed lodged against one wall, stools, baskets, grinding stones for preparing corn meal, and other items for cooking.

Among the Bamiléké, the compound or palace of the king or *fon* (or some other such notable), usually has a central avenue with the fon's house (or that of the head of the family) at the end of it. Along both sides of the avenue are the houses of women, and the outer walls of the houses are part of the compound's or palace's enclosure. The spaces between houses are filled with sun-dried mud bricks or raffia palm matting.[16]

In the southern forest region, most houses are rectangular with two-sided thatched roofs. The men do the main construction work on the houses, working with wood and raffia palm ribs. The women then fill the spaces between the ribs with mud. After the mud has dried, each house is painted green, blue, or orange and occasionally is decorated with pictorial designs. On average, each house is about 25 feet long and 12 feet wide and contains three to five rooms.

In recent years, residential architecture in this and other parts of Cameroon has undergone significant modifications to take into consideration new materials and building techniques, as well as changes in economic conditions of families. For example, as household incomes have increased, many people have switched to using independent contractors for the construction of their homes. Hence, professional masons and carpenters have become important in the housing construction industry. In addition, professional builders are more likely to use so-called modern building materials, which include cement bricks for walls, cement for floors, and aluminum sheets for roofs. Also, many of the professionally constructed homes have windows and shutters. In urban centers such as Douala and Yaoundé, homes may have indoor plumbing.

Among the Pahouin of the forest region, houses are built primarily with wood (with two-sided roofs covered with corrugated iron sheets) and either lined up along a road or grouped together around a central square. Men's houses are placed closest to the square, and women's houses are behind the men's. Stables and granaries usually are not part of forest architecture.

Among the fishermen of the Wouri and Sanaga Rivers, houses constructed of raffia palm ribs and leaves are used as temporary shelter during the height of the fishing season (December to May) when they spend a lot of time away from home. These structures are close to the fishing areas and are abandoned after the season is over.

In the extreme southern tropical forests, the Bakas (or Pygmies) usually dwell in tiny huts that are constructed by partially burying strong, leafy tree branches into the ground in the form of a circle. These branches are then tied together at the top with vines. Construction of each hut takes about a day and they are used for a little more than six months and then abandoned.

Traditional architecture in Cameroon contrasts greatly with that brought by the Germans when they annexed the territory in 1884. During their stay in Cameroon (1884–1916), the Germans left behind impressive buildings and significantly influenced housing construction throughout the country.

However, their influence was most felt among the country's public infrastructures and palaces. Important architectural landmarks from the German era include the majestic former prime minister's office in Buea; various government offices in Limbe, Yaoundé, Douala, Buea, and Bamenda; many military forts, several of which can still be seen today; and palaces, including especially those of King Manga Bell of the Duala and King Njoya of the Bamoun—the latter was destroyed and can be seen only in pictures. Despite French and British efforts to erase the German presence in Cameroon, many of these architectural landmarks remain.[17]

Royal Architecture in Cameroon: The Palace at Foumban

The most important symbol of the sovereign in the Cameroon grasslands was his palace or royal residence. Colonization contributed significantly to the destruction of many of the region's palaces, especially those of kings that were considered recalcitrant and unwilling to cooperate in the transformation, and subsequent reconstitution of their societies in line with the German, British, and French civilizing missions. In fact, by the end of 1910, the magnificent palace of King Njoya (of the Bamoun) at Foumban had been completely destroyed. However, photographs and detailed plans of the structure exist.[18] The palace covered more than 70,000 square meters and housed at least 3,000 people when King Njoya was the sovereign.[19] Of these, 1,200 were the king's wives and 350 were his children. Also residing at the palace were approximately 2,000 individuals who served the king in various capacities. Construction of the palace took place in the 1860s or 1870s for King N'sare and was located in the center of Foumban, the kingdom's capital. Work on the structure was a joint effort of all of the people of Bamoun, who, by custom, were expected to assist in the construction and provide the necessary materials for it.

The palace, which was divided into three main sections had three main entryways: the non-royal court officials' entry (left), the royal entry (center), and the princely entry (right). Bodyguards were stationed within chambers adjacent to these entryways. The non-royal functionaries included civil servants attached to the palace, various court officials, and other palace-based regulatory bodies. Toward the back, the interior of the palace was subdivided along its horizontal axes into several upper and lower sections.

Most of the upper (front) court of the palace was devoted to governance. Here were the gathering courts (e.g., the great hall, which was used for gatherings and feasts; a court performance preparation area; and a princely gathering court). Toward the back and to the right were the courts of law and taxation or tribute and the prison. On the left were special areas for punishing those convicted of royal infractions. Immediately behind this section were the throne room, the royal library, and secretarial offices. The king spent most of his day in this area receiving official visitors or dealing with affairs of the kingdom.

The extremely important and religiously critical palm wine was kept in a room adjacent to the throne room. Next to the storage house for the sacred palm wine and the throne and accessed only via a well-guarded chamber was the royal cemetery. Across from the royal burial ground was a non-royal area, which was used by the palace's most important regulatory society—the *mbansie*. The power of the palace resided in three important centers: the throne room, the royal cemetery, and the *mbansie*. However, apart from the royal cemetery and the throne room, the *ngu*—the chamber that housed the royal ancestral skulls and relics—was considered the most sacred section of the palace. The *ngu* was behind the king's bedroom and separated from it by a narrow passageway. Other important chambers within the palace included the residence of the queen mother, whose job was to supervise the ruling sovereign's wives and daughters and provide the king with constructive criticism. The queen mother's court was located in the non-royal section to underscore the fact that she served as an intermediary between the royals and the subjects.

Cities and "Modern" Housing

In virtually all of Cameroon's cities and towns, one can find what is often referred to as "modern" housing—modified traditional architectural styles that have borrowed significantly from other cultures. These structures combine various regional elements, and the architecture reflects European (especially German, British, and French), and, depending on the region, Middle Eastern (specifically Arabic/Islamic) influence. The development of this unique architectural style that came to dominate housing structures in Cameroon's urban areas began in the nineteenth century with the establishment of permanent European settlements in the Cameroon coast and the subsequent founding of what would eventually become large metropolitan areas. Among the earliest structures were churches, government offices, and houses for Europeans. Since most of the earliest missionaries to establish worship centers in Cameroon included several freed slaves from Jamaica, the early buildings also reflected not only European but also West Indian architectural styles.

Establishment of the colony of Kamerun saw rapid expansion in the construction of houses to meet the needs of a growing population of German bureaucrats, planters, and missionaries. German builders took into consideration the landscape, materials available, climate, traditional architecture, Western European styles, and the technology that they could easily access to produce a synthesized form of architecture often referred to as "German tropical architecture." Some of these buildings are still functional and have become important parts of Cameroon's history.

After World War I, Cameroon was partitioned into French and British spheres of influence. From the end of World War I to the beginning of World War II, there was very little economic activity in British Cameroons and, as a consequence, there was a break in architectural developments and only French architectural styles reached the colony in the 1920s and 1930s.

The end of World War II brought about a new awareness and appreciation of the various forms and expressions of Cameroon art and culture. Such appreciation, however, did not translate into new architectural forms reflecting local culture, because the country's building projects remained under the control of European architects and firms. Buildings produced during the postwar period reflected "pseudo-African attributes" as stylistic elements and did so until almost a decade after independence. Various ministerial buildings in Yaoundé represent examples of this type of urban architecture.

Although by the 1990s, Cameroon could boast of several indigenous architects and architectural firms, no truly individual style adapted to the various urban centers has yet emerged. This is primarily because building contracts continue to be awarded almost exclusively to foreign firms. In addition, many traditional houses, which used to differ significantly from one region to another, are now more uniform. Natural materials for roofing are giving way to corrugated iron sheets, just as regional building materials are being replaced with cement (or concrete) blocks.

Once the exchange economy became established in an area, houses of the emerging entrepreneurial class began to reflect the new architectural styles. Hence, in many places where the cash-crop economy had developed, traditional building styles gave way to more modern ones, with concrete blocks and corrugated sheets replacing traditional materials. In recent years, many homes, primarily in the urban areas, have been built with concrete and steel. During the oil boom of the mid-1980s, there was massive expansion in building, especially in such urban centers as Douala and Yaoundé. A uniquely modern Cameroon architecture, however, has not yet fully developed, and building construction has still not fully taken advantage of the country's rich artistic resources.

Within the urban areas, homes are usually two or more stories in height and are frequently larger than those in the rural areas. Homes owned by rich entrepreneurs or top-level civil servants and politicians usually have additional structures (located at the back) called "boys-quarters," which may house such domestic staff as drivers, cooks, gardeners, and security guards. Such houses may have gates manned by security guards (called "night-watchmen"), who depending on the level of crime in the area, may work around the clock.

In Cameroon's urban centers, modern homes are designed for the single family, defined in the Western (and not traditional) sense as wife, husband, and children. The interior consists of a master bedroom exclusively for the wife and husband, several rooms for guests, a living room, a kitchen, and at least two bathrooms (one for the exclusive use of the wife and husband and the other for children and guests). The living room is considered the most important place, for it is where the family gathers on a regular basis and receives visitors, including relatives from the village. It is here where one usually finds such items of modern living as the television, videocassette recorder and/or DVD player, hi-fi system, art, high-quality furniture, and decorative items. In some urban houses, one may also find bookshelves containing encyclopedias, children's literature, and magazines, including religious tracts.

In virtually all of Cameroon's cities are areas "reserved" for the rich. Some of these areas trace their origins to the so-called government residential areas or GRAs, which during the colonial period were reserved for the exclusive use of the Europeans. After independence, these GRAs became residential areas for top civil servants and the country's political elites. Within these neighborhoods most of the houses are similar to structures found in wealthy neighborhoods in Europe and North America. Utility or even investment is often not the primary objective of owning these homes. Impressing neighbors and proving to the public that they have achieved success and prosperity are usually more important to many owners of these very expensive homes. Most rich people prefer to use imported materials (e.g., marble) for construction even though more suitable local materials are available.

Traditional religious buildings, Christian churches, and mosques are the most important buildings in most Cameroon cities and are usually located in very prominent places. In some towns, these buildings are also the largest and most visible. In addition to churches, public buildings (including offices for civil servants) are also placed in prominent locations. Hotels, offices of insurance companies and banks, as well as the headquarters of major multinational firms also dominate the architecture of Cameroon's major metropolitan areas.

As the rate of rural-to-urban migration has increased significantly, especially after Cameroon became a net exporter of oil in the mid-1980s, adequate housing has become a major problem for most of the country's urban centers. In such cities as Yaoundé and Douala, housing has become so expensive that it has become virtually impossible for the poor to secure decent and affordable housing. As a consequence, the occupancy rate of many apartments has increased significantly, with overcrowding becoming the norm. In the poor sections of town, it is fairly common to find people sleeping outside in the open air because the houses, most of which are poorly constructed and do not meet minimum standards for safety, are too hot because there is no air conditioning. Rentals are available in virtually all urban areas but can be quite expensive. Many poor people turn to makeshift structures, many of which are constructed illegally and have no access to basic services such as water and sewage disposal. Many of these crowded informal settlements, which litter most urban areas, have become breeding grounds for many diseases, including HIV/AIDS, malaria, and tuberculosis.

In addition to creating housing shortages, migration from rural areas to the urban centers has significantly increased the demand for public services such as sewage disposal, police protection, water, electricity, and education. Given the fact that many urban areas in Cameroon have relatively inefficient and not fully functioning sewage disposal systems, sanitation has become a major problem for many cities. The continued increase in informal housing, which usually does not have any type of plumbing, has exacerbated the sewage disposal problem and contributes significantly to poor sanitary conditions in many parts of Cameroon's cities. The hope among most Cameroonians is that public policy will be directed at not only dealing effectively with the housing shortage but also with significantly improving the provision of various services to inhabitants of the urban sectors.

NOTES

1. Monica B. Visonà, Robin Poynor, Herbert M. Cole, and Michael D. Harris, *A History of Art in Africa* (New York: Harry N. Abrams, 2001), p. 338.

2. Richard Bjornson, *The African Quest for Freedom and Identity: Cameroonian Writing and the National Experience* (Bloomington: Indiana University Press, 1991).

3. Suzanne P. Blier, *The Royal Arts of Africa: The Majesty of Form* (New York: Harry N. Abrams, 1998), pp. 169–172.

4. Ibid., pp. 185–188.

5. Ibid., p. 188.

6. Jean-Baptiste Bacquart, *The Tribal Arts of Africa* (New York: Thames and Hudson, 1993), p. 108.

7. Ibid., p. 108.

8. Ibid., p. 108, for a picture of the mask (#8).

9. Ibid., p. 109.

10. Ibid., pp. 108–109.

11. Ibid., pp. 104 and 107, for examples of Kaka masks and figures.

12. Ibid., p. 106.

13. Harold D. Nelson, M. Dobert, G. C. McDonald, J. McLaughlin, B. Marvin, and P. W. Moeller, *Area Handbook for the United Republic of Cameroon* (Washington, DC: U.S. Government Printing Office, 1974), p. 102.

14. Nelson, et al. (1974), p. 102.

15. Ibid., p. 103.

16. Ambe J. Njoh, *Urban Planning, Housing and Spatial Structures in sub-Saharan Africa: Nature, Impact and Development Implications of Exogenous Forces* (Aldershot, England: Ashgate, 1999), pp. 40–45.

17. Nnamdi Elleh, *African Architecture: Evolution and Transformation* (New York: McGraw-Hill, 1996), pp. 286–292.

18. Visonà, et al. (2001), pp. 339–340; Blier (1998), pp. 176–177.

19. Blier (1998), p. 176, for a plan of the palace at Foumban.

Akwa high street, Douala. © Ernest V. Mbenkum (www.cameroonincolour.com)

Busy people on street, Ndotki, Douala. © Ernest V. Mbenkum (www.cameroon incolour.com)

Boys, Beedi, Douala. © Ernest V. Mbenkum (www.camerooincolour.com)

Street traders, Bonaberi, Douala. © Ernest V. Mbenkum (www.cameroonin
colour.com)

Street vendors, Ndotki, Douala. © Ernest V. Mbenkum (www.cameroonin colour.com)

Church, Bonaberi, Douala. © Ernest V. Mbenkum (www.cameroonincolour.com)

Tribal masks for sale, Douala. © Ernest V. Mbenkum (www.cameroonincolour.com)

Artisan booth at cultural festival, Douala. © Ernest V. Mbenkum (www.cameroonincolour.com)

Lions sculptures on roundabout, Douala. © Ernest V. Mbenkum (www.cameroon incolour.com)

Sculpture of giant, Rond Point, Douala. © Ernest V. Mbenkum (www.cameroon incolour.com)

The Chief's compound in Bandjoun is one of the most impressive buildings in the traditional Bamiléké style. The decorated columns tell the long history of the Bandjoun dynasty. Traditional Bamiléké family houses often use the same type of carvings and construction in a much smaller scale. The main building is used for the King's court and for the different religious ceremonies carried out by the secret societies. The current king lives in a modern house just next to the main building. The forest behind the compound is taboo and very few people are allowed to go there. © Jacob Crawfurd (www.crawfurd.dk)

Fruit seller in the trade city of Bafoussam in the Western Province. © Jacob Crawfurd (www.crawfurd.dk)

Wearing traditional clothing at cultural festival, Douala. © Ernest V. Mbenkum
(www.camerooincolour.com)

Cameroon village scene. © Jacob Crawfurd (www.crawfurd.dk)

Woman fishing beneath the Lobé Falls. © Jacob Crawfurd (www.crawfurd.dk)

Girls washing at a stream that runs through the village of Bafang. © Jacob Crawfurd (www.crawfurd.dk)

Children playing a game, Douala. © Jacob Crawfurd (www.crawfurd.dk)

Girl twirling a hoop in the coastal town of Kribi. © Jacob Crawfurd (www.craw furd.dk)

Village children catching fish and shrimp where the Lobé River runs out in the Atlantic Ocean. Many locals come to this bay in the weekends for swimming, fishing and relaxing. © Jacob Crawfurd (www.crawfurd.dk)

Dancers at cultural festival, Douala. © Ernest V. Mbenkum (www.cameroonin colour.com)

Costumed dancers at cultural festival, Douala. © Ernest V. Mbenkum (www.came roonincolour.com)

Mun Dum Cultural Dance Group at cultural festival, Douala. © Ernest V. Mbenkum (www.camerooincolour.com)

5

Cuisine and Traditional Dress

CUISINE

CAMEROON CUISINE differs by region. Although the country's cuisine and eating habits differ significantly from those in the West, like other practices in modern Cameroon, local cuisine has been affected significantly by external influences, which were brought about by colonialism, Christian missionary activities, the spread of Islam, and, in recent years, globalization. For example, traditionally, Cameroonians drink water at meals. However, in recent years, soft drinks such as Coca Cola, Pepsi Cola, and locally produced sodas such as Champagne soda, have become popular as table drinks, especially among teens. As a result of the influence of French colonialism, imported wine is a popular lunch and dinner drink in the French-speaking part of the country, especially among urbanites.

The one-course meal, with large servings, is quite popular and standard in Cameroon. Soup (also called stew or sauce), which is prepared with and without vegetables, may be consumed with rice, yams, cocoyams, plantains, potatoes, cassava (including the grated form called *garri*), maize (corn), and millet. Many starches are pounded and turned into what is generally called *fufu* and eaten with a stew. Depending on the wealth status of the family, the stew or soup may contain beef, poultry, or fish. In recent years, many families, especially those that reside in the urban centers, drink wine and/or beer, as well as various types of sodas, with their meals instead of the standard water. In rural areas, locally produced palm wine is preferred to imported beverages as an alternative to water at the lunch or dinner table. The drinking of palm wine, however, in most rural regions of the country is limited to men, with women only occasionally indulging in the practice and usually during special ceremonies. Children rarely drink palm wine.

Drinks are usually served at room temperature and without ice. In urban areas, drinks might be chilled. Among Muslims, tea is preferred to coffee, and occasionally beef is eaten. However, pork is prohibited. Pork is quite popular in the southern part of the country, where the fat is used as a seasoning.

Cameroonians use the fingers of the right hand to eat their meals. Although the use of knives, spoons, and forks is becoming common among urbanites, many Cameroonians still view their use as a sign of elitism. In fact, many people believe that the use of silverware prevents the individual from effectively extracting all the pleasure from the food. Foods such as *fufu* and pounded yam are better enjoyed when consumed with the fingers.

Cameroon does not have a single national dish, although the ingredients used to prepare dishes are similar, and some foods like *fufu* are quite popular. In Cameroon, *fufu* strictly refers to the dumplings produced by boiling cocoyams, then pounding them in a mortar until they are soft and resemble mashed potatoes, and shaping them into balls. One at a time, pieces of *fufu* are pinched off, dipped in soup, and swallowed. Many other starchy preparations in Cameroon resemble *fufu* and have been mistakenly called *fufu* (e.g., starches made from maize, a staple food among the Bali-Nyonga and various other groups in the grasslands, or starches made from cassava, which are popular among various forest groups).

Recipes and the way foods are prepared usually differ from region to region based on customs, religions, and the availability of foodstuffs. For example, seafood recipes are popular in the coastal communities and the areas around Lake Chad. Recipes that use plantains are common among the plantain growing regions of the south. In the western highlands where a variety of yams and cocoyams are grown, recipes emphasize these foodstuffs, and in the north, millet, rice, and sorghum dominate recipes.

Most dishes include stewed vegetables, seasoned with salt, red pepper, and palm oil. Chicken is considered a delicacy consumed primarily by rich families. Although beef is considered a luxury, especially in rural areas, "bush" meat (e.g., snake, monkey, wild fowl, crocodile, deer, porcupine, squirrel, and various rodents) is widely consumed. Sauces or stews are present in virtually all Cameroonian meals.

In urban areas, breakfast may include tea or coffee, bread, and fruit. In rural areas, breakfast usually consists of leftovers from the previous evening's dinner. While most people in the rural areas eat breakfast, lunch is not an important meal. Eating between meals is quite common, especially in urban areas where snacks may be purchased from street vendors who sell everything from raw sugar cane to fried fish. Among rural farmers and others who live in the countryside, the tradition is to eat one big meal in the early evening and then relax (e.g., tell stories and socialize; men may drink palm wine and reminisce about the past) before going to bed.

Among the relatively well-to-do urban elite, three meals (breakfast, lunch, and dinner), as well as between-meals snacks, which include various fruits, are becoming standard fare. The urban bureaucrat who sits at a desk all day and rarely exercises tends to consume more food than the farmer who maintains a physically demanding daily schedule. Such dietary habits have resulted in a relatively high incidence of high blood pressure and obesity among urban dwellers.

Women and girls do most of the cooking for the family. Some men do cook, although they usually make light and simple dishes. Grilling meat, especially game meat, is common in rural areas. Along the nation's highways, it is common to find vendors at strategic bus stops selling roasted and/or grilled game meat to travelers. Although most Cameroon families do not eat in restaurants, preferring instead to take their meals at home, unmarried men sometimes frequent restaurants. A type of restaurant called the "chicken house" has become common in the urban areas. These establishments sell baked fish and chicken (and only in rare cases, stewed meat), along with beer, and men (including married men) often take their girlfriends to these establishments, even after having eaten dinner at home with the family. The "chicken houses" are considered places where people go to socialize, drink beer, and discuss anything from soccer games to politics. Commercial eating places in the country's urban centers range from the roadside stand, where one can purchase simple meals such as rice and beans, to five-star restaurants that serve traditional, as well as international, cuisine. Specialized eateries that serve such foods as pizza, hamburgers, Chinese food, and Indian food, just to name a few, can be found in the major urban centers.

Most families sit either on the floor or at a table and eat with relatives. Dining tables are more common in urban areas and among relatively well-to-do families. Depending on cultural practices, men, women, and children may be segregated from each other during meals (with each group occupying a separate section of the house's dining area); in some parts of the country, men may be served their dinner before everyone else is allowed to eat. In general, elders and heads of household are expected to eat before anyone else and usually leave food on their plates for the young. In most Cameroonian societies, visitors are invited to eat with the family, and, in anticipation of the possibility that unexpected guests may have to be fed, more food than is needed to feed the immediate family is usually prepared. Affection for and respect for guests is expressed through generous portions. Within some groups, the visitor or guest must finish all the food offered to him or her, as a sign of respect. In others, however, guests are not expected to finish all the food offered. In cases where visitors or guests are highly respected individuals, they are expected to reciprocate with gifts, either immediately after a generous meal or at a later date. After the meal is completed, the children usually join the women in tidying up.

In rural households in which the man has multiple wives, the eating arrangements can be quite complex. In one variation, each wife, who usually has her own house in which she lives with her children, prepares food for herself, her children, and her husband. She then dishes out the right portion for her husband and either carries it to his house or gives it to the eldest daughter to take it to the husband's house. The food is placed in the husband's house at a previously designated spot for him to consume at his leisure. The wife then sits down to eat with her children. To avoid wasting food, the first wife, who traditionally is considered the de facto head of household, designs a schedule that allows only one wife to provide the husband with food each day. In another variation, the man's first wife designs a schedule for the husband to eat meals with each of his wives (and their children) on a daily or weekly basis.

The use of bottled or canned infant formula is limited and found only among highly educated urban women. Breast-milk remains the food of choice. During the weaning period, mothers usually use traditional methods to introduce solid foods. The mother chews "adult" food in her mouth until it is ready to be swallowed and then spits it out and places it in the child's mouth. During colonialism, this process was condemned as unsanitary and backward. However, it remains quite popular, especially among rural women, who, for various reasons, either cannot afford modern alternatives or have no access to them. Perhaps more important is the fact that many modern food alternatives have introduced health risks and dangers that are actually greater than those associated with the traditional practices. For example, without refrigeration in most of the country, bottled food (and various liquid formulas) cannot be safely served to children, and using local water to prepare powder formulas is known to have subjected infants to various waterborne diseases, some of which have proven fatal.

In rural areas and among the urban poor, cooking is done on a hearth, using wood for fuel. Most middle-class families, especially those in urban areas, cook with electric and gas ranges in a kitchen. Cookers that use kerosene are quite affordable and are common among low-income households in the urban centers. Depending on the region, rural homes may consist of a single room with a cooking hearth in the middle of the room or in one of the corners. In some rural areas, cooking is done in a shed located next to the wife's house. Quite often, the main cooking area may consist of three stones, arranged in a triangle, which serve as a tripod to hold the pot. Firewood is placed in the spaces between the stones and under the pot. Both traditional and modern kitchens have facilities to boil, fry, roast, grill, steam, stew, and bake.

Cooking in rural areas relies on and utilizes local materials very effectively. For example, palm oil produced locally is used to deep-fry foods; or food is baked by wrapping it in moistened plantain or banana leaves and burying it in hot coals. Likewise, most of the utensils used for cooking are made from materials collected from the immediate environment. Mortars carved from local wood are used to pound yams, cocoyams, nuts, and other plants; pots used for cooking and water storage urns are made from local clay; local blacksmiths produce various kitchen utensils; and bowls made of local wood and also from clay are used for serving meals. Throughout the country today, however, plastic and aluminum utensils, the bulk of them produced in the industrial centers around the Douala-Edea area, have become very popular. Even in rural areas, plastic buckets and aluminum basins are gradually replacing gourds as vessels for fetching and storing water.

Cameroonians are efficient eaters. When an animal is slaughtered, virtually all parts of it are consumed—the head, skin, feet, the intestine, and other innards are prepared and eaten. Even the fat derived from the pig is used as seasoning in various dishes. In the northern part of the country, where firewood is extremely scarce, many people use (cow) dung for heating.

Although Cameroon is self-sufficient in food production, many imported foodstuffs are sold locally. Among these are yams from the Calabar region of Nigeria; rice from Asia; fruits from several parts of the world; canned foods from Europe, especially France, Germany, and the Netherlands; flour from the United States; and spices from around the world. Within the country there is significant trade in foodstuffs. Items produced in the south travel to markets and trading posts in the north and vice versa. For example, smoked and dried fish produced along the Atlantic coast travels north and into the interior of the country. Bananas, kola nuts, and plantains produced in the south are sold all over the country, and maize (corn), yams, cassava, and other tubers produced in the grassfields are distributed throughout the country. Peanuts (groundnuts) and cattle produced in the north travel south, east, and west.

The most important crops in Cameroon are tubers (several varieties of yams, cassava), grains (corn or maize, millet), fruits (bananas, plantains, papaya, oranges, guava, melons), and vegetables (okra, "bitter-leaf" or spinach). Most of these crops are grown by small-scale farmers, most of whom are women. In the south, most people cook with palm oil and use hot red pepper for seasoning. In the north, cooking is usually done with peanut oil. Both palm oil and peanut oil are produced locally—peanuts are produced in the savanna and other parts of the country, and palm trees grow throughout most of the south. The Cameroon Development Corporation, which inherited the former German plantations, is a major producer of palm oil. The staple foods in Cameroon vary by region but include millet, cassava, groundnuts (peanuts), yams, rice, potatoes, beans, and plantains.

Millet dominates the diet of northerners. Among the people of the western grasslands, maize (which is usually turned into flour and used to produce a type of *fufu* or is eaten as "corn-chaff"—a stew of beans, corn, and spices cooked with palm oil), yams, cocoyams, *garri* (grated cassava that is dried over a fire), and several varieties of beans dominate the diet. Among southern dwellers, plantains, cocoyams, yams (forest varieties), and rice are popular. In some regions, rice is eaten only during special occasions (such as Christmas and marriage ceremonies).

Diet and Nutrition

Because of the climate and a short growing season, as well as general poverty, northerners are the most nutritionally insecure in the country. In fact, according to a survey conducted in the 1960s, the people who live in the hills of Diamaré and Margui-Wandala in the extreme north of the country are among the poorest fed in the country.[1] This part of the country regularly suffers from droughts and, hence, the land is difficult to cultivate. Food shortages are common and persist throughout the year. The region's staple food is millet; meats and fish are rarely eaten. Although the people keep goats and chickens, these are not usually eaten—the goats are not milked or killed for food; instead they are used as sacrifices in important ceremonies such as funerals. Chickens are slaughtered and eaten only in ritual sacrifices, and the eggs are hatched to produce other chickens.

The people who inhabit the northern flood plains usually have enough food to eat. However, they suffer shortages during June and July, when the heavy rains make growing food virtually impossible. Millet and maize are the staples, although occasionally people eat rice. From time to time, cassava, yams, and sweet potatoes are eaten. Groundnuts are widely grown in this area of the country, but they are not eaten; instead they are grown for export to other parts of the country or abroad. Locally made millet beer is popular.

The people of the flood plains raise cattle but do not slaughter it for meat. Instead the cattle are kept as a store of the family's wealth. In fact, within this region of the country, a family's status in the community is often determined by the number of cattle it owns. The most important source of protein is fish harvested from Lake Chad. The men drink a lot of milk year round and especially during the *gourouna* ritual.

Among the peoples of the Adamaoua Plateau, millet and sorghum are the main staples. Cassava, yams, and sweet potatoes are also consumed. Among the Fulani, the standard dish is *mbusiri,* which is a mixture of milk and either maize or millet flour. Fulani women often prefer cassava, which they purchase from Baya farmers, because it is easier to prepare than maize and millet. Milk is the Fulani's main source of protein and is used fresh, curdled, or in the form of butter. Butter is popular among the sedentary Fulani, whereas the nomadic cattle-rearing Fulani usually prefer fresh milk.

The Fulani, who are cattle owners, usually do not slaughter the cattle for food. Only sick and dying animals are eaten—healthy animals are considered important investments and sources of family wealth. So-called town-Fulani (i.e., those who reside in the urban areas) purchase meat for their meals, usually from Hausa traders. For religious reasons, most of the people who reside in this part of the country do not eat pork.

The diets of the forest peoples of Cameroon consist primarily of roots and tubers, notably cassava and yams, as well as plantains. Although many people eat bananas, these are considered food for the poor. Ripe bananas are usually eaten as a snack; only poor families boil green bananas and eat them or pound them into a paste or *fufu* and eat them with a stew. Cassava, which can be converted into a flour called *garri,* has virtually no known nutritional value but is nevertheless very popular, probably because it stores well. Plantains are eaten in various forms, but never raw. They can be boiled and eaten with a stew; sliced and stewed with various vegetables; fried and eaten with baked beans; and ground, mixed with various vegetables (e.g., spinach), and then stewed. The plantain is a useful tree crop among the peoples of the southern forest region. Its fruit is an important source of food, and its leaves are used for (1) wrapping food for storage and baking, (2) covering food placed in pots for cooking, (3) serving food, and (4) shelter from rain. Locally produced butter (derived from various nuts—notably those of the palm tree) provides the fat in the diets of the southern forest peoples. Vegetables such as "bitter-leaf" (a type of spinach), various fruits, legumes, rice, as well as maize (most of it imported from the grasslands), are also consumed.

Although the forest peoples usually have enough to eat, they have been known to suffer from nutritional deficiencies, especially of protein. In the past, game animals served as the main source of protein for the forest peoples. However, as a result of population pressures, excessive exploitation of the region's environmental resources (including the cutting down of trees for export to Europe), and recent conservation efforts mounted by the government with the assistance of international conservationists, access to productive hunting grounds has become difficult. In fact, game animals in this region are now limited to monkeys, rodents, bats, and birds. Most of the beef eaten by the forest peoples is purchased from local butchers who are supplied by Hausa herdsmen. Some families keep goats, sheep, pigs, and chickens, which are usually allowed to roam freely throughout the village. Mushrooms gathered in the forests, snails, termites, grasshoppers, crickets, and other insects are also eaten. Fish and other products of the sea are important sources of protein in the diet of the forest peoples. Crayfish and prawns are popular among the Duala and other peoples who inhabit the coastal regions.

Although the western highlands are densely populated, the people usually have enough to eat. Shortages, however, seem to appear before the harvest. Diets often are unbalanced. The high population density has significantly reduced the amount of land available for wildlife, and, as a result, hunting is no longer an important activity. Meat can be purchased from Fulani herdsmen. In the 1970s, the government, with the aid of the United States, initiated a fish farming process in which various villages were provided with fish ponds and were taught how to farm fish. Convincing the people of this region to include fresh fish in their diet turned out to be a bigger problem than teaching them how to raise them. Most western highlanders' experience with fish has traditionally been with dried fish imported from Nigeria and sold in the urban markets. Yams, plantains, cocoyams, cassava, and maize are popular food staples. Palm oil, and to a certain extent, peanut oil, are the main oils used for cooking.

People who live in the urban areas have a large variety of foods available in the various markets. Each urban center usually has one large market where one can find a variety of both locally grown and imported foods. However, because of cultural, traditional, economic, and religious reasons, some urban residents are unable or unwilling to take advantage of the variety of foods available to them. First, many young immigrants to the urban areas usually prefer to save their money so they can return to the village and secure a wife. Second, the demands of urban living often force young people to sacrifice adequate nutrition in favor of buying the latest imported fashions. Third, many immigrants refuse to adapt to urban cuisine and insist on retaining the eating habits that they grew up with. These foods may be hard to find in the urban area and hence are very expensive. For example, many urban Hausa often insist on eating only millet and maize, which are usually quite expensive in the urban centers of the south. Fourth, religion and tradition may prevent some people from eating certain foods (e.g., Muslims do not eat pork; among some western highlands groups, only men can eat chicken). Finally, just before the harvest, food is usually very expensive in the urban areas, making it difficult for lower-level wage-earners to maintain a balanced diet. In the past, the government has attempted to resolve this problem by maintaining stocks of cereals, cassava, and other foodstuffs, which can be released into the economy at appropriate times to prevent shortages.

Various taboos have a significant impact on the ability of Cameroonians to maintain balanced diets. As already mentioned, women among various western highlands groups are not allowed to eat chicken. Pregnant women, who must increase their protein intake, are actually prohibited by taboo in various societies from eating eggs and meat because of the belief that the child's health may be affected by such consumption. Taboos in the north prevent people from eating meat derived from monkeys, horses, and dogs. Among the Dourou and Baya of the Adamaoua Plateau, local taboos prohibit the eating of monkey and snake meat. Throughout most of the savanna region, many people do not eat fruit for fear that planting a tree that bears fruit negatively affects one's life force.[2]

Maintaining a balanced diet is quite difficult, either because of existing taboos and/or cultural and religious beliefs and practices. Since independence, the government has made efforts to institute programs to teach nutrition, especially among students. Hence, courses on science, agriculture, home economics, and hygiene are encouraged. The hope is that the knowledge gained from school would help these students, especially the girls, go on to raise children who take balanced diets seriously.

Globalization and other influences continue to change the Cameroonian diet. Today, as already mentioned, wines and sodas have already replaced water during mealtime in some families, especially in the urban areas. In addition, bread, tea, cakes, and, to a certain extent, coffee, have been added to the diets of many families as a result of contact with external forces, notably European colonialism. Some of the items were introduced into the country through foreign aid, notably from the United States. In fact, the popular "puff-puff," which is made from imported wheat flour (the flour is mixed with water into a paste and then rolled into a ball, deep fried, and sprinkled with sugar), emerged in the 1970s after massive donations of wheat flour arrived from the U.S. government. Many imported food items that first came into the country as luxuries for the rich elite and were consumed primarily by wealthy urbanites have today become quite popular among the general population. Hamburgers, pizza, hot dogs, and other foreign fast foods are popular, especially among young urbanites.

Beverages

Wine made from palm trees has been an important part of the traditions of many groups in Cameroon for centuries. Cameroonians also made alcoholic beverages from maize, bananas, and sugar cane. Production or "tapping" of palm wine is carried out primarily in the south, where the palm trees grow in the wild. Palm wine is made by tapping the palm tree's sap. The freshly tapped wine is usually very sweet and contains very little alcohol; however, as it ferments, it becomes less sweet and becomes more alcoholic. The palm wine is usually harvested in the mornings and is supposed to be taken to the market for sale the same day. Quite often, however, some tappers are unable to sell all of their stock on time. Deterioration can be rapid, especially since most of it is unrefrigerated. Some tappers add saccharin to their stocks to sweeten it and make it appear fresh. Palm wine connoisseurs, however, find this practice repugnant and would not knowingly purchase such adulterated wine. Many people brew spirits illegally and sell the liquor in bottles that do not indicate its purity, quality, or alcohol content.

Cameroon is renowned for its brewing expertise. In fact, in recent years, many beers have found favor with connoisseurs in Europe and the United States. Important breweries include Guinness Cameroun (Douala), Nouvelles Brasseries Africaines (Douala), Société Anonyme des Brasseries du Cameroun (Douala), Union Camerounaise de Brasseries (Douala), Brasseries du Camer-oun (Yaoundé). Extremely popular beers include "33," Beaufort, Guinness, Mutzig, Castel, and Isenbeck.

Drinking of alcohol by Muslims is strictly prohibited on religious grounds. Among other Cameroonians, however, drinking is considered an important pastime and a way to entertain friends. Drinking establishments abound, with some specializing in serving palm wine and others serving a variety of both imported and domestic brands of beer. The "off-license" is a special store that sells beer for consumption off the premises and, hence, does not provide areas where clients can sit and enjoy their purchases. In bars and nightclubs, customers can sit and enjoy their drinks. In the rural areas, palm wine dominates beer and other alcoholic beverages. While the consumption of alcoholic beverages is quite widespread, drunkenness is severely frowned upon. In urban areas, drunks are often picked up by the police and taken to jail to spend a day or two sleeping it off. Women usually are not expected to drink or smoke cigarettes in public. Such behavior is associated, in many societies, with prostitutes.

Nonalcoholic beverages are quite popular, especially among young people. These include various fruit punches, juices produced from local fruits (e.g., mango, guava, orange, and pineapple) and various sodas. Coca Cola and Pepsi products are quite popular. Cameroon is a major producer of coffee, tea, and cocoa. However, the consumption of these products is not widespread. The consumption of tea and coffee is associated with educated elites, although many people in the north regularly drink tea and, to a lesser extent, coffee. Various cafés that serve tea, coffee, and hot chocolate can be found in the major urban areas. These beverages are usually consumed with bread. Cocoa is converted into candies and sold locally, with most consumption limited to young people.

Cuisine and Ceremonies

At virtually all traditional ceremonies in Cameroon, food of some kind is consumed. At traditional weddings, for example, food plays a critical part and, in some cultures, the ceremony is concluded with a large feast that is open to everyone, including uninvited guests. In many public ceremonies, men and boys feast together, separate from the women. Most of the country's traditional ceremonies often coincide with changes in seasons and with the beginning and/or end of the harvest. Feasting increases significantly during the harvest season and decreases during the planting period, although some societies engage in light feasting to seek ancestral intervention to guarantee a good rain for their crops. In the days when interethnic wars were common, it was standard practice to send soldiers to the front with a feast and celebrate the end of the conflict regardless of the outcome.

Virtually all of the country's various groups engage in some kind of religious animal sacrifice. Such sacrifices are usually performed for various reasons and may include thanks for (1) a good harvest; (2) protection from enemies; (3) rain; (4) high fertility rates among the group's women; (5) sons; (6) a successful hunt; and (7) return of a "prodigal" son. Sacrifices can also be used to thank or express gratitude to ancestors or gods for the group's overall prosperity.

Animal sacrifices find more favor among followers of traditional religions. These rites represent a sign of respect and devotion to their gods. During such sacrifices, certain parts of the animal (e.g., the heart, kidneys, liver, and gizzards) that are believed to have significant spiritual powers may be extracted and consumed by priests or those performing the ceremony.

In virtually all societies in Cameroon, marriages, christening or naming ceremonies, and burials are associated with large and complex feasts. In fact, among the Widekum people, funerals are considered celebrations, with associated feasting expected to send off the recently deceased on the journey to meet his or her ancestors. During such a ceremony, elaborate dishes are prepared, and, depending on the status of the deceased, the ceremony could last as long as two weeks, with relatives and strangers congregating at the home of the deceased to eat, dance, and celebrate. Birth and naming celebrations are often combined and celebrated together, with dancing and eating going on all night, and, depending on the parents' status, the process could last for weeks.

Traditional doctors often prescribe the consumption of certain foods to sick people, because it is believed that these foods have medicinal qualities and can cure illness. It is quite common for such doctors to prescribe the consumption of certain parts of an animal as a cure for various illnesses. In addition, the doctor may gather a variety of plants and boil them to produce a concoction that is given to the sick. Traditional doctors often prescribe the consumption of various foods as cures for fevers, dysentery, diarrhea, and various psychiatric problems.

Cameroonian Cuisine in the United States

Since the mid-1980s, a significant number of Cameroonians have migrated to the United States. Among them have been entrepreneurs who have brought the country's cuisine to their new country. Of course, Cameroonian food, like that of many other countries and communities in West Africa, resembles in a significant way Caribbean and southern U.S. cuisine (especially Gullah and deep Gulf Coast soul food). Its roots date back to the late sixteenth century when European traders (including those who dealt in slaves) brought yams, rice, peanuts (groundnuts), and black-eyed peas to the Americas and returned to the West African coast with cassava, plantains, corn (maize), okra, tomatoes, coconuts, string beans, and chilies, all of which became important ingredients for the cuisine that emerged in this region of Africa.

Cameroonian restaurants and grocery stores can be found in major U.S. cities, especially where there are large concentrations of immigrants. Houston, Atlanta, and Washington, D.C. offer authentic Cameroonian cuisine at various restaurants owned and operated by immigrants. Although these restaurants make an effort to serve authentic Cameroon cuisine, many of them continue to refine traditional meals to meet health concerns and changing tastes of American-born consumers.

TRADITIONAL DRESS

Despite many years of colonialism and European influence, Cameroonians have kept their traditional dress. Most Cameroonians still wear traditional clothing or some modified form of it on a regular basis. Although most civil servants and business executives wear Western attire to work, they return to traditional attire at home and for various ceremonies. During the tenure of President Ahmadou Ahidjo (1961–1982), even civil servants could be found wearing traditional dress (usually the *boubou* or some variant of it) to work. Ahidjo was most often attired in traditional dress and wore Western-styled suits only occasionally.

Cameroon does not really have a national attire. Dress varies widely, ranging from skimpy attire won by inhabitants of the remote hill regions of the north to the latest French suits preferred by the educated elites who roam the urban centers in the south.

Among the Fulani and other groups that have adopted their clothing styles, the *boubou* (an ample cotton garment that is comfortable even in the high desert heat of the north) is common. Traditional rulers (the *lamibé*) and other important dignitaries of the north wear the *boubou* with a turban, which is either white or indigo. Fulani men also strap to their upper arms a dagger that is encased in a decorated sheath. In addition, an amulet in the form of a small, rectangular satchel and containing verses from the Koran, is hung from the neck, arm, or belt.

Married women in the north wear a three-piece costume that consists of a *pagne* (a rectangular piece of cloth that is wrapped around the body from the breast area down to the ankles), a large veil (which covers the shoulders and the upper part of the body), and a scarf (which is made of the same material as the *pagne* and covers the head). Women from less well-off households usually adorn themselves with only the *pagne* and the scarf. Other adornments for Fulani women include anklets, bracelets, earrings, and necklaces. The earrings are worn in a series of holes along the earlobe. Occasionally, a silver ring or a piece of wood is inserted in an opening on the right side of the nose. While the men shave their heads, women usually braid their hair and grease it with butter.[3]

In the west and south, men wear Western-style shorts, shirts, and caps, most of which are used clothing imported from the United States. "Flip-flops" and sandals are quite common. These may be made of plastic or leather. Quite often, the men purchase so-called Arab slippers, which are produced by the Hausa or Fulani and sold in shops in the urban centers. Women wear the *pagne* but often without the veil used to cover the upper part of the body. However, a scarf usually covers the head. While northern women use the scarf to cover their entire head, including the ears and sometimes the nose, southern women may expose several parts of the head, including the ears, chin, nose, and mouth. In addition, like northern women, some southern women may wear the *pagne* without a garment to cover their shoulders and hands.

In the south and west, many urban women prefer European cotton dresses or mixed styles that include a blouse *(buba)* and a piece of cloth (called a wrapper) wrapped around the hips. The *buba* is a traditional blouse that is worn only with the wrapper and is actually a smaller type of *boubou* specifically designed for women that extends only to the waist. It has a rounded neck; a slit in the middle, directly under the chin; and tubular sleeves. The version of the *buba* common among women in the south, west, and east of

Cameroon originated among the Yorubas of Nigeria. Professional women in the south and west also wear Western-style blouses and skirts and jackets. In recent years, stockings, as well as high-heeled shoes, have become popular among these women. Although they indulge in a variety of hairstyles, the braided style is very popular—the braids are tiny and are usually arranged in intricate patterns. African American hairstyles can be found among many urban women, especially those who have studied or lived in the United States. Hair straightening is gaining ground among highly educated urban women; however, braiding remains the standard for most of them. Wigs are also worn, although in the past they have been associated with prostitutes.

Cameroonians like to dress well. It is not unusual for people, especially in the south and west, to spend a significant part of their incomes on clothes. During Christmas, a husband is expected to buy new clothes for his wife and children. Among the educated urban elites, such purchases must include the latest fashions from Paris, London, and more recently, New York. During the colonial period, clothes and fashions from Lagos (Nigeria) were highly regarded.

Depending on the region, clothing for preschool children may range from none at all to Western-style shorts and shirts, with cloth diapers serving as underpants. In rural areas, most preschool children are likely to wander around without any clothes or with a piece of cloth wrapped around the waist. Mothers or sisters carry babies on their backs, and hold them in place with wrappers. The wrapper is wrapped around the baby and secured by tying the two ends into a knot over the carrier's stomach—the baby's feet protrude on either side of the carrier's waist.

Since independence, clothes have been used to make important political statements. In fact, during the Ahidjo years, *danshikis, boubous,* and other garments carrying the president's or the single party's (CNU) image were quite popular. Today, the tradition continues as many people use what they wear to advertise their political affiliation to one of the many political parties that dot the landscape.

Cameroon's Variant of the Poncho

Various forms of the poncho can be found throughout the country. Among the Fulani in the north, one can find the *danshiki*—several adaptations of the *danshiki* are found among the various groups of the Western grasslands, with some of them called gowns. While the *danshiki* usually covers the body from the shoulders to the waist, the *boubou,* which is quite popular among the Fulani, runs from the neck to the ankles. It is a roomy garment that is worn mostly by men with or without a pair of trousers. While educated urban dwellers and the youth may wear the *boubou* with Western-styled trousers or pants, *boubou* purists only wear pajama-type pants (usually made of the same material as the *boubou*). The dress is usually complemented by a dome-shaped hat, which is made of the same material as the *boubou.*

The Wrapper and the Loincloth

For practical as well as economic reasons non-tailored clothes are quite common among Cameroonians. In the western grasslands, as well as in many parts of the forest regions, men wear wrappers (called loincloths) in the form of a toga. It is common for men in the western grasslands to wear a toga-style loincloth without a shirt. During various ceremonies (e.g., dances to celebrate the death of a loved one), both male and female performers dress in wrappers of various sizes, colors, and quality.

The quality of wrapper worn by a Cameroon woman is determined by her class and wealth. While poor rural women may wear locally produced or handwoven pieces, usually without a blouse (the wrapper is tied immediately below the armpits to cover the body from the breasts to the ankles), rich urban women are likely to adorn themselves with expensive imported materials, complete with a blouse. Among the rural populations, wrappers are not worn for fashion. They are a relatively affordable way to cover the body and protect it from the elements and come in handy when carrying infants and children. However, in the urban areas, women have transformed the wrapper into an important piece of fashion. Usually, an urban professional woman may adorn herself with three wrappers of matching colors—one to serve as a scarf used to cover the head; the second, which is the largest piece, is tied around the body, usually beginning at the waist and covering the thighs and most of the legs down to the ankles; and a third piece, which can be worn as a stole or used to help hold the larger wrapper in place. A *buba,* made of the same material as the wrappers, is usually worn with this ensemble.

Wrappers are very important in Cameroon and can be found among virtually all groups, from the southern forest regions to the northern arid areas, and from the east to the west, along the border with Nigeria. However, how the cloth is used differs by region. Grasslands uses of the wrapper are affected by contact with various groups from neighboring Nigeria, notably the Yoruba and Igbos. In the north, the uses of the wrapper are influenced by Fulani culture and customs.

Adornments

Adornments among Cameroonians are informed by culture, traditions, religious practices, and climate. Usually men wear hats or caps (Muslim men wear turbans) and women headties (also called "tiehead"). In the western grasslands, a man's ceremonial dress is not complete without an elaborately decorated hat. Most men's hats are made of the same material used to produce their gowns. Straw hats are rare; in recent years, Western-style baseball caps have been worn by urban youth. High school students can be found wearing caps carrying the names of various U.S. colleges and universities. Many of these can be purchased from stores that sell second-hand clothes imported from the United States. Educated urban elites, many of whom have lived in Europe or North America for many years, may wear hats of Western design, even including variations of the American cowboy hat.

Professional and other elite women can be seen sporting European hats. However, Muslim women, regardless of their educational attainment, wear a veil that covers the head and the face. Scarves of various qualities and prices are used by women to cover their hair. Some scarves are used to complement an elaborate hairstyle and, hence, do not cover the entire head. Common among these are the Yoruba-inspired scarf, which consists of a band of cloth about six feet long and one foot wide. It is usually wound twice around the head and then tucked in at the side, with allowance for admirers to see the wearer's beautiful hairstyle.

Young girls learn from their mothers how to braid their hair. Although professional hairstylists abound in Cameroon, especially in the urban areas, most Cameroon women learn how to braid and style their hair from their mothers and do it themselves. The occasional trip to the hairdresser, however, remains a fact of life, especially among professional and other elite women. In urban areas such as Yaoundé and Douala, one can find modern salons that provide both Western and traditional hairstyling services, including hair stretching, extension weaving, and wigs. Most northern women adorn their hair with various ornaments, including beads but must cover the hair with a veil when they travel out of the home.

Women and young girls wear necklaces, bracelets, earrings, and other body adornments. Young men may wear necklaces, many of which are religious symbols —the cross is very popular. Muslim men may hang from their neck, arm, or belt an amulet in the form of a small, rectangular satchel and containing verses from the Koran. Nobles and other traditional elites may wear jewelry (e.g., ivory bracelets) that reflects their position in society. In some regions (e.g., western grasslands), women wear "necklaces" of various materials around their waists and under their clothes—these are considered part of the wearer's undergarments and, hence, are not visible to admirers other than the husband. Women traditionally complement their fashions with a handbag, and many Cameroon men, especially those in rural areas, carry straw bags for utilitarian purposes. In the urban areas, men carry Western-style attaché cases. Shoes, some of which are imported and others produced locally, are worn for fashion and to protect the feet from the elements. Rural inhabitants, however, do not wear shoes on a regular basis but rather on special occasions, such as attending church, participating in a wedding ceremony, and going to the weekly market.

The European Influence

Through colonialism and Christian missions, Europeans have had a significant impact on Cameroonian traditions. In fact, women's dress styles in today's Cameroon are heavily influenced by what is going on in the fashion capitals of Europe and the United States. In addition to the fact that many of the popular *bubas* that one finds in the urban shops in such cities as Douala and Yaoundé are produced with European fabrics, many women now prefer wrappers made of fabrics imported from Amsterdam. Urban women frequently wear Western blouses, stockings produced with imported lace, dresses made of imported materials, and imported underwear. In fact, among young women, undergarments marketed by Victoria's Secret are quite popular.

Men's fashions have also incorporated ideas from Europe. In addition to the fact that the *boubou* is being made with Western fabrics, Western variations of the *boubou* and *danshiki* have gained popularity. Of course, many Cameroonians wear European-style pants, shorts, and shirts. In the colonial days, European fashions were worn primarily to attend (Christian) church, school, and participate in European types of economic activities (e.g., to work in a government office, a bank, or an insurance agency). Today, European-style clothes are quite common in Cameroon and can even be found in rural areas. In virtually all schools in the country, students are required to wear uniforms, all of which are European-style clothes—pants or shorts and shirts for boys and skirts and blouses for girls. Although most government offices do not have a dress code, most workers wear European-style clothes to work. Private businesses usually have dress codes, with men executives required to be attired in a business suit and necktie. Although traditional attires are still very popular for weddings, many educated and urban couples, especially those who plan to marry at a Christian church, choose to wear Western-style clothes for the ceremony. Even some funeral homes are now adorning the deceased with Western-style clothes for the final voyage to meet their ancestors.

NOTES

1. Harold D. Nelson, et al., *Area Handbook of the United Republic of Cameroon* (Washington, DC: U.S. Government Printing Office, 1973), p. 106.
2. Nelson, et al. (1974), p. 108.
3. Nelson, et al. (1974), p. 105.

6

Gender Roles, Marriage, and Family

TRADITIONAL VIEWS on gender, marriage, and family in Cameroon have been affected significantly by migration, colonialism and the institutions it brought to the country, globalization, and foreign religions. Cameroonians who travel to the West to obtain university training often return home to reject the large extended family and favor the small, monogamous nuclear family. Plural marriage, in which the husband has more than one wife, is frowned upon by individuals with a Western education and those who belong to various Christian churches. In fact, young girls who have completed the Western-style high school are not likely to consider marriage to a man who already has a wife. Despite all these changes and influences, most Cameroonians continue to favor large families, with lots of children. Polygyny (one man married to two or more women) is quite common, especially in the rural areas and among some rich urbanites. In the grasslands, virtually all kings (*fons*) have many wives. In fact, the late Sultan Njoya of the Kingdom of Bamoun was said to have had at least 1,200 wives and 350 children.[1]

Although the family is recognized as a universal social institution, its definition differs from society to society. While in Western society, the family usually consists of a mother, father, and children, membership in the unit as understood by Cameroonians may include an entire village. Members of a family are related by blood, marriage, and adoption. Members share various duties, including the ownership and maintenance of a home or homes, creation of wealth, production and rearing of children through sanctioned sexual relationships, and the support and protection of one another.

In Cameroon, each family is known and identified by a name, occupies a geographic residence or compound (comprised of several houses), and belongs to either a traditional or "modern" religion or both. Members of families also may be identified by facial marks and titles. It is the job of the family to prepare the children to be productive citizens. Family members instruct children in the customs and traditions of the group and help them acquire those skills that they need to survive and prosper. In rural areas, the family functions as a production unit, creating wealth and providing for the needs of all members. Farming is the most important occupation, with women and girls engaged primarily in the production of foodstuffs and the men and boys dedicated to the production of cash crops (e.g., coffee, cocoa, bananas, and palm oil and kernel). The cash crops and surplus foodstuffs are sold and the proceeds used to purchase goods that the family cannot produce itself (e.g., salt, clothes) and, in recent years, to provide a Western-style education for the children.

Both the traditional and modern Cameroonian family serves as a form of welfare and insurance to elderly, needy, unemployed, and sick members. In rural areas, which are often underserved by the state, families provide everything from health care to protection from opportunistic neighbors. In urban areas, where the demand for public goods and services often outstrips supply, families stand ready to serve the needs of members who migrate there from the rural areas in search of opportunities for economic advancement.

The Cameroonian family is also a social organization, providing members opportunities to participate in such activities as recreation, religion, education (especially in traditions and custom), and general socializing. The family creates the opportunities for ceremonies that are important to its members (e.g., birth and christening celebrations and leisure, education, and various traditional and modern sporting activities). The family also defines roles based on gender, age, and social standing, maintaining discipline and compliance to rules. Throughout most of Cameroon, patriarchy, which grants men (and male children) more authority, is dominant.

The Cameroonian family is formed by marriage, is usually larger than the nuclear family in the United States or Western Europe, and often contains members of several generations. It is common to find people who claim to be united by one ancestor (usually male) living in the same family. Hence, one may find grandfathers, grandmothers, fathers, mothers, sisters, and brothers living together as a family.

LINEAGE

When individuals are joined in a marriage, the relationship is called affilial, and when they are joined by blood, it is called consanguineous. In the latter relationship, the emphasis is on ancestry—a family tree can be constructed to show how one generation is related to the previous one. One can trace descent four ways. In Cameroon, the most common way to trace descent is through the male ancestors, usually the father. Second (and less common) is matrilineal descent, which traces descent through the mother. These two methods are examples of unilineal descent, where descent is determined by just one parent. The third method, which is common in the United States, is bilineal and traces descent through both parents. The last type, which is common among some northern Muslims (specifically the Hausa), traces one's ancestors through grandparents in both the father's and mother's families. Regardless of how descent is determined, members of a line of descent are known as a lineage. Most Cameroonian lineages share or claim a common ancestor. When two or more lineages claim a single ancestor, they are called a clan. This can occur when a member of a clan or lineage breaks away and relocates and, hence, becomes the founding ancestor to his new offspring. In most Cameroon societies, members of the same lineage are forbidden to marry one another.

When a man and woman get married and begin a nuclear family, they are still considered members of the larger family, which is the lineage. Those who are economically successful are expected to share their wealth with less fortunate members of the extended family. Upon the death of such a person, cousins, nephews, and others may challenge the deceased's sons and daughters for a share of the wealth left behind. Traditionally, a man is expected to treat his children and those of his sisters or brothers equally and, when possible, provide for all of them without discrimination. Hence, it is not unusual for children from poor parents who have a rich uncle (from either the mother's or father's side) to expect that uncle to provide for their education. Such children, of course, are expected to use the wealth that they generate from the skills obtained through education to provide for other less fortunate members of the family. In this system, many young people, whose education has been paid for by the family, often return from the United States and other Western countries with different ideas about family claims to their earnings. During the last several years, there has been a significant level of resistance from these foreign-educated elites to share their wealth with members of their extended family, many of who contributed to the education.

Throughout most Cameroonian societies, men are favored in inheritance, especially with respect to access to land and other environmental resources, as well as with where one can live and engage in agricultural pursuits. In Cameroon's patrilineal societies, when a woman marries, she becomes a permanent member of the husband's lineage. All the children born, regardless of their gender, belong to the father's kinship group. Among educated men, the wife is expected to take the husband's last name. However, in rural areas, married women take special names that identify them as such but that may not be related to the husband's. Among the Moghamo people (of the Widekum ethnic group), married women take names that identify them as married as well as with their fathers. Success for a man within most societies in Cameroon is still identified with his ability to support his family and provide for all the needs of its members.

MARRIAGE

All Cameroonian groups consider marriage one of the most important social institutions. It is the main structure for producing children, expanding the lineage, creating new households, and maintaining the customs and traditions of the group and ensuring that they are passed on to future generations. Although reproduction is considered a critical reason for marriage, love and affection are also important. Through marriage, individuals gain respect and social status. Throughout the country, single men and women are pressured by their families to get married. Married women typically forgive their husbands for various lapses in judgment rather than divorce them. However, men can be very hard on wives who engage in adulterous relationships—inflicting punishment that ranges from beatings to divorce.

In rural farming areas, a premium is placed on children, who are expected to help on the farm, do household chores, and take care of younger siblings. Given the high infant mortality rates in the rural areas, having many children also ensures that the family has surviving children. A married couple who are unable to reproduce will seek assistance from virtually all available sources, including consulting traditional or "witch" doctors, religious leaders, and modern medicine in order to improve their chances of conceiving. Because of the emphasis on having children, daughters of women who have proven themselves to be fertile are expected to be as fertile as their mothers; they are considered excellent marriage material and are courted by many families for their sons. If a child is sick, the family may suspect someone in the community of bewitching the child. Under such circumstances, the family may appeal to ancestral spirits to intervene and save the child and, at the same time, impose punishment on the offending party. Children are the center of most Cameroonian families and are loved and taken care of by all family members and not just by their biological parents. Quite often, a couple may send some of their children to live with relatives who have not been fortunate enough to have children of their own. Under such an arrangement, the children eventually come to regard the people they grow up with as their real parents. This is acceptable behavior in most societies in the country.

In Cameroon, a marriage brings together more than just a man and a woman. It joins together their lineages and clans and forms alliances between different kinship groups. The importance of family among Cameroonians is exemplified by the fact that most of the major ceremonies that take place among the various ethnic groups (marriage and death celebrations are the most important rites) center on the family unit. Young people often consider the impact of their behavior on the family before they engage in any activity. When a couple is making the decision to seek a divorce, they usually take into consideration the impact of their action on the larger family. They may seek advice, counsel, and intervention from various family members and may choose to stay together for the sake of family unity. An individual's success or failure in many pursuits is generally believed to be influenced significantly by the type of family to which he or she belongs.

Traditionally, many communities in Cameroon have engaged in arranged marriages in which the daughter is engaged to be married to a man chosen by her parents, with the choice based primarily on the quality of the expected husband's family and not necessarily on any personal traits exhibited by the young man in question. In such a marriage, the emphasis is on the union between the two families. Hence, dating as done in Western societies, is not part of the process. Parents may encourage their daughters to marry important dignitaries—such as kings, chiefs, princes, priests, and other high-ranking individuals within the society—even if these individuals are already married and, hence, would be accepting these girls as additional wives. Such marriages can form strategic political or economic alliances that can place the girl's family in a position to receive favors from the sovereign or dignitary.

In recent years, arranged marriages have become less common, especially among girls whose parents are highly educated and live and work in the urban areas. However, even if the boy and the girl make the decision by themselves to get married, families are still expected to be involved and make certain that their son marries a girl from the right family or that their daughter's husband comes from a respectable and highly regarded family. Families may check the medical history of a prospective spouse for their offspring to make certain that the marriage does not introduce hereditary diseases into their lineage. When a man and woman decide to get married, they share their decision with their immediate and extended families and usually wait for them to grant their consent and blessing—the latter is considered critical for procreation since many people still believe that a marriage not blessed by one's parents is likely to result in childlessness. Parents and other family members charged with the decision to grant the couple consent to marry would investigate to determine such things as the ethnicity, village of origin, religion, and occupation of the prospective spouse in order to help them make their decision. They also would seek information about the prospective spouse's family to make sure it is a good match. Generally, most Cameroonian parents wish their children to marry someone from their own ethnic group.

Cameroonians love their marriage partners, but they do not show love in the same manner as in the West. Unlike Westerners, most loving Cameroonian couples do not hold hands and kiss in public, dine out in restaurants, and attend various activities such as movies and concerts together. Instead, spouses are expected to reveal their love for each other by being responsible and respectful, working hard to bring up the children to be moral and respectful citizens, maintaining fidelity, and caring for members of the extended family.

Traditional marriages in Cameroon rarely end in divorce. In rural areas, where most people still marry through the traditional system, the extended family works hard to ensure that marriages survive. In many of these communities, a couple that has problems but chooses to stay together is viewed more favorably than one that solves its problems by divorcing. Despite the social stigma associated with divorce, children of divorced parents are usually not viewed in the same negative light as their divorcing parents. Among many groups, in the case of a divorce, the father automatically retains custody of all the children. While the infants and toddlers may stay with their mother, they are expected to return to their father's house as soon as they are able to. Of course, during the time of their absence from their biological father's home, he still retains significant control over their upbringing.

In the urban areas, where most couples are likely to marry either in church or at the court house and where couples are influenced significantly by practices brought to the country by European colonialists and other more recent visitors, divorce has gradually lost its social stigma and is more acceptable. One can now find many unmarried people living together in the urban areas, and divorce has become fairly common. Even women can now file for divorce from their husbands and later remarry. Modern marriage counseling centers and the various churches have become involved in helping urban couples improve their marriages and avoid divorce. Sometimes struggling urban couples are advised by friends and relatives to return to the village to seek the counsel of elders to resolve their differences and save their marriage.

Traditional marriages in Cameroon have rules for divorce based on such circumstances as adultery, abandonment, neglect (including the husband's inability to meet the needs of his wife), and behavior considered damaging to the family unit or lineage. For example, if a spouse engages in criminal activities and brings shame to the family, that may constitute grounds for divorce. Although adultery on the part of the wife is usually considered grounds for divorce, the same behavior by the husband may not necessarily elicit a similar response from family members. In urban areas, however, women who catch their husbands cheating often have the right under the law to file for divorce and many of them do. When marriages are contracted through Christian churches or the courts, rules for divorce follow the French and British legal systems. The Islamic parts of the country have rules for divorce based on adultery, mutual incompatibility, and the husband's failure or inability to meet the basic needs of his wife.

Although divorce has become more acceptable in urban Cameroon, the rate is still not as high as that in the United States and other Western countries. Granted, children are highly valued, and, as a result, when a couple is unable to produce offspring, there usually is significant tension within the marriage. However, divorce is not usually the outcome; instead the husband may decide to take another wife with the hope of producing children with her.

Marriage Forms

Although monogamous marriage is practiced among the urban educated elite and Christians, polygyny is widespread among traditionalists and Muslims. Many Cameroonian men, especially those who reside in the urban areas, are known to keep mistresses, especially when their marriages are troubled or have not produced offspring. The desire to have a son (or, in some instances, any child at all) is so strong in some men that many resort to taking a second wife when the first wife is unable to conceive. In doing so, many of these men are forced to abandon their Christian faith. Depending on the ethnic group from which the man hails, bringing a child born out of wedlock into the patrilineage may be quite problematic.

It is generally believed that about one-third of the married population in Cameroon is in polygynous relationships. The institution continues to survive because Islamic laws and the customs and traditions of various ethnic groups in the country allow it. To date, the modern Cameroon state has made no effort to outlaw the practice. The country's rural agrarian economy supports and encourages the practice of polygyny because farming requires a significant number of field-hands. Large families are required to tend the fields, harvest the crops, and perform other activities necessary to keep the rural economy functioning properly. In addition, because the infant mortality rate in the rural areas is relatively high, one way to improve the probability that the family will have grown children is to have many. Having many children also increases the likelihood that the father will produce an heir to keep the kinship line viable and going and that grown children will be able to provide for his care and that of his wife or wives in their later years. Among many grasslands groups, in which pregnant and nursing women are forbidden to have sex, marrying another woman provides a partner for a man who does not want to wait three or four years to resume sexual relations. Wealth in many of these societies is counted not only according to the size of a man's herd of animals and land possessions, but also in how many people are in his family. Hence, many chiefs (*fons*) in Cameroon, for example, desire more wives and children because of the prestige that accompanies a large family. Some men boast about their virility and contributions to a large kinship group.

It is often argued that, in regions of the country where there are more women than men, polygyny allows every woman who wants to marry the opportunity to do so. In most rural areas, men can remain unmarried, but it is taboo for a woman to remain single. In these societies, being a second wife is more respectable than being single. Women can marry at a younger age than men. Hence, it is fairly common to find older men with much younger wives. However, polygyny is constrained significantly by its economic aspects—marriages in Cameroon, even in urban areas, still require the payment of the bridewealth. Marrying more than one wife implies that the man must be able to secure the resources needed to pay the parents of his new bride, as well as provide for her and her children. Various traditional institutions must approve such marriages before they can be considered legitimate. The approval process involves making certain that the prospective husband is able to support the family he is creating.

Another form of polygyny that is practiced is referred to as widow inheritance, whereby a man marries the wife of his deceased brother. The woman is not forced into the marriage but sees it as a form of insurance against uncertainty. The marriage generates various benefits: she and her children will be well cared for; the lineage will be retained, and the children will continue to live with the family and in the village; and she is not likely to be separated from her children.

Managing a polygynous household is quite difficult. The husband must not show favoritism or discrimination in the division of marital resources. He must treat all his wives and their children with respect and not give any one of them any reason to feel discriminated against. The first wife, of course, exercises a certain amount of power over younger ones. However, tradition places constraints on her activities and makes it difficult for her to practice any form of favoritism or become vindictive. The husband is supposed to watch the activities of the first wife, who is the de facto manager of his compound, to make certain that she does not bring strife and chaos into his household. If the family is managed properly and according to tradition, the wives support one another in raising the children, feeding the husband, and taking care of the family's interests. If, however, it is poorly managed, the husband can lose his wives and place his children in jeopardy.

Most groups in Cameroon strictly prohibit marriage between members of the same kinship. However, among nomadic Fulani in the north, intermarriage among clan members is allowed. In an effort to perpetuate their nomadic lifestyle, these Fulani may reject people from sedentary populations as partners. Among Fulani nomads, a younger brother can marry his deceased older brother's wife; the older brother, however, cannot marry his younger brother's wife. After the death of a wife, the bereaved husband can marry her sister, as long as she is single.

Bridewealth

Cameroonian marriages usually involve the transfer of assets from the man's lineage to that of his future wife. This bridewealth is unlike the dowry practice of other cultures, in which wealth is transferred from the woman's lineage to that of the prospective husband. Further, bridewealth in Cameroon societies is not viewed as payment for services to be received from the future wife, nor is it interpreted as the purchase of a wife. Its purpose is to (1) cement the new relationship between the two families; (2) indicate the seriousness and commitment of the man and his family to the pending relationship; (3) inform the community at large that a legal relationship has been entered into; (4) clear the way for the couple to freely engage in socially accepted and approved sexual practices; (5) ensure that the offspring of the relationship are legal members of the man's lineage; and (6) provide nominal compensation to the woman's family for raising her into a moral, responsible, and respected adult. Of course, a daughter's marriage and departure from home implies that the family will now lose her labor services; hence, a certain level of compensation is considered appropriate. In cases where the girl has achieved a significant level of modern education at the family's expense and has accumulated skills that will make her a high wage earner, the level of compensation is expected to be a little higher.

Within some societies in Cameroon, if a divorce occurs, the bridewealth, especially if it is significant, might have to be paid back. If a wife divorces her husband and marries someone else, then the new husband or the woman's family is expected to help repay the first husband. Of course, repayment terms may be negotiated to allow the woman's family enough time to secure the needed resources. In determining the amount to be reimbursed, reductions are made for each child born in the marriage. The knowledge that the bridewealth might be refunded provides a certain level of stability in marriages and forces couples to work harder to sustain their relationships.

Bridewealth, as a proportion of the family's annual income, can be quite high, especially among rural households, which depend on subsistence agriculture for a living. One of the motivations for arranged marriages has been the desire by families, especially those that have many boys, to deal with the issue of bridewealth. Shortly after the birth of a son, the father may immediately set out to find a bride for the son. Once such a bride is secured, negotiations can proceed with the girl's family and the amount of the bridewealth set. The boy's family can begin to transfer resources to the girl's family on a yearly basis, with the expectation that, by the time both the boy and the girl reach marriage age, the boy's family would have transferred enough resources to the girl's lineage to secure the deal. The alternative, especially in urban areas, is to postpone marriage until the young man or his family can accumulate the resources needed to complete the deal.

The nature of the wealth transferred from the man's family to the woman's differs by region and is determined by what is available locally. Traditionally, resources transferred include items of economic and social importance, such as food staples, cattle, pigs, goats, and other domesticated animals, ivory, gold, clothes, kola nuts, and palm oil. The exchange of cattle is common among the pastoralists of the north. In rare instances, land may be used. Using cash for this purpose is a modern development.

Bamiléké Families

Among the Bamiléké of the western grasslands, descent is traced to both the father's and mother's lineage. However, affiliation through the father is more visible and important. Within Bamiléké societies, patrilineal descent is intrinsically tied to various sacrifices (especially to the spirits of ancestors) and the possession of skulls and inheritance. A son chosen by his father to take over for him when he dies is expected to inherit the skulls of his ancestors and his father's title and all the duties associated with it, which include raising all the children, taking care of the old and the sick, and providing for the effective functioning of the family.

The Bamiléké patrilineage is relatively small because the sons who are not chosen by their father as heir must leave to establish their own lineage somewhere else. Although these sons are still required to offer sacrifices to the spirits of their fathers and grandfathers, they are not required to go any farther back in the lineage. Only the chosen heir maintains distant ancestral ties. The skulls retained by the heir indicate the number of traceable generations. If a family decides to move, the skulls in its possession are carefully transferred through a special ceremony to the new location. Children are important not only to continue the lineage but also to take possession of the skull of the father, worship him, and ensure his status as an ancestor.[2]

In Bamiléké tradition, a purely sentimental affiliation is maintained with the mother's lineage. It does not confer any rights or privileges. The matrilineage is comprised of all the people descended through women from a common female ancestor. Since all female descendants of the matrilineage are considered his sisters, a man must not marry within this group. No specific taboos exist against marriage within a patrilineage, although most Bamiléké who share a common male ancestor four generations back will not intermarry. Whereas members of a patrilineage live close to each other and regularly commune with each other, those of a matrilineage are not close and may, in fact, belong to different chiefdoms.

Bamiléké women also choose an heir from among their daughters and bequeath to her their skull and personal belongings. The wife of a chief or king would include land in the inheritance. The daughter who is chosen to inherit buries the skull of her mother and grandmother besides her bed and regularly makes sacrifices to them to seek their intervention to ensure good health, fertility, a good harvest, and prosperity for the family. The other sisters are expected to assist the chosen one with her chores, as well as provide the goat meat and palm oil that she needs to carry out the sacrifices.

Like most women in the grasslands, Bamiléké women do most of the agricultural work, especially that associated with the production of food. Bamiléké men must pay bridewealth to the family of the woman they intend to marry. Such payment, in Bamiléké tradition, entitles the prospective husband to certain rights, including the wife's offspring and the fruits of her labor. The bridewealth payments are seen as compensation to the woman's family for the loss to her lineage of her economic contributions and her reproductive potential.

The Bamiléké also engage in a special kind of marriage called *nkap* that does not involve any transfer of bridewealth. The woman is given away in marriage by her father or legal guardian, and the new husband is required to provide only nominal gifts and services. He receives the rights to the woman only as a wife, but her procreative ability is retained by her father or legal guardian. Hence, if the marriage produces daughters, the father cannot arrange their marriages or receive any bridewealth. The legal guardian may choose to give away his grand-daughters in marriage under the *nkap* system, a process that allows him to continue to increase his capital stock of marriageable women.

Bamiléké kings or *fons* derive significant power from the *nkap* institution, using it to build alliances and increase the power and influence of their kingdoms. One Bamiléké *fon,* who is said to have ruled over a chiefdom of 20,000 people, had 1,500 female wards and was linked through the *nkap* institution to virtually all of the people in his jurisdiction.[3]

Christianity and other European influences have had a significant impact on Bamiléké society. In addition, population pressures and inheritance rules have forced the migration of many Bamiléké to other parts of the country, and many of them have settled in the large urban areas of Yaoundé and Douala. Although some of these urbanized Bamiléké (many of whom have become economically independent of the traditional system) have strayed from and rejected traditional practices such as the *nkap* and are no longer willing to subject themselves to the control of the *fon,* they still maintain ties with their homeland, visit occasionally, and continue to honor their ancestors.

Gbaya Marriage

The Gbaya are a fiercely independent people who, as a linguistic and social group, extend from central Cameroon through the Central African Republic into northern Congo. Within Gbaya society, a girl becomes marriageable at between 12 and 16 years of age. Young men are expected to marry when they reach 18 years of age. However, colonialism and modern education have altered some traditional ideas about the appropriate marriage age for both young men and young women. Young men are able to complete high school before they marry; hence, those who attend school may marry in their early twenties. However, since most girls only complete primary school, many of them are ready to marry in their late teens.

Boys choose the girl they want to marry and indicate their intention to the girl's parents by bringing them a gift. Items preferred as gifts include chickens, fish, and liver. If the girl's parents determine that the new suitor will make a good husband to their daughter, then the girl's mother will prepare the gift and it will be consumed by the girl's parents. Traditionally, the boy is not allowed to partake of the gift. If the girl's parents determine that the boy is not a suitable partner for their daughter, then the gift is returned and the boy must look for a wife elsewhere.[4]

If the gift is accepted, indicating that the courtship may begin, then the boy and his family are instructed to begin transmitting the bridewealth to the girl's family. The wealth to be transferred consists of such items as pans, cloth, goats, tools, spears, and other valuable items (which in recent years have included cash). The gifts are divided between the girl's mother and father.

It is common for a boy to choose a girl who is much younger than him and has not yet attained marriage age. Under such circumstances, he is still expected to approach the parents and offer the usual gifts. If they are accepted and permission to marry is granted, the process of transferring the bridewealth to the parents begins and it continues until the girl has attained marriage age. At that time, the young man will begin the *kofe* or "brideservice," a process that requires him to perform various services for his future in-laws. During this period, he is called a *wi-kofe* or one who asks for or seeks a wife. He is expected to work in the fields, gather firewood, participate in the hunt with the girl's father, visit the girl's family, and help his future in-laws carry out other chores. He remains in the service of his future wife's family for about a month or two to allow the girl's father to judge and determine whether he is a hard worker and a person who is likely to be a good and productive husband. If he lives close to the girl, then he will stay at home and commute. However, if his village is far away, making commuting difficult, he will reside with the girl's family while he works for them. During the period of service, he and his bride-to-be will be allowed to visit regularly. The girl will cook for him and they will eat together, and her parents, especially her mother, will watch them interact and determine whether he is a kind and loving person.

Failure to perform the required tasks and spend time with the girl's family, as well as treat her kindly and lovingly, will jeopardize the relationship and put into question his suitability as a husband. The parents may decide to cancel the "engagement" and send the young man back to his family and make arrangements to return the bridewealth that has already been paid.

A Gbaya girl is allowed to have more than one suitor at the same time. All such suitors make their intentions known and provide the girl's family with the necessary gifts. Once they are approved by the father, they can begin to transfer resources to the girl's family for the bridewealth. The girl eventually chooses one of the suitors, and, after her father's approval, the chosen one will continue to make payments. The others will have their bridewealth returned by the parents, and the unsuccessful suitors will search for a wife elsewhere. If the man chosen by the girl is not acceptable to her parents, she must choose someone else.

The Gbaya are an adaptive and resilient group of people and have changed along with the times. As a consequence, Gbaya girls have been granted greater say in whom they choose to marry. The father still plays an important role in the marriage of his daughter, but decisions are now more likely to be reached by negotiation instead of through parental commands.

Once the amount of the bridewealth to be paid by the prospective husband has been agreed upon and recorded in a book, a first installment is expected. A record of the transaction is kept with the girl's family and a duplicate is supplied to the young man. When payments are made, they are recorded in both books. Such records are expected to help the young man determine how much is left to pay, and, in the case of a divorce, the record can be used to calculate the amount of the refund. All the resources transferred, including money and the various gifts, are recorded in the book. Young men usually seek the assistance of their fathers and other relatives in meeting these obligations. Tradition mandates that older members of the family, especially the men, assist the young man in meeting his bridewealth obligations. Educated girls command a higher bridewealth because they are thought to be more economically viable than their uneducated counterparts.

The bride is also expected to spend time with her future husband's family, helping with household chores and getting acquainted. She will help prepare meals, clean the house, fetch water, sweep the yard, and engage in other activities that will convince the man's family that she will make a good wife and take care of her husband well. By the age of marriage, girls are expected to have learned from their mothers how to perform these tasks.

When a young man has decided to take a wife, he must begin the construction of a house in which he and his new wife will live. Thus, while he is performing services for his future in-laws, he is also working on the construction of a new house. Meanwhile, the girl will stay with his parents and eat her meals there. After the house is built, a feast is prepared to be eaten by all invited guests, excluding the girl—she must not partake of this meal. After the feast, the young woman and man will both go to the new house and settle in, officially becoming husband and wife. Hence, in Gbaya society, there is no official public marriage ceremony. Those who want their marriages recognized by the state may later engage in civil marriage at the nearest town hall, but this ceremony need not be undertaken immediately.

Gbaya couples usually do not spend enough time together before marriage to know each other well. The process of getting to know one another is expected to be accomplished after marriage. Emphasis before marriage is placed on family compatibility. The young man spends most of the courtship period trying to prove to the girl's family that he comes from a good family and that he will make a good, loving, and protective husband to their daughter. At the same time, the girl also tries to prove to her prospective in-laws that she hails from a good family and that she will make a good wife and mother. Once they are married, they then must concentrate their efforts on learning to know each other and develop their love so as to make the marriage work. This process is referred to as *mboo-zu* or "molding one's head; submission."[5] The wife is expected to submit to her husband; however, in Gbaya tradition, this does not mean that she must do everything that is dictated to her by him. On the contrary, it means that the wife should be patient, kind, supportive, and helpful and take good care of her family. The husband must submit to his wife and bring harmony to the family. *Mboo-zu* is achieved when the husband and wife are both patient, kind, generous, and bring harmony to the family.

If a conflict arises in marriage, *mboo-zu* is endangered. When the husband and wife talk, settle their differences, and make things right again, then there is *mboo-zu*. If, for example, the husband is the offending party and he refuses to apologize and discord remains in the family, then there is no *mboo-zu* and the wife may be forced to return to her parents to await the husband's apology. Her parents may encourage her to return to her husband and try to resolve the issue and restore *mboo-zu*. The man's parents, especially the father, may intervene and encourage their son to reach out to his estranged wife and make things right so that *mboo-zu* can return to the household. Unless there is mutual respect in the house, there will not be *mboo-zu*. *Mboo-zu* can also be absent if there is discord between the parents and the children. The children are expected to obey their parents, respect them, and work and get along with each other. When children are recalcitrant, refuse to do their chores, disrespect their parents or elders, and fail to work together peacefully, there is no *mboo-zu*.

Although both the mother and father are responsible for disciplining the children, most of the job falls on the mother, who spends more time with the children than the father does. The children learn the customs and culture of the Gbaya from their parents. At an early age girls begin to learn to be good wives and boys get instruction on how to become good husbands.

Within the Gbaya family, there is a strict division of labor. The father clears the land and prepares it for cultivation while the wife plants, tends, and harvests the crops. (The husband often helps with harvest.) Women usually work on the farm all day, returning home in late afternoon to cook food for the family. The evening meal is the main meal of the day and is prepared while the husband is still out in the field working. After the food is ready, the mother and children will sit down to eat, saving part of the food for the husband to eat when he eventually returns. Usually, when the children are younger, the whole family will eat together. However, after the children are old enough to eat by themselves, then the father will eat with the boys and the wife will eat with the girls. When people come to visit, men will usually eat together, and the women will gather in another part of the house to eat.

The Gbaya suffer from relatively high rates of divorce, especially among young couples. Each type of divorce is given a name, depending on whether the wife has left the husband or the husband has sent her away. When the wife leaves the husband, this is called *gbia koo*. One example of a reason this situation might occur is if a Gbaya husband shows interest in another woman or commits adultery, his wife will leave him and return to her parents. The woman's father will fetch the husband and his parents and all of them will go to the chief for a hearing on the matter. If, during the hearing, the husband decides to take responsibility for his actions and promises to remain faithful to his wife and respect her, then he is given a reprieve and his wife is returned to him so that they can try to bring back *mboo-zu* to their home. If, however, he is unwilling to change, his wife will not be returned to him and he will not be entitled to a refund on the bridewealth that he paid when he married her.

Other reasons for the *gbia koo* include (1) alcohol abuse, (2) abandonment, (3) failure to provide for the family, (4) cruelty, and (5) poor treatment. Sometimes if a man takes a second wife and the two women cannot get along, one may leave, usually the first one. Of course, some first wives may make life so miserable for the second one that she eventually leaves.

In most cases of *gbia koo,* the husband is entitled to a refund of the bridewealth that he paid. The refund does not include the services that he provided for the girl's parents while they studied him to determine whether he was a suitable husband for their daughter. If the divorce is because of adultery on his part, he is not entitled to any refund. Such cases usually end up in court, with the chief of the village serving as the magistrate to adjudicate the case and determine whether a refund is due and how much the refund should be. The decision of this court is binding.

If a married woman becomes interested in another man, she must first leave her husband before she can marry the second man. The new husband must go through the same process that is required of all men who want to marry—seek the approval of the woman's parents; provide the woman's family with services; and, if approved by the father, pay the necessary bridewealth. After the woman has left her first husband, she returns to her family and her father is required to refund the bridewealth to the first husband. If the father does not have the resources to make the necessary refund, he may wait until the new husband has completed his obligations to him and then use those resources to effect the refund.

Ndaka koo is the second type of Gbaya divorce. Literally, it means "chasing away one's wife." The most cited reason for the *ndaka koo* is adultery on the part of the woman. Adultery is considered to include sexual intercourse with other men and flirting or showing interest in other men in such a way that the woman no longer performs the traditional functions of a wife, including taking care of her husband and children. When the husband first notices such behavior, he will scold and cajole her, invite her to repent and mend her ways, and bring harmony back to the house. However, if she refuses to comply and continues to create disharmony in the house, the husband will eventually send her away.

Wives may also be sent away by their husbands for being stubborn, engaging in constant quarreling, challenging the husband's authority, and refusing to take care of the husband (including refusing to cook for him) and the children. Generally contributing to driving away *mboo-zu* from the household is considered a valid reason to send the wife away. When the husband sends his wife away, he usually is not certain whether he will get a refund on the bridewealth he paid to her parents before the marriage. In cases where the wife has become so difficult that the husband's welfare is threatened, he may send her away and not seek to recover the bridewealth. On some occasions, the father of the woman may voluntarily return the resources, especially if he discovers that the divorce is the fault of his daughter. Some husbands may take the case of the refund to the chief for adjudication. If the chief determines that the woman's behavior was the cause of the divorce, then he will rule that the woman's father should refund the bridewealth. Under these circumstances, the father will try to get his daughter to return to her husband—usually the husband will take her back and try to resolve their marital problems. However, if she refuses to cooperate and continues to behave in a disruptive manner, the husband may send her back again. This time he is not likely to accept her back if her father returns her to him.

A common reason for divorce in Gbaya society is the failure of the woman to bear children. Children (especially boys) are expected to take care of their aging parents; girls are released from this duty when they get married because they are expected to help care for the parents of their husbands. If a family has only girls, then the parents will be taken care of by male relatives. If a Gbaya woman is unable to bear children after three to five years of marriage, there is a very good chance that her husband will send her away to her parents and marry someone else. Such a woman is usually branded as infertile and may find it difficult to find another man willing to marry. The parents, however, will still make an effort to secure another husband for her.

When a Gbaya man with two wives converts to Christianity, he may decide to send the second one back to her family. Under these conditions, he is not entitled to a refund. In addition, he is expected to pay the parents of the wife he is sending away some money to help resettle her.[6]

Yua koo, or "fleeing one's wife," is the third type of divorce and describes the abandonment of a sick wife or one who is afflicted by a terminal disease. Of course, wives also flee husbands who are suffering from incurable diseases. Sometimes when a husband abandons a sick wife, expecting that she will eventually die, he is not likely to take her back if she recovers, because by the time she gets well he must have married someone else.

After the birth of a baby, the husband's mother usually comes to see the baby and stays for a while to help take care of both the baby and the mother. As soon as the baby is strong enough to travel, the mother will take the baby to her parents for a visit—such a visit may last as long as six months and is quite agreeable to the husband.

Births are considered very important blessings to the husband and his lineage. After a birth, the husband will usually send gifts to his wife's family to thank them for their daughter's fertility.

Marriage and Family among the Fulbe

The Fulbe practice polygyny—the cultural practice that allows men to marry more than one woman at a time. Most Fulbe are Muslims and, under Islamic laws, a man is compelled to treat all his wives equally and with dignity. Implied in this dogma is that polygynous men must secure the resources needed to provide for the material needs of all their wives—a process that can be quite difficult given the economic constraints that these men face. Thus, in addition to the fact that polygynous men must carefully balance their emotions and behaviors so as not to show favoritism toward any one wife, they must also work hard to produce enough wealth to meet the needs of all the wives.[7]

Fulbe men expect their marriages to produce many children. Hence, a Fulbe wife who is unable to reproduce is usually insecure and suffers from severe emotional stress, especially if the other wives are fertile. In Fulbe society, a married woman without children is likely to take her meals alone (while other wives eat with their children), must complete all her errands and chores by herself (e.g., there is no child to send to fetch water or firewood), and her ability to negotiate with her husband is severely constrained—if she had a boy to carry on the family name, for example, her ability to influence the husband's decisions would be strengthened. In addition, when she leaves her husband to visit her parents, no children are left behind who might irritate the husband and make him want her to return home as soon as possible. So when she is away on a visit, her husband is unlikely to miss her because he can find comfort in his other wives and there are no children to remind him of her absence.

Among the Fulbe, cloth is an important symbol of wealth and is used to convey social and economic status, as well as affection. Women adorn themselves with blouses, wrappers, and wraparound skirts made of locally produced or imported cloth. Married men are obliged by tradition to give their wives cloth on a yearly basis. The main wedding gift is a suitcase packed with several yards of cloth. How a bridegroom feels about his bride and her family is gauged by the quality, quantity, and price of the cloth that he offers her at their wedding. A suitcase full of expensive and highly valued cloth, preferably imported from Nigeria or The Netherlands, would please the bride and her family very much. Such a wedding gift implies that the man is caring and wealthy and has the ability to take care of his wife and the children she will produce for him. A gift of cheap cloth is a sign that the future husband is poor and cannot support a family or does not care about the bride and her family. Gifts of cheap cloth are considered an insult to the bride and her family and could constitute grounds for dissolving the marriage. Under such circumstances, the parents of the bride would send the suitcase back to their prospective son-in-law.

Each year the husband must give his wife a length of cloth, usually for her to wear to the feast that marks the end of Ramadan, Islam's holy month. Failure to provide one's wife with cloth can constitute grounds for divorce. The amount of cloth given and its quality depend on the husband's economic status and his love for his wife. A man who has more than one wife must be very careful to make certain that his yearly gifts of cloth do not reveal favoritism for one wife over another. When the women visit their friends during the holiday, they usually adorn themselves with outfits made of the cloth that they recently received from their husbands. During such visits, the women have the opportunity to publicly display symbols of their husband's economic status, as well as his generosity and love. A woman who expresses disproval to her friends of the quality of the cloth given to her by her husband brings shame to her household and dishonors her husband.

For a Fulbe woman, being married is very important because marriage changes her social status significantly and influences how she is treated by others in society. Women, depending on various factors, are classified as (1) virgin; (2) married; (3) free; and (4) postmenopausal. A free woman (*azabaajo*) is said to be "between husbands." She is not a virgin but is available for courting and marriage. Such women take lovers who ply them with gifts that may constitute an important part of their income. Some free women (usually relatively young divorcées), however, may prefer to remain celibate and stay with their parents while they are courted by prospective husbands. During this time, they live modestly, do not openly associate with men, exercise significant restraint, and expect men interested in them to contact them through their parents. Some of them may engage lovers but only under the most secret of conditions in order to maintain their public image and enhance their chances of securing a good husband. Despite the fact that many of these women behave quite modestly and live exemplary lives, men consider them available for sexual relationships. In general, most of these women prefer to be patient, trying to avoid men who are only interested in casual relationships, while they wait for men who are serious about marriage and the establishment of a permanent relationship. Free women who seek casual relationships with men suffer severe public criticism and could be labeled a prostitute, a designation that significantly reduces the woman's chances of ever securing a husband. Married women see free women—particularly those who engage in casual relationships—as a threat to the institution of marriage, especially because many men, despite publicly condemning the free women's lifestyle, are attracted to these women. Of course, given the high divorce rate among the Fulbe, most women during their lives would, at one time or another, be an *azabaajo* and suffer from its indignities. For most women, however, such a status is temporary and they are expected to soon find husbands and gain the respectability and protection that comes with marriage.

Men quite often speak of the *azabaajo* as individuals without honor and lacking in morality. Yet when a man breaks some traditional codes, he is not treated in the same manner. Although his behavior may be called to question, he is not treated as one without honor or someone whose very being embodies immorality. When an *azabaajo* engages lovers who give her gifts, she places herself in a position to be seen by the public as a prostitute. Yet her behavior and activities may be her way to search for a husband to gain the respectability that she lost through her divorce. However, society, especially men, does not see this as a legitimate and morally acceptable way for her to exit the insecure unmarried life and enter the more respectable and secure one of marriage. The men who visit the prostitutes do not usually suffer from similar censure by society.

Within Fulbe society, the life of a free woman is considered to be full of sin and immorality—it is assumed that a free woman engages regularly in sex with many men. Tradition, however, forbids sex outside marriage. Hence, free women (many of whom are summarily called prostitutes) are encouraged by their relatives and friends to work as hard as possible to secure a husband, who can restore them to respectability and allow them to live the kind of life that is sanctioned by Islam. All women of marriage age within Fulbe society, then, are encouraged to give up their single or free status and secure a husband as soon as possible, not only to avoid public criticism and condemnation but also to ensure their security.

A respectable status for single women in Fulbe society is that of *puldebbo,* which is usually accorded to postmenopausal women who have given up sexual relations with men and all the social problems associated with such relations. Such women would have grown children. While sexuality seems to play a very significant part in how the Fulbe define the status of a woman, fertility may actually be the defining factor. Hence, the social categories for women might be further defined in terms of a woman's fertility: a virgin/child is potentially capable of producing a lot of children; a married woman (or *debbo*) is ready to produce children for her husband; a prostitute/free woman's *(azabaajo)* fertility has been interrupted by divorce, but she is waiting and ready for the chance to resume reproduction; a *puldebbo* is no longer fertile and is identified with her sons's lineage and their fertility.[8]

Within Fulbe society, while both the *azabaajo* and *debbo* are assumed to be fertile, only the fertility of the *debbo* is considered useful and important for the patrilineage. The fertility of the *azabaajo* is considered a waste because it cannot be used effectively to produce or build a family or contribute to the patrilineage. These women are viewed as disruptive, undisciplined, and not functioning in ways that contribute to the building of harmonious families and communities. Like the *azabaajo,* the postmenopausal woman (or *puldebbo*) is considered to have useless fertility because her reproductive days are long gone and she can no longer contribute to the patrilineage. However, the *puldebbo* is well regarded and respected within society for her accomplished fertility (her grown sons) and retains her standing within society as one who has contributed to sustaining the patrilineage. Postmenopausal women need not leave their husbands; nor do they need husbands to retain their respectability. They gain and retain respectability and legitimacy through their sons, who will grow into men and contribute to the patrilineage.

In Fulbe society, both men and women must marry. Each completes the other, and hence, marriage is a very important institution. Although one can find many men in their early to late twenties in Fulbe country who are not yet married, these typically are men who, as a result of economic hardships, are still trying to secure the resources that they need to marry and establish a functioning household. Older men who have never married are usually considered to be insane and incapable of taking care of themselves, and they depend on their brothers.

Men are not expected to cook for themselves—this is the job of the wife. A man who cooks for himself is seen as usurping the job of a woman. Fulbe women prepare for their husbands a staple dish called *nyiiri,* which is a thick millet porridge. While most Western societies consider the honeymoon sexual encounter between the new wife and husband to consummate the marriage, in Fulbe society, consummation is marked by the husband's consumption of the new bribe's first *nyiiri.* Until a young girl can fully prepare the *nyiiri* dish by herself (usually one suitable for feeding a household of several people), she is not considered ready for marriage.

Fulbe men become adults through marriage and fatherhood. To remain social adults, they must continue to convince their wives to cook for them. A man should be able, on a regular basis, to invite friends to eat with him at his home. If a woman does not cook for him and he cooks for himself, he is called a *samarooka*—a gender role that is neither fully male nor female. A Fulbe man who is temporarily thrust into bachelorhood because his wife has left him must either immediately secure another wife or hire a woman to cook for him. With the wife gone, his compound is empty—it is without food, water, and the mother of his children. He may be forced to call on relatives to help or hire outside help. Without such help, he cannot invite friends to his home for a meal, and his social position suffers.

FAMILY AND GENDER ROLES

In Cameroon, the extended family is the norm. A Cameroon household may consist not only of the mother, father, and children, but also of uncles, nephews, cousins, aunts, and children of friends and relatives. Hence, people rarely complain of loneliness. In the rural areas, joint economic activities integrate members of the family and hold them together. Within the family, there is strict division of labor, with each person given well-defined tasks to perform. For example, the mother works in the fields producing food for the family; the elder children may help her in the fields or baby-sit younger ones and fetch firewood and water for cooking, bathing, and washing clothes; and the father is expected to provide important cooking ingredients such as palm oil, meat, and salt, as well as buy clothes and other important household items. In the old days, many men hunted to secure the meat for their families. Today, most men farm cash crops that they sell in the marketplace and then use the money to buy meat and household items. Some men are employed in wage labor and purchase household necessities with their wages. In each household, strict rules regulate how family property is used and how that property will be divided upon the death of the head of household—usually the father.

The typical nuclear Cameroon family has, on average, five or six children. A newly married couple's most important objective is to have a child. When the wife is pregnant, there is celebration: the wife is proud of her fertility, and the husband celebrates his virility. This makes the marriage stronger and cements the relationship between husband and wife. In traditional societies, diviners are usually summoned at this time to determine (1) the sex of the child, (2) whether there are likely to be any problems with the pregnancy, and (3) what action to take to make certain that all problems are minimized and ensure the birth of a healthy baby. If necessary, ancestral intervention is sought on behalf of the unborn baby and the mother.

An expectant woman's mother or an aunt is likely to come and live with her and care for her until she delivers the baby. During this time, the mother of the pregnant woman will reinforce what she had taught her daughter about childbirth and child care and help her prepare effectively for the upcoming birth. All the necessary items to receive the child are secured at this time. Depending on where the couple lives, delivery can take place in a hospital or health clinic with a modern midwife in attendance or at home with the help of a traditional midwife. In general, husbands and other male members of the family are not allowed to participate in or witness labor and delivery.

After a successful delivery, there is celebration among immediate family members. At an appropriate time, a larger celebration is held that might last several days and involve dancing and the consumption of large amounts of food and drink. When the child is strong enough to be taken on trips, the mother will visit her birth home and share her joy with relatives. In traditional families, such visits could last several months, giving the mother an opportunity to visit many relatives and allow them to see the child and rejoice with her.

The next step is to name the child. Within some groups, names are predetermined. For example, the first child of a couple takes the name of the father's father if it is a boy and that of the mother's mother if it is a girl. Then the second child will take the name of the mother's father if it is boy and that of the father's mother if it is a girl. Muslims and Christians draw names from their holy books. However, within most Cameroon societies, the Christian name is used only as a first name. Other names must be related to the family. A boy may be given the first name of his grandfather on his father's side (e.g., Fotoh) and he will be known by that name as he grows up. If he is baptized into a Christian church, then he may take another name, which then becomes his first name (e.g., Gideon). Then, when he attends school, he will take the family name as his last name (e.g., Mukum). Hence, on official school lists, he will be known as Gideon Fotoh Mukum. When some Cameroonians grow up and become interested in reasserting their traditions and identifying more with their clans, they either drop their Christian names or rearrange their names to make their middle names their first names.

Muslim names are usually associated with important events such as the feast celebrating the end of Ramadan; days of the week; and the holy book (Qur'an). Names associated with the Prophet Mohammed are quite common, as well as those associated with the prophet's wives or daughters.

Cameroon mothers usually breast-feed their children and wean them after three or four years. Although bottle-feeding children with formula is becoming common, especially in urban areas among elite women, breastfeeding remains the norm. Most women are full-time homemakers. In traditional households, sexual intercourse is not allowed during pregnancy and during the breast-feeding period. It is generally believed that sex can introduce diseases that will contaminate the breast milk and sicken or kill the child.

Most women carry their babies on their backs, secured by a piece of cloth called a wrapper. The children usually sleep in the same bed with their mothers until they are weaned. Then they may sleep with older children and interact more with them. At this time, they begin to learn the rules related to social behavior; boys begin to spend more time with their fathers, and the girls spend more time with their mothers and learn to cook and keep house. Even in the urban areas, where the girls are more likely to be in school, they are still expected to assist their mothers in preparing meals, washing dishes, and keeping the house in order. Where there is no indoor plumbing, the girls will also fetch water. The boys fetch firewood and do yard work.

Raising children is the job of the entire village. All members of the village are supposed to look out for all children and assist them when necessary. In rural areas, children are expected to be invited to eat when a family sits down to eat, even if those children are not members of the family. If some-one else's children come to play with your children and it is time for dinner, the traditions of most groups in Cameroon require that those children be invited to share your family's meal. A family that treats the children of other people poorly could summon the wrath of ancestors upon itself. Children are expected to respect and honor not only their parents, but all elders in the village. Occasionally, families will send some of their children to live with relatives, not necessarily as a form of discipline, but to help relatives who do not have children experience the joy of living with children or to deal with unexpected changes in the family's economic situation. It is common for rural families to send children to live with relatives in the urban areas, where there are better opportunities for economic and educational advancement for the child. Children can also be sent away to live with relatives or attend a boarding school for disciplinary reasons. Many of these schools are run by missionary societies and are well known for maintaining a rigorous regime of discipline, hard work, and learning.

Despite so-called modern influences, the division of labor by gender remains strong in Cameroon. Among sedentary northerners, men are farmers, and the women help with the harvest. In the western grasslands and southern forest regions, women are primarily farmers of foodstuffs, while the men cultivate cash crops. Among nomadic groups, the men keep livestock, and the women maintain the animal shed and sell dairy products. Among Fulani boys and girls, roles are blurred because they perform similar tasks; however, as they become teenagers, division of labor along gender lines emerges, and they are also segregated at play. The girls milk cows, churn butter, prepare cheese, and sell various products at the market. The boys perform security duties, watching over the cattle and the clan, and perform other duties to maintain the integrity of the group. In the grassfields, both girls and boys may be seen fetching water and firewood together; however, as they become teenagers, the girls begin to specialize in more domestic activities (e.g., cooking, clean-ing house, doing laundry, watching over younger siblings, and helping their mothers on the farms), while the boys move on to various outdoor activities (e.g., clearing fields for cultivation; helping their fathers in the coffee farms; felling trees for firewood; protecting their sisters from males outside the family and making sure that their virtue is not compromised, and repairing and maintaining their mothers' homes).

Grasslands women—especially those of the Bamiléké, the Widekum, Bali-Nyonga, and other so-called *graffi* groups—are great traders. Many of them often travel great distances in search of profits. In fact, throughout the country, Bamiléké and *graffi* women are well known as aggressive traders who can be found in most of the urban markets of the country selling both domestic and imported wares.

Both men and women can perform religious roles. The Muslim imams and religious scholars are mostly men. Although women play a very important part in Christian churches (serving as elders, choir directors, organists, and Sunday school teachers), church leadership is still dominated by men. In traditional religions, men remain dominant, although women have very important positions. Since independence, women have made significant inroads into the modern professions, as well in the political arena. Most of this progress can be attributed to increased opportunities for the education of women, especially at the higher level. Cameroon women can now be found in virtually all continents reading for degrees in disciplines ranging from art to wildlife management. However, some occupations that involve significant levels of physical exertion, such as hunting, blacksmithing, carving, and the building trades, remain male dominated. The kitchen remains dominated by women, even in commercial establishments.

Division of labor in the modern economy tends not to be based on gender. Most schools in Cameroon admit both boys and girls, and women can be found in virtually all industrial concerns and public offices in the country. However, men occupy the top of the managerial ranks. The continued marginalization of women is due to two important factors. First, emphasis on the education of women, especially at the postsecondary level, is a recent development. Second, traditionally, the education of boys has been given priority in most Cameroon societies. Given the fact that most people have viewed a girl's main occupation to be child bearing, investment in the education of girls has been considered a misallocation of resources. Thus, until the government began to provide free elementary schools, most parents did not consider money spent to educate their daughters a good investment.

THE FAMILY AS INSTRUMENT OF SOCIALIZATION

In Cameroon children are taught the customs and traditions of their parents to help them become responsible and productive members of society. Most of this teaching is undertaken through socialization within the family, village, and kinship group. Urbanites often return home during the holidays with their children to interact with other members of the kinship group. Also, urban parents may send children to live on an extended basis with relatives in rural areas so they can become more familiar with the traditions and customs of their ancestors and learn discipline and the value of hard work.

As they grow up in large families and mingle with relatives, children come to appreciate the importance and reality of the extended family. They see how their parents take care of their grandparents and other aged members of the family and come to understand and appreciate the role that they, too, will have to play one day. Children attend various ceremonies and see the roles played by their parents and understand that someday they, too, will be required to assume those roles. Eventually, through this interaction, the children come to recognize their important role in this cycle of life to sustain the kinship group. Their ancestors represent the past, their parents represent the present, and they represent the future. Through socialization, they learn the importance of continuity and eventually come to cherish and respect the role that they must play.

In the years before formal educational institutions were introduced in Cameroon, most teaching and training of children took place in the home and the village. Subjects covered included everything from customs and tradition to economic occupations such as hunting and gathering. While all groups taught their offspring their customs and traditions, other subjects covered in the instruction of children differed by region. For example, in the coastal regions, while home instruction of boys may emphasize fishing, hunting, and other sea- and forest-based occupations, instruction of the children of northern nomads will focus on raising cattle and the nomadic lifestyle. Children usually become apprentices to their parents, older siblings, and relatives. If a child is interested in an occupation that is not practiced at home, the parents might take him or her to where the training can be obtained. In doing so, the parents must make certain that the trainer chosen is one who would treat their children professionally and give them the necessary and appropriate training. Formal education is usually obtained outside the home and at schools provided by either the state or voluntary organizations such as churches and mosques.

Among all ethnic groups in Cameroon, there is unanimous agreement that elders and the aged must be treated with respect and allowed to maintain their dignity. All groups have rules governing the treatment of elders. Among most grasslands groups, children are not allowed to make eye contact with their elders, and a child cannot call his or her mother by her given name—the child must use special names that roughly translate into "mother."

Taking good care of the elderly and aged ensures continuity for the group. An important problem that societies have with rules is compliance and the costs associated with making certain that no member of the group engages in opportunistic behaviors. To minimize opportunism, societies impose sanctions against those who violate rules and statutes. Hence, children who disobey their parents and their elders, in virtually all societies in Cameroon, are punished, sometimes quite severely. In addition to sanctions that can be imposed by the living, violators can also be punished by ancestral spirits. Since elders are soon to be ancestors with the power to mete out punishment, anyone who disrespects elders and treats them poorly is risking inviting the wrath of ancestral spirits. Among many groups, the elders and the aged serve as mediators between deceased ancestors and the living. Before engaging in many activities, the blessings of elders is usually sought. Elders also assist in taking care of children and, since they are no longer working, they have the time to devote to the care of the younger ones. They resolve many family conflicts, discipline children, tell stories that help children learn the culture and customs of the group, and contribute significantly to the maintenance of strong and viable families.

To prevent people from looking at themselves solely as individuals and pursuing only their self-interest, emphasis is placed on the family's membership in the village and kinship group. It is important that individuals, in their daily activities, consider the impact of such actions on the welfare of not only themselves and their families, but also on the village and kinship group of which they are members. Economic independence, made possible by employment opportunities in the modern sector, has led many urban dwellers to think of themselves more as individuals and less as members of a village and kinship group. Slowly, but steadily, group interests are being eroded, as well as the sense of responsibility to one's kinship group. However, in both modern and traditional societies in Cameroon, individualism as it is practiced in the capitalist centers of the West, is still rejected. Most people still define identity in terms of membership in lineage, clan, and community. Despite the enormous demands of modernization, a culture of community, sharing, philanthropy, and togetherness remains strong among most of the country's various groups.

Coming-of-age transitions are very important among Cameroonian groups. Each transition is celebrated with special ceremonies that bring the community and kinship group together. After the various initiation activities to welcome a boy into adulthood, the process is usually concluded by a marriage, forming a new household, which increases the size of the clan and enhances the likelihood that children will be produced to add to the kinship group. The transition of girls to adulthood also results in marriage in many groups. Despite recent criticisms of the practice, some groups still engage in female circumcision (clitoridectomy). In those places where circumcision is practiced, failure to do so can stigmatize the girl and jeopardize her chances of marrying into a respectable family. Boys who are not circumcised may also be ostracized and find it difficult to secure a marriage partner. Female circumcision, now generally referred to in the West as female genital mutilation, can create many health problems, including inability to properly function sexually, difficulty bearing children, and increased risk of contracting many diseases. Due to the work of human rights and women's health organizations, the practice is dying out in many parts of the country.

Non-kinship groups are quite important in the country, although most of them have been replaced by institutions brought by colonialism and the exchange economy (e.g., Boy Scouts, labor unions, and other professional organizations whose membership is not based on kinship). Modern schooling has replaced adulthood initiation ceremonies in many groups. In the grassfields, the enormous powers that used to be exercised by kings *(fons)* are now performed by civil servants and politicians. The need to train people in traditional forms of administration and governance has fallen significantly as the kingdoms and chiefdoms have been incorporated into the modern Cameroon state. Various secret societies have survived, although their objectives have changed significantly. Today, many of them are used to enhance the economic and social activities of their members and provide them opportunities for advancement. In many areas of the country, modern medicine has replaced traditional medicine, although some modern medical practitioners have begun to take advantage of some traditional practices in the treatment of their patients.

THE FAMILY AND SOCIAL CHANGE

Colonialism and its accompanying institutions, as well as modern forms of globalization, have had a significant impact on gender roles, family, and marriage in Cameroon. The exchange economy introduced by colonialism keeps expanding and having an impact on rural areas as they continue to be incorporated into the modern industrial sector. Wage labor has gradually replaced many traditional occupations (e.g., hunting and gathering), and, in the process, it has enhanced the economic mobility of many people. Many Cameroonians now travel far away from home to work and in the process meet people from other ethnic groups. People who travel out of Cameroon to study and work may meet people of various ethnic and racial backgrounds. Today, various social changes are threatening the traditional extended family in favor of the nuclear family, especially among urban dwellers. In addition, other changes are being noticed: (1) a reduction in the average family size (fewer children); (2) increased rates of participation in the labor market by women; (3) the emergence of new child-rearing practices, most of which emphasize a Western-style education; (4) rural-urban migration; (5) more participatory ways of managing the household; and (6) increased opportunities for economic advancement, even for women.

Western education, the demands of living in the urban areas, and other factors have made the monogamous marriage the preferred social arrangement among many of the educated elite in Cameroon, as well as the younger population. Of course, Christians are encouraged by their religious leaders to practice monogamy. In today's urban centers in Cameroon, people derive prestige from living in large beautiful homes in nice neighborhoods, driving expensive imported cars, and wearing the latest fashions and fancy jewelry. This lifestyle costs a lot of money. A man who marries several wives cannot afford to maintain such a lifestyle, especially given the economic constraints that most Cameroonians face today. In addition, having a smaller family allows the father to educate his children at elite private schools and even send them abroad for higher education, significantly increasing their chances of being economically successful. Among rural inhabitants, the average number of children in families has also declined, due in part to improvements in access to modern health care, reductions in infant mortality rates, and increased survival rates for children.

As the nuclear family has gained currency among many groups in Cameroon, the extended family has continued to decline. Throughout most of the country, younger couples are no longer required or obliged to live with members of the extended family or even stay in their ancestral village. Kinship groups are no longer united by religion, occupation, or culture. One, however, should not interpret these developments to mean that the institution of the extended family has died in Cameroon. Cameroonians continue to regard themselves as members of a wider kinship group, even if the members of that group do not all live in the same area.

The functions of the modern nuclear family in Cameroon are significantly different from those of the traditional extended family. Unlike the traditional extended family, which functioned as a unit of production, the modern nuclear family does not specialize in the production of foodstuffs and other consumption items. The exchange economy and the use of money have made specialization possible, and other people and organizations have taken over the production of food and other consumables. In the area of law and order, professional police organizations, provided by the modern state, now police many communities. Governments at the federal, state, and local levels now provide communities with public goods and services that were previously provided by families and kinship groups.

The working mother is a new phenomenon and one that worries a lot of traditionalists. It is argued that most modern women—who typically live in the urban areas and work either in business or in the public sector—do not spend enough time with their husbands and children. The demands of their professions are so significant that many of them neglect their families as they struggle to advance at work. Many of these families have turned to maids and other hired domestic help to take care of their households. Improved opportunities for women in the economy have changed the dynamics of the family —decision making, especially with respect to the allocation of resources, has become more democratic. Traditional values of patriarchy have been eroded as women have attained significant levels of participation in the management of the household. In addition, children in these households are also granted the right to participate in determining the types of professions that they would like to enter when they grow up. Such autonomy for family members has produced undesirable consequences such as premarital sex, a growing problem that is especially alarming because of the HIV/AIDS pandemic.

Educated elite families in Cameroon have altered traditional rules of inheritance and now allow their daughters to inherit. Daughters are now as welcomed as boys, especially given the fact that with improved economic opportunities for women, the latter are now capable of taking care of their aging parents. Many elite women are now using hyphenated last names to show that they belong to two families. This is especially common in situations where the woman's family is well known and is politically, socially, or economically prominent.

One of the most important agents of socialization in modern Cameroon is Western education. Skills acquired in schools in Cameroon or abroad are considered very important for success in the modern sector. Schools are an important arena within which people learn not only the skills that they will need in the workforce, but also develop values, friendships, and associations that will serve them throughout their lives. Some of the values acquired in school are now being blamed for some of the country's moral problems. In fact, in recent years, many religious leaders and traditional elders have publicly expressed their anger at Western fashions (which they believe are corrupting the youth), foreign films, literature, and ideas (which they believe have destroyed the country's moral compass). High divorce rates, truancy, out-of-wedlock pregnancies, and increasing rates of sodomy are all blamed on the corrupting influences of foreign cultures, most of which, it is argued, are transmitted through modern education.

Despite all these changes, many long-established cultural practices have been retained. Whether living in the country or abroad, Cameroonians remain family-oriented, spend a lot of time with their children, share their income with members of their extended families, adore and respect their elders, and remain committed to the institution of marriage. Most of them still prefer to identify themselves with their village and kinship group. The individualistic lifestyle has still not been accepted by most Cameroonians, even those educated in the capitalist West.

NOTES

1. Monica B. Visonà, Robin Poynor, Herbert M. Cole, and Michael D. Harris, *A History of Art in Africa* (New York: Harry N. Abrams, 2001), p. 340.

2. Harold D. Nelson, M. Dobert, G. C. McDonald, J. McLaughlin, B. Marvin, and P. W. Moeller, *Area Handbook for the United Republic of Cameroon* (Washington, DC: U.S. Government Printing Office, 1974), p. 87.

3. Nelson, et al. (1974), p. 88.

4. Alice Eastwold, "Gbaya Marriage," in *Grafting Old Rootstock: Studies in Culture and Religion of the Chamba, Duru, Fula, and Gbaya of Cameroon,* ed. Philip A. Noss (Dallas, TX: International Museum of Cultures, 1982), pp. 33–34.

5. Ibid., p. 36.

6. Ibid., p. 39.

7. H. A. Regis, *Fulbe Voices: Marriage, Islam, and Medicine in Northern Cameroon* (Boulder, CO: Westview Press, 2003), p. 43. Most of this section on Fulbe marriage and family is based on the excellent work done by Regis among the Fulbe of the far north of Cameroon.

8. Ibid., p. 50.

7

Social Customs and Lifestyle

AMONG THE MOST IMPORTANT and widespread social customs in Cameroon are ceremonies and rites that celebrate various aspects of life, sporting events, and activities that promote nationalism in an effort to create a national identity and build a united and peaceful country. Current lifestyles in Cameroon reflect many years of traditional practices, as well as the influence of external factors such as colonialism, Christianity, Islam, and globalization.

Cameroonians are generally very friendly and outgoing. Although kisses are uncommon as a greeting, salutations that communicate warmth and a sincere sense of caring are very common. People hug, shake hands, and hold each other openly. Even men may hold hands in public, and this show of friendship does not have any sexual connotations. Speaking loudly in public is not considered rude or vulgar, although in certain situations (e.g., during a funeral or when one is in the presence of a king or other traditional ruler), such behavior is not welcomed. Kissing, especially in public, is not common. During the Ahidjo years, Cameroonians rarely discussed their political views openly; however, they engaged freely and frequently in open discussions of other issues. While domestic politics were off-limits, Cameroonians engaged freely in the discussion of everything from the "wages of sin" to the costs and benefits of polygynous marriages. Popular topics for discussion, especially among urban dwellers, included soccer (and other sports), international affairs, and popular music. Global racism, Marxism, colonialism, neocolonialism, HIV/AIDS, human rights, feminism and gender politics, ecosystem degradation, structural adjustment programs, and study abroad remain important topics of discussion on university campuses throughout the country. Cameroonians are quite knowledgeable about other parts of the world and pride themselves on being able to intelligently discuss international affairs with foreign visitors.

Whether riding in a bus or airplane, standing in line to be served at the bank or at a restaurant, Cameroonians will openly discuss many topics. Since multiparty democracy returned to the country in 1990, citizens can now openly examine domestic affairs without fear of retribution. Religion is a favorite topic of conversation—many believers are not afraid to proselytize. Some can be quite aggressive as they try to convince others to accept their brand of religion.

Community life, even in the urban areas, is important to Cameroonians. They enjoy social gatherings, ceremonies/celebrations, and parties, especially those that include dancing, eating, and drinking. Within virtually all groups in the country, occasions that mark important events in one's life (e.g., birthday, christening, marriage, and death) are cause for party and celebration, providing friends and relatives the opportunity to enjoy each other's company, dancing, good food, and music. A family whose child has just returned from studies abroad may invite friends and relatives to their home for food, drink, and celebration. Rich and successful individuals often celebrate their achievements by giving a party and hiring a live band to play at the party. In addition to inviting many people to celebrate, the host may parade men and women of high social (and/or political) status (to emphasize the kind of company that he keeps), and provide the guests with large quantities of expensive and sumptuous food and drink. Imported items, such as French and Italian wines and spirits, Cuban cigars, Russian caviar, and assorted other expensive consumables may also be provided guests. Rich urban Bamiléké throw elaborate parties to mark virtually all important events in their lives. Other groups do likewise and feed the celebrants well, allowing them to drink and dance all night. In the rural areas, all-night parties are quite common and are used to mark important occasions, including birth and death celebrations, christenings, weddings, and school graduations.

Access to telephones and other modern forms of communication is still limited to a small minority of people, most of whom reside in the urban areas. However, Cameroonians are quite adept at face-to-face communication. This type of communication is so important in the country that many people still believe that, even when one can afford a telephone or have access to a fax machine or e-mail, face-to-face communication should be chosen because it is more polite and courteous. When an issue is important, most parties involved prefer face-to-face contact to other forms of communication. Hence, a man living in an urban area, for example, may travel more than a hundred miles to meet with the parents of his wife to discuss pending marital difficulties and seek counsel instead of, say, sending e-mail or writing a letter.

Appearing in person and presenting the problem gives the other party the impression that you consider the issue important.

During an appearance before an elder or someone in a position of authority, a younger person or one of lesser rank usually avoids eye contact. This is considered a sign of respect. In addition, the younger person or one of lower rank usually allows the elder or person of higher rank to dominate the conversation or discussion. In addressing an elder or person of higher rank, the younger or individual of lower rank usually speaks in the third person, saying "they" and "he" instead of "you." Where intervention by a third party is being requested, gifts are usually given. These gifts need not be expensive, since the purpose is to show respect for the recipient. Hence, a few kola nuts, a bottle of wine, a pouch of cured tobacco, and so on are usually considered appropriate.

Cameroonians, especially elders, are good storytellers. Stories are used to teach lessons and help people deal with various daily problems. Hence, in sending away a child from the village to the urban area to attend high school, village elders may use stories to help the child cope with the demands of city living. The main objective is to help the child hold on to his or her values (those instilled by his or her parents) while adapting to the new environment. Such stories are also used to help young couples meet the challenges of marriage, motherhood, fatherhood, and raising children. Through the use of proverbs and idioms, elders instruct the young in the challenges facing them in life. In the instance where elders or parents must help a child with a very delicate issue (e.g., the death of a relative), stories laced with proverbs and idioms can be very effective. For example, to deal with children who continuously lie or tell fibs, a variation of Aesop's fable of the boy who cried wolf is used effectively to help the child learn the importance of telling the truth.

Taboos are important in most traditional societies in Cameroon. These are actions and activities that are not allowed in certain well-known circumstances. For example, in most communities in the grasslands region, no one is allowed to shake hands with the wife of the *fon* (king); males cannot sit on the same bench with the wife of a *fon;* subjects cannot shake hands with the sovereign or speak in their presence unless they are specifically asked to do so; when the sovereign enters the room, everyone must stand and remain standing until he has taken his seat; no one, except the sovereign, can sit on his stool; and after age of maturity (12–16 years) boys can no longer sleep in the same room with their mothers. Although many of these taboos help maintain peaceful coexistence, educated citizens tend to ignore them. In addition, since many of them are associated with traditional religions, those who convert to Christianity often ignore them. However, many of these so-called modern citizens have come to realize that, although they can ignore these taboos when they reside in the urban areas, doing so in the rural areas can endanger their lives and make it quite difficult for them to function effectively among rural folk.

SOCIAL RELATIONS

Within all Cameroon groups and communities, interpersonal relations are governed by a code of conduct (often unwritten) that emphasizes respect, especially for elders; kindness to others, especially children; and acknowledgment of achievement. Hence, a son respects his parents; a junior sister respects her elder sister; in polygynous marriages, a junior wife respects the senior wife; and, at work, junior staff are expected to show respect to the senior staff. Students respect their teachers; they rise to attention when the teacher enters the classroom and wait until they are instructed to sit down before they do so. Respect based on age, however, is complicated by other determinants of respect, which include wealth and titles. For example, a *fon* (king), regardless of his age, must be treated according to the dignity of his office and position.

Cameroonians can show respect by the way they greet each other, as well as by the forms of addresses that they employ. For example, one is expected to bow to a chief or *fon*. Elders should not be addressed by their first names. In most cultures, morning greetings are compulsory. In such greetings, it is customary to inquire about the health of not only the person being encountered but also of his or her family. Usually, the younger person is expected to greet the older person first. Among the Widekum, every occasion has its own appropriate greetings, so, in a day, one may be greeted a number of times. People of the same age and social status may shake hands; however, a younger person is not expected to shake hands with an elder. No one can shake hands with a *fon*. Both women and men must bow before the *fon* and talk only when requested to do so by the sovereign. In some grasslands cultures, one must cover one's mouth when talking to the sovereign. In the kingdom of Foumban, citizens who address the king must bow their bodies at an angle with their hands pressed together and positioned below their chin so as to prevent the speaker's saliva from touching the king. In addition, citizens addressing the king must stand at a pre-approved distance away from the king, speak in a well-tempered voice, and avoid looking directly into the king's face. It is forbidden to be so close to the king as to touch his body or his shadow. Explicit and well-developed protocol regarding one's appearance before a king, as well as speaking and seating during an audience with a king, exists among the Fulani, Bamiléké, Bali-Nyonga, Widekum, Bamoun, and various hierarchically organized cultures in the grasslands.[1]

Among most groups in Cameroon, failure to greet another person (be they a friend or stranger) or respond to a greeting is considered a serious infraction of social customs. An entrepreneur who exhibits such behavior could forfeit the opportunity to engage in trade, because many people would avoid doing business with him or her. All engagements, whether professional or social, are opened with greetings. Some greetings are elaborate and others are short—the nature of each greeting is determined by the occasion or circumstances under which the greeter and the recipient meet. For example, two fellows from the same village who meet in an urban center after having not seen each other for a while might turn a simple greeting into a long conversation about memories of home and the challenges of urban living. On the other hand, a student from a rural village who is visiting an uncle in the city and runs into his teacher (who is probably taking a refresher course at a local university) may nervously sputter "good morning sir," wait for the teacher to answer, and quickly move on.

Cameroonians, regardless of which group they belong to, love titles—both traditional and modern. Hence, it is not unusual for people to insist that they be addressed with their occupation before their names. For example, Geneticist Mary Api Ngu instead of Ms. Mary Api Ngu; Principal J. Mba Mbaku; and Parliamentarian Samuel Ebong Ateng. Individuals who have completed the pilgrimage to Mecca are addressed as Alhaji (for men) and Alhaja (for women). In some professions (especially music), individuals may appropriate various titles to enhance their public image. For example, musicians have been known to appropriate such titles as King, General, Commander, and Professor. Many people who have earned or have been given honorary titles will parade them and make sure that everyone around them is aware of these titles. Hence, calling a man Mr. or a woman Mrs. is often not enough. A business card is usually quite elaborate. For example, Dr. Emmanuel Mba Ngo, BSc., MSc., Ph.D., Fellow of the Royal Society of Chemists, Member, American Chemical Society, followed by a summary of the individual's life achievements. Individuals who have traditional titles such as "chief" (whether inherited or honorary) would include them. Even in social situations, individuals often insist on being addressed by their titles. Hence, it is fairly common to hear university professors being addressed as Professor so-and-so, instead of by their regular names, even outside the university campus.

Young people are quite aggressive as they seek to earn those titles they are later to parade and that will validate the level of their success. Competition to train at the nation's universities or go abroad to read for degrees is very intense. Those who are lucky enough to enter the university will do whatever it takes to succeed—most of them continue their studies until they can get the terminal degree in their chosen field of study and, if possible, secure a job as a professor. Even if they give up teaching and take another job, they will still insist on being addressed as professor, a title that comes with a great deal of social respect. In addition to using titles to show off their success, many successful people also live in fancy houses (staffed with many servants, including a security guard), ride in expensive chauffeur-driven cars, and maintain a long list of influential acquaintances.

Although many Cameroonians, especially the young, have become quite aggressive as they search for opportunities to improve themselves economically and socially, most Cameroonians are respectful and tend to engage in a much less aggressive form of competition. Integrity and honesty are expected of all people at all times. In fact, one of the features that attracted many of the early Christian missions that expanded inland from the Cameroon coast was the premium that many groups placed on morality and integrity. Traditional religions place a high premium on ethical behavior, personal responsibility, respect for one's ancestors, and integrity in one's dealings with others. Children are taught at home that hard work, good character, and honesty will bring prosperity, friends, and blessings from ancestors. Hence, people are generally expected to be honest; work hard; be kind to everyone, including strangers; avoid opportunistic behavior; be generous, especially to members of one's family and friends; help the less fortunate; and avoid bringing shame and public ridicule on one's family, village, and lineage. Fornication, adultery, theft, cheating, refusing to meet one's public obligations (e.g., paying taxes), cruelty to children (as well as to animals), and disrespect of elders are all strictly discouraged. All citizens are encouraged to be generous and give gifts, especially at special occasions—to show appreciation for being included in the ceremony or celebration, to reciprocate a previous gift or favor, to help the host with the cost of the event, and to solicit or court the friendship of people in positions of authority. When someone is in need and requests help and one is in a position to help, it is generally expected that one will do so. In case of an emergency or a life-threatening situation, those in the vicinity are expected to offer to help even if help is not solicited. Cameroonians expect everyone to have compassion. In fact, many grasslands groups believe that the souls of people who are callous and have no compassion will not be able to reunite with their ancestors and will remain in limbo for all eternity. Human life, it is argued, is to be cherished and placed ahead of money and other material belongings. The Widekum believe that their ancestors return to earth occasionally to dwell among them and determine the level of their compassion. Those individuals who show a lot of compassion are guaranteed passage to the ancestral home when they die, and those who are without compassion are sentenced to a hopeless existence in the afterlife. Ancestors return to earth disguised as ordinary people, so one cannot risk being callous, even to strangers because one of them might be an ancestor on watch.

CEREMONIES

In Cameroon, ceremonies in both villages and urban centers and among both traditional and modern religions are an important part of life. Most of them are associated with rites of passage and various religious events. Through these activities, members of the various groups reaffirm their commitment to each other and the group, help younger members become familiar with customs and traditions of the group, and have fun. At these ceremonies, participants sing, dance, eat and drink, engage in merry making, and generally enjoy themselves. For example, Christmas celebrations help Christians reaffirm their faith in their savior, provide opportunities for believers to rediscover others, and help new members integrate themselves into the family of believers. Ramadan offers similar opportunities to Muslims.

Virtually all life transitions are marked by some sort of ceremony. One of the earliest transitions is, of course, birth, and this is marked by elaborate celebrations. The naming celebration takes place within a few weeks after birth. Some cultures combine the naming ceremony with the celebration of the birth itself and have one elaborate party to which the entire extended family is invited. Each participant is expected to bring possible names for the baby, and, from among these, one will be chosen. However, among most grasslands groups, the choice of a name for the child is predetermined by traditional practices. Among the Moghamo, for example, if the first child is male, he will take the name of his paternal grandfather.

All names have special meanings. Some traditionalists consult oracles before the child is conferred with a name. The oracle supposedly determines the link between the child and an ancestor. If the child is the reincarnation of a particular ancestor, according to the oracle, then that child will be given the name of that ancestor. With the spread of Christianity throughout Cameroon, many children now routinely receive Christian names, although this practice is limited to those households that have accepted and embraced Christianity. Even in Christian households, children are still given traditional names that reflect their membership in the family and the lineage. For example, a child born to a family in Guzang (a Widekum village in the North West province), whether to a Christian or traditional household, will be assigned a name based on tradition (e.g., Mukum). Then, at baptism into, say, the Presbyterian Church (a predominant church in this village), the child will take or be given a Christian name (e.g., Jonathan). Upon entering school, the child will take on the family name (Mba) and be known officially as Jonathan Mukum Mba.

A young person's transition into adulthood is usually marked by a community-wide ceremony. The initiation ceremony often serves a dual purpose: to test those being initiated and to mark their exit from one stage of life into another. In the past, some groups have sent their sons when they attain the age of 15 years to live an isolated existence in forests adjoining the village for a whole year and return to the village for the final part of the initiation, which involves dancing, drinking, and the official reception of the young men into the circle of adults. Those who return successfully from the extended stay in the woods are accepted as adult members of society and granted permission to marry. Those who fail to return are considered not fit to take their place among their kinfolk as adults and are not mentioned anymore—death under such circumstances is accepted as a natural selection process that enhances the quality of males available to the lineage. In the days when interethnic wars were common, this process was considered critical to the cultivation of the warriors needed to maintain the integrity of the group and ensure the defeat of its enemies. However, since the late 1880s, Christian missionary groups, with the help of the colonial government, have effectively eliminated these extreme initiation rites and replaced them with what they consider "civilized" and more humane activities. The most popular of these is scouting. Scouting is popular among groups that have embraced Christianity and in the process marginalized their traditional religious practices. Wrestling, also a traditional sport, remains quite popular, even among groups that have adopted the various rites introduced by Christianity.

Initiation ceremonies remain popular, especially in the rural areas. In addition to offering youngsters the opportunity to be ushered into adulthood, they also serve as conduits through which the customs and traditions of the group are reinforced and members allowed to take pride in the achievements of their forebears. Successful participation in the ceremony also indicates to society that the individual is ready to marry and establish an independent household. Among some groups, males are circumcised at this time and their sexual identity confirmed, allowing for the differentiation of sexual roles. As the new adults join peer groups, they do so with pride in their successful passage from childhood to adulthood. Now they are ready to begin life as productive members of the community.

While birth is the beginning of one's life on earth, death represents the end of that life and the beginning of a new one, marked by a long journey to the ancestral resting place. Burial and the various ceremonies associated with it prepare the deceased for the journey to meet ancestors. The kind of preparation undertaken and the nature of the burial ceremony are determined by the status of the deceased in the family, village, and lineage. Burial for a king is significantly different from that for a commoner. In the grasslands, burial ceremonies for important dignitaries (e.g., *fon,* chief, or subchiefs) can last as long as three weeks and involve various types of celebrations. If an individual commits suicide, no public ceremony is offered for burial and the burial is carried out in secret. Among the Moghamo, those who commit suicide are said to insult and degrade their families, as well as bring the wrath of ancestors on themselves and their relatives. Instead of celebrating the death passage and wishing him or her a safe journey to ancestors, family members will perform the burial in secret and usually not in the traditional burial place. They will live with the shame of this act for the rest of their lives and hope that future generations will eventually forget about this relative and the shame that he or she brought to the family.

All groups have rules that regulate the preparation of bodies for burial. Although modern funeral homes exist in the country, most people still prefer to prepare the dead for their long journey to meet ancestors in the traditional way—which, of course, differs widely throughout the country. Preparations of the body of a sovereign for burial are more elaborate and must be carried out according to traditional protocol. Some cultures (e.g., Bamiléké in the western grasslands and the Maka in the east) practice divination and perform public autopsies to determine the cause of death. Among these peoples, such autopsies are used to determine whether death was caused by witchcraft. Among the Moghamo, an oracle is usually consulted, especially in the case of the death of an important dignitary or one who has left behind a lot of property, to determine the cause of death. Public wailing, usually by women, is used to announce a death. Among many Moghamo villages, drums announce a death.

Most grasslands groups bury their dead quickly and then engage in the "cry-die" or mourning period a week or so after burial. The length of the public mourning period is determined by the importance of the deceased with ceremonies for important dignitaries lasting as much as three weeks. In addition to the daily celebrations involving dancing, eating, and wailing, close relatives of the deceased are expected to shave their heads. It is important to note that, despite the fact that women cry at these occasions, the public mourning is not considered a sad event—it is actually a celebration and send-off party in which the soul of the deceased is set on the journey to its ancestors to begin a new life. About a year after burial, elaborate celebrations take place to honor the deceased, who is now an ancestor.

Among the peoples of the forest regions of Cameroon, death provides their most important ceremonies. Spirits that dwell in the forest and have significant impact on the lives of the peoples of the region participate in death ceremonies—they come as dancers wearing raffia masks. As with other groups, the length of the celebration depends on the importance of the recently deceased. Ceremonies for important dignitaries can last many days and involve many activities.

Burial rituals differ by region. Among most grasslands peoples, burial of important dignitaries is in a grave dug in the main house. Non-dignitaries are usually buried in a specially designated place in the compound. In the various grasslands palaces, special places are set aside within the complex for burying kings and storing their skulls. Those who have accepted Christianity are buried at a church-owned cemetery, usually located in the same area as the worship center. In the urban areas, public cemeteries are provided because burial in the home is prohibited by law. Many urban dwellers, however, take deceased relatives back to their villages to be buried near their ancestors. Among Catholic Ewondo, ancestors are buried in elaborate tombs in the courtyard. The Fulani, like other Muslim groups around the world, believe in an afterlife characterized by significant material rewards for those who live according to the laws of Islam and keep all of Allah's laws.[2]

FESTIVALS

Most of Cameroon's cities and villages hold some kind of annual festival to mark an important date in their history or some occasion uniquely associated with the locality. For example, the city of Buea holds an annual celebration in honor of Mount Cameroon, its most important and enduring attraction. In addition to bicycle races and marathons to mark the celebration, there is also dancing and feasting.

Although festivals may have historical importance, they are also opportunities for people to get together and enjoy themselves through dance, song, drink, and merry making. Perhaps more important is the fact that these festivals, such as the annual harvest thanksgiving festival, bring the various peoples in a community together and give them the opportunity to meet and interact with their neighbors. In some festivals, school children engage in various competitive activities and allow parents to take pride in their performances. Communities have an opportunity to take pride in their achievements and then vow to do even better in next year's competitions. Festivals reinforce participants' sense of belonging and help them improve their relations with their neighbors.

In some festivals, the history of the village, lineage, or group is displayed for all to see. In festivals in Foumban, Nso', Bali-Nyonga, and various other grasslands kingdoms, an effort is made to glorify the achievements of ancestors and help younger members of the groups learn about their history and traditions. Quite often, ancient conflicts are reenacted, although such reenactments may sometimes not be very accurate—the group is always portrayed as victorious. The victory of ancestors is then marked by elaborate celebrations, which include dancing and feasting.

Some groups use festivals to punish individuals convicted of criminal activities. Such condemned criminals are paraded for all to see, publicly shamed, and forced to endure public condemnation and scorn. During the parade of criminals, the crowds may join in song to condemn the convicted felons and instill the fear of ancestors in them. The hope is that after such a public display, these people will return to their homes and, from then on, live exemplary lives, respecting all the customs and traditions of their ancestors.

Bountiful harvests provide opportunities to celebrate and rejoice. Yam, maize, and groundnut festivals are common. Villages hold celebrations and offer sacrifices to ancestors and pray for future abundance. During such celebrations, the people usually promise their ancestors that they will use the abundant harvest generously and take care of the less fortunate among them. In recent years, especially with the reintroduction of multiparty politics, many politicians have become interested in these festivals, because they provide excellent opportunities for securing votes. Hence, many politicians return to their villages of origin during festival time to participate and give their constituents the opportunity to see and interact with them. Some of them may even help defray the costs of the festival. Although many of these harvest festivals have their origins in traditional rites designed to thank ancestors for blessing the people with a good harvest, many Christian religions have joined in the celebrations. In fact, throughout the grassfields, Christian churches hold celebrations to mark the harvest and raise money for charity work. Crops are brought to church on Sunday by members of the congregation and are auctioned off to raise funds to finance the church's outreach missionary activities.

Since the early 1970s, the Cameroon government has become involved in promoting some of the more prominent festivals in the country. In fact, various agricultural shows directed by the government and held around the country, usually in November, are adaptations of the traditional harvest festivals. These government-sponsored programs function basically as the traditional harvest festivals, except on a much larger scale and involve a larger variety of crops. In addition, sports competitions and political issues (e.g., national integration and unity) are emphasized in the government festivals. Various foreign dignitaries are invited and given the opportunity to see the country's achievements in agriculture and arts and crafts during the previous year. Of course, government-sponsored festivals also offer participants the opportunity to enjoy themselves.

NATIONAL AND RELIGIOUS HOLIDAYS

All holidays in Cameroon are opportunities for celebration and merry making. There are both religious and secular holidays and people enjoy taking the day off and spending it with family or returning to their village to meet extended family and celebrate. Even when the holiday is unimportant to them, they still celebrate and enjoy themselves. Hence, individuals who have not accepted Christianity still celebrate Christmas and take the days off from work to join the various parties within the community.

Secular holidays in Cameroon include New Year (January 1); Youth Day (February 11); Labor Day (May 1); and National Day (May 20). Many books on Cameroon erroneously give January 1 as the country's date of independence. On January 1, 1960, the UN Trust Territory of Cameroons under French administration was granted independence and took the name *La République du Cameroun.* The following year, the UN Trust Territory of Southern Cameroons under British administration opted to achieve independence by uniting with *La République du Cameroun* on October 1, 1961, to form what is now the Republic of Cameroon (although the original arrangement was a federation). Hence, Cameroon does not really have a single independence day since different parts of the country gained independence at different times. The government is aware of this problem and designates May 20 as the country's National Day. (May 20, 1972, was the day the Ahidjo government unilaterally abrogated the federation formed in 1961 and introduced a unitary form of government, which has survived.)

Celebrations include government-sponsored parades in which public officials participate and members of political parties dressed in commemorative cloth with party insignia join in the festivities. School children are especially important participants in these festivities. In metropolitan areas such as Yaoundé and Douala, school children may be joined by dance troupes brought in from many parts of the country.

Religious holidays include Christmas, Ramadan, Ascension Day, Festival of Sheep, Good Friday and Easter, and Assumption. As mentioned, many Cameroonians, even if they are not members of the religion whose holiday is being celebrated, often join in on the fun and enjoy themselves. Unlike secular holidays, religious holidays are rarely celebrated with street parades. Instead, celebrations are held indoors, usually at churches. Some Christians, however, may put together a parade that reenacts the entry into Jerusalem of Jesus of Nazareth shortly before his crucifixion.

Easter (Good Friday and Easter Monday) is an important holiday for Christians. It commemorates the death and resurrection of Jesus. During this period, Christians engage in activities to renew their faith, provide opportunities for new members to experience the warmth and fellowship afforded by membership in this religion, and help the less fortunate. The various events end on Monday with singing, dancing, feasts (mostly on the grounds of the church), and testimonials from believers. Christmas, which is celebrated on

December 25 each year, is marked by long prayer and meditation sessions, which start on the night of December 24. On Christmas day, a long church service is followed by various celebrations. Although many people exchange greeting cards, elaborate gifts are usually not part of the celebration. The next day, December 26, is called Boxing Day and is also a holiday; it is a day of relaxation and family get-togethers. In some communities the Christmas celebration extends to New Year's Day—January 1—which is also a public holiday.

Muslims celebrate Ramadan and Eid-el-Fitr around November. The exact dates of these holidays are based on the Islamic lunar calendar and vary from year to year. Ramadan is a 30-day period that starts when the full moon appears. This is one of the most important events for Muslims. Participants are required to abstain from sex, food, and drink during the day. In the evenings, the fast is broken and participants consume a variety of fruits, topped with a large meal and desserts.

Young Muslims prepare for Ramadan by bringing together various musical instruments, which are used on the day the moon is sighted. Early in the morning following the sighting of the moon, the young people play the instruments and sing around the city to wake up people so they can prepare for prayers and officially start the event. In addition to singing, young boys and girls play approved games and may be rewarded with presents, which are later shared with friends and family.

The end of Ramadan is marked by Eid-el-Fitr. Believers organize special prayers, which are conducted on specially designated grounds, to thank Allah (God). This event provides Muslim dignitaries an opportunity to display their grandeur and generosity. Throughout the north, many nobles will ride elaborately decorated horses back to the palaces where they are received by poets, singers, and drummers. A parade usually honors the ruler, an address is presented, and feasting follows. Virtually all Muslim households participate in the feasting. Participants, following Islamic tradition and teachings, will usually begin the day with the giving of alms and the care of the less fortunate. Once this activity is completed, the people then dress in new and beautiful clothes and head for the designated prayer ground. After they complete their prayers, they return home to eat, visit with friends, and engage in merry making.

Another major Islamic holiday is the Eid-el-Kabir, which is held for two days in June and marks the end of the hajj, when believers perform the pilgrimage to the holy city of Mecca. Rams are killed for this holiday. Other fun activities are added to make the festival enjoyable for all participants. Equestrian races and the display of beautiful and elaborately decorated horses are quite common. In September, Muslims celebrate the Eid-el-Maulud to mark the birthday of the great Prophet Mohammed. This celebration is marked by prayer, helping the poor, and various equestrian activities.

Amusement and Sports

Cameroonians love sports and enjoy various forms of amusement. Children, as well as adults, compete in games, storytelling, and wrestling. Today, many of these activities are now supplemented by radio and television programs, as well as by movies shown at commercial cinema houses. Despite an influx of American entertainment programs, many films, television, and radio are still based on traditional stories. These are used not only to entertain the various audiences but to preach morality, teach culture and customs, and encourage national integration and peaceful coexistence of population groups. Religious programming continues to gain popularity in the country, and churches have become quite adept at entertaining while instilling in their viewers some moral teaching.

All groups have stories that fit virtually all occasions. The Widekum, for example, have stories that teach morality, help young people learn about their ancestors and their achievements, prepare young people for adulthood, and provide travelers with the tools to deal more effectively with the challenges that they would face on their travels. Usually, tales for children use animals, fairies, and tricksters to help the young learn important values. A popular tale among the Widekum is a variation of Aesop's story of the boy who cried wolf. As with the ancient Greek tale, the Widekum story is designed to help children learn the importance of telling the truth, as well as the dangers of telling fibs. Tales for more mature youngsters and adults deal with life's travails and are designed to help people deal more effectively with the challenges that they face on a daily basis. The main purpose is to help someone live a moral and upright life, one that would find favor with ancestors. Hence, such stories teach the listener how to avoid bad luck, destructive vices (e.g., sex outside marriage), loss of faith, and various other activities that might reduce one's quality of life and place one's soul in danger.

Children usually play outside and inside the house. They use clay, mud, cornstalks, paper, leaves (especially those of plantains and bananas), and various other items found in their environment to make toys and other play things. Adults participate in various activities, including boxing, basketball, football (soccer), netball (mostly played by young women), table tennis, lawn tennis, handball, field hockey, hunting, and fishing. In many villages, primary and secondary schools provide the arena within which some of these games are played. Competitions that take place between schools from different villages are usually well attended, as villagers show up to support and cheer their team to victory.

Wrestling is an old sport in Cameroon. Many groups have developed it into part of their initiation ceremonies and use it as a test for transition into adulthood. Among the Bakweri, wrestling is an important activity during major celebrations. Villages compete for important prizes, including "bragging rights" for the upcoming year. Children and adults also compete for individual prizes. Many wrestling competitions are accompanied by tug-of-war events in which one village competes against another. Both the wrestling matches and the tug-of-war are incorporated into festivals marking important events in the group's evolution (e.g., the installation of a new king or chief).

The most popular sport in Cameroon is soccer. It is said that soccer is the only thing on which all Cameroonians unanimously agree. While they may disagree on many things, including especially political issues, when the national team is competing in the Olympics or the Africa Cup, Cameroonians leave behind their political and other disagreements and support the national team. When the national team plays outside the country, few Cameroonians are able to accompany the team to provide the necessary support. However, people gather in living rooms and sports bars throughout the country and watch the game on television or listen to it on radio and cheer on the team while they drink beer. If the team wins, there usually is a big celebration afterward. In certain circumstances, as was the case when Cameroon won the Olympic gold medal in soccer at the Sydney games in 2000, celebrations may spill into the streets. More organized celebrations, supported by the government, usually follow the victorious team's return to the country. If the game is played locally, then many people will go to the stadium to watch and support the national team. Others, unable to attend in person, will cheer from their living rooms.

Soccer is so popular that, as one travels throughout the country, one can see youngsters playing the game, some of them using locally produced balls. Some people think that soccer has become a religion practiced by most of the population. Today, talented Cameroonian soccer players play and make large fortunes in Western Europe and North America. However, when called upon, they usually return home to help the national team, the Indomitable Lions, in international competitions such as the World Cup, the Africa Cup, and the Olympics.

Cinema

Cinema complements television as a modern source of leisure. Although most films shown at cinema houses and theaters are imported from abroad, locally produced films have found an important niche in the market. Such films capture indigenous cultures, social values, and various challenges facing the different groups that inhabit the country.

Cinema was brought to the country by European colonialists (notably the French and the British). Most of the early films shown in the country were documentaries designed to inform the indigenous peoples of the superiority of European culture and entice them to accept that culture. Films were often used to persuade people to adopt new values and new ways of doing things. They spread knowledge about inoculations against certain communicable diseases, encouraged people to send their children to school, and explained unpopular measures that were taken by the colonial government.

In 1939, Britain established the Colonial Film Unit and located a branch in Nigeria to serve British interests in West Africa. The unit was used effectively to mobilize African support for Britain in World War II. In 1955, the Overseas Film and Television Center was established to replace the Colonial Film Unit. It produced many movies specifically for Africans. Many of these early efforts were not of very high quality. In each film, Africans were presented as backward, unsophisticated, childlike, superstitious, uncivilized, and without compassion. The Europeans, specifically the British, were presented as highly educated and sophisticated people, whose primary objective was to rescue Africans from their own savagery and bring them into the modern age. Most British colonial activities in the area of education and the arts in West Africa, however, were limited to Nigeria and, to a certain extent, the Gold Coast (Ghana). The British Southern Cameroons were totally neglected. While there was more activity in the UN Trust Territory of Cameroons under French administration in the area of education and the arts, much of that effort was devoted primarily to the development of literature. Little was done to help develop an indigenous filmmaking industry.

After reunification in 1961, the government did not actively promote the development of a local film industry. Instead, cinema was restricted to local consumption of materials imported from France. A few large French firms, with the help of the government, dominated the market and provided European and American films in large urban theaters, and cheaper Indian, Chinese, and Egyptian films were shown in smaller theaters. These films glorified violence, romantic love, and wealth. Although public officials, religious leaders, and the country's intellectuals criticized these cinematic imports for their corrupting influences on society and failure to portray indigenous cultures in a positive way, the audiences loved them because they, like soccer and pulp fiction, offered opportunities to momentarily forget their crushing poverty and material deprivation.

Today, a handful of filmmakers have emerged in the country and some of them have even managed to develop an international reputation. However, there is still no formal film production infrastructure. There are many highly talented local producers and actors; however, the government is not actively promoting the development of a viable film industry, especially one that would produce films that make effective use of local resources and provide viewers with positive images of local cultures and traditions. Since most of this talent is bilingual in English and French, it has the opportunity to make important contributions to the development of film in the country and region.

The first full-length Cameroonian film was *Muna Moto,* produced by Dikongué Pipa and presented to the world in 1975. Since then, he has made other films, which include *Courte Maladie* and *Badiaga.* Presently, the country's most prolific film producer (who is also an accomplished actor) is Alphonse Béni, who plays Inspector Bako in the highly acclaimed *Cameroon Connection.* Other filmmakers include Arthur Si Bita (*Les Coopérants*), Jean-Pierre Bekolo (*Quartier Mozart, Aristotle's Plot*), Daniel Kamwa (*Pousse-Pousse, Le Cercle des Pouvoirs*), Bassek Ba Kobhio (*Le Grand Bland de Lamarene*), Jean-Marie Teno *(Clando, Chef!),* Eloi Bela Ndzana (*Djamboula*), François Woukoache (*La Fumée dans le Yeux*), and Olivier Bile (*Otheo, l'Africain*). Several of these films have been entered into international competitions.

Like most Cameroon literature, locally produced films are dominated by cultural issues, the impact of colonialism on the various societies, and the assimilation of Western cultures. Others such as *Le Cercle des Pouvoirs,* critique post-independence government incompetence and corruption, as well as the failure of indigenous rulers to deal effectively with mass poverty and deprivation. Many Cameroonians are confident that the country's film industry, even though it is still in its embryonic stages, can produce films that can help correct the negative images of Cameroonian (and African) customs and culture presented in foreign films and present audiences with a more wholesome and positive view of the people and their cultures.

Foreign films, regardless of the violence and profanity that they portray, continue to be popular and dominate, as they have done for more than 40 years, cinema houses in the various urban areas. In most of the north, Indian films are very popular. Among young people, action films (especially so-called police films such as the James Bond series), including war movies, command a lot of respect. Many of these young people enjoy the violence and the drama. Young girls, however, prefer movies about romance and are less likely to attend films that portray significant levels of violence.

Since the mid-1980s, the viewing of movies has expanded significantly in Cameroon as a result of the arrival of videos and VCRs. Most of the videos being viewed, however, are imported, mostly from France and the United States. In recent years, however, videos produced in neighboring Nigeria have started to arrive in Cameroon markets and are gradually providing competition for the European imports. Like soccer, these movies provide Cameroonians not only entertainment but a way to escape, if only temporarily, their pressing social and economic problems.

Notes

1. Suzanne P. Blier, *The Royal Arts of Africa: The Majesty of Form* (New York: Harry M. Abrams, 1998), pp. 167–168.

2. Melvin Ember and Carol R. Ember, eds., *Countries and Their Cultures: Afghanistan to Czech Republic* (New York: Macmillan Reference, 2001), pp. 393–394.

8

Music and Dance

MUSIC AND DANCE usually go together in virtually all parts of Cameroon. Both music and dance are integral parts of all religious ceremonies and social occasions. For example, initiation rites, births, weddings, funerals, sporting events, and several ceremonies are usually each associated with a particular dance and corresponding music. Traditional music does not have a written score; it is transmitted orally from one generation to another. The singer usually commits the songs to memory. Except for the solo troubadour who accompanies himself on a harplike instrument, traditional vocal music is sung by a song leader who alternates with a chorus.[1]

To understand a piece of music, one must focus on the sound, the instruments that produce the sound, and the composers of the music. In order to understand and appreciate Cameroonian music, one must, in addition, take into consideration the belief systems and rituals of the community. In Cameroon, music and dance are used to express various emotions, as well as the values of the society.

Instrumental music is dominated by percussion instruments, which include xylophones (with calabash or leg resonators), bells (traditionally worn by dancers around their ankles), rattles, clappers, scrapers, and several types of drums. The talking drums, which can produce a variety of tones, are important. The pitch of each drum can be varied by increasing or decreasing the tautness of the tension cords that are attached to the skin membranes that cover both ends of the drum. Whistles, flutes, bamboo horns, and various stringed instruments with calabash resonators, are also used to produce music.[2]

Like many other aspects of Cameroon culture and customs, dance and music were affected by colonialism and its institutions. In fact, a lot of traditional dances are no longer performed, having been banned either by the colonial government because they were considered threatening to the colonial enterprise or by Christian missions because they were judged offensive, pagan, or immoral. Because most traditional music and dance were associated with certain ceremonies and rites, they died out when the colonial authorities banned many of these practices. The ones that survived eventually lost their ritual functions and eventually came to be used primarily for entertainment and recreation. In some regions of the country, some songs and dances were incorporated into Christian ceremonies.

Music and dances from other countries have been imported into Cameroon. Among them are *maringa* (from Ghana in about 1850), the *ashiko* (from Nigeria in about 1925), and the *abele* (also from Nigeria). In Cameroon today, Congolese dance music is very popular. Modern music in the country has been influenced significantly by both European and African traditions. Among the most popular forms of music today are *makossa* and *bikutsi,* which have become internationally famous. Cameroon musicians, such as Manu Dibango, Francis Bebey, Dinal Bell, Prince Ndedi Eyango, and Anne-Marie Nzie, are world famous.

Western music has become quite popular, especially among young people who live in the urban areas. In addition, many Cameroonian musicians have adapted imported forms to create a blended style that appeals to many people in the country. In fact, some of the most successful local artists are those who combine Western and African traditions to create innovative genres. Of course, famous Cameroonian musicians such as Manu Dibango play to sellout audiences in Europe and North America. In record stores in the metropolitan centers of the West, one can find recordings by Cameroon's major artists.

Although many Christian denominations have tried to ban or restrict the use of traditional music in their worship services, new songs and forms of worship music influenced by traditional music continue to evolve and gain popularity in worship services. Most of this blended music has found its way into commercial recordings, some of which are used in Catholic and Protestant worship ceremonies.

MUSICAL GENRES

Cameroonian music can be classified in many ways: (1) era (traditional or modern), (2) origin (local or foreign), (3) type (instrumental, vocal, or mixed and also solo or group), (4) structures, (5) repertoires, and (6) functions.

One can classify traditional Cameroonian music according to its audience. A musician may target an audience or be required to play to a specific group of listeners. For example, the musician may be contracted to compose music and play at the court of a king to entertain him and his guest on the occasion of his birthday, enthronement, or some other important event in his life. A songstress may sing to a bridegroom or a couple at their wedding. Of course, others in attendance may also enjoy the music.

Cameroonians love music and, quite often individuals, especially in the rural areas, may sing while they perform various activities. For example, children may sing as they go to the watering hole to fetch water or on their way to school in the morning; women may sing as they cultivate the fields in mid-afternoon; laborers may join in song as they complete various tasks at an industrial work site; prisoners in a chain gang often use song to provide the rhythm for their work; and a young girl picking wild flowers for her mother's kitchen table may sing to the butterflies and birds that fly by. This type of spontaneous singing usually does not involve instruments, although some singers are known to use things they find in their immediate environment (e.g., sticks, spoons, pot covers, etc.) as makeshift instruments.

Women often sing as they do housework, play with their children, or make crafts. Girls who baby-sit or take care of younger siblings sing lullabies to the babies in their care to help the child go to sleep or stop crying. Some people sing when they are happy; others when they are sad. Whistling a tune is a very popular way to deal with sadness among many people in the grasslands.

Group music is an important form of performing music. Here, several people join together to sing (with or without instruments) for an audience that usually dances as well. This type of music is very popular at festivals and celebrations such as weddings and christenings. Quite often, the singers will also be the dancers, as in the case where children playing sing to themselves. In place of instruments, some groups clap their hands or tap their feet to provide the rhythm needed to enhance the singing. Instruments popular with groups include drums, flutes, trumpets, cymbals, and several types of stringed instruments.

Court Music

Grasslands royal courts have historically been well known for supporting the arts. Such support extended to music, which was performed at the royal court for the king, members of the sovereign's household, important officials and dignitaries, chiefs, subchiefs, and various types of visitors. Some of the music was specifically developed to be played at special occasions, which included the enthronement of a new king, the funeral of a king, ceremonies to reaffirm the institution of kingship, and special celebrations to mark the birth of the king's first son, who was expected to become the heir to the throne.

Musicians who played at the royal court were usually housed within the palace, some of them on a permanent basis. The costs of their training were taken care of by the king, and many of these musicians trained their children to take over for them when they retired. As a result, playing at the royal court often became a family affair. Children trained within the palaces in the instruments and musical traditions of their parents and at court expense were expected to remain in the service of the king for the rest of their lives, unless they were specifically discharged by the sovereign. Playing at the royal court was considered the most prestigious gig that a musician could ever hope to have. Thus, it was not likely that a trained musician would voluntarily leave the comfort of the royal court in search of economic opportunities in the larger community.

Music at the royal court was always associated with power. Those who played the music enjoyed a certain level of power and were well respected throughout the kingdom. The music itself was reserved specifically for royal use. Certain instruments used in the production of music were reserved for either royal use or for producing music only in the court.

Court music combined vocal and instrumental arrangements and reflected the range of activities that took place in the palace. During times of peace, certain kinds of music were played to reflect tranquility at the palace and provide its inhabitants, especially the king, with the right sounds for sleep. In the morning, musicians provided the king with the right wake-up music, and, as the day dawned, court music was changed to suit the various activities of the sovereign and his consorts (e.g., eating breakfast, performing administrative tasks, receiving visitors, visiting with his children). All of the music was designed to enhance the welfare of the king. The activities of the court musicians, then, had to take the well-being of the king into consideration.

Court music was also used to announce disasters, such as the outbreak of a war or the death of a sovereign or some other important member of the royal family. In some cases, royal musicians accompanied the army into battle and played for them while they faced the enemy. This was especially true in cases where the king decided to follow his soldiers into battle.

Music for Entertainment

Virtually all forms of entertainment in Cameroon involve music. Cameroonians like to listen as well as dance to music. Even in cases where music is used specifically for rituals, there may still be some aspect of entertainment in it. In fact, various grasslands rituals involve musical productions that are quite entertaining and, in recent years, the entertainment aspects have come to dominate the ritualistic ones. Music associated with burial rituals, especially for important dignitaries, is quite popular. Those who attend these funerals do not go there to grieve but to dance, rejoice, and wish the deceased a joyous journey to the place where the ancestors live and watch over the group.

Work Songs

Individuals or groups, especially those engaged in manual labor, usually find it helpful to sing while they work. Hence, work-synchronizing music is common, especially among industrial workers. Of course, rural farmers use songs to relieve the boredom of routine labor; children sing as they perform various chores; and individuals engaged in various professions also sing as they carry out their duties. In the rural areas, women who work in the fields all day sing to relieve boredom and increase productivity; blacksmiths sing to the rhythmic pounding of the hot iron rod; and women who make pottery sing as they carefully mold the clay. Young men who take care of cattle, goats, sheep, and other domesticated animals sing as they sit on a hill and watch their animals graze. In the marketplace, some merchants sing to advertise their wares and attract customers. In recent times, many merchants have turned to piped-in music, from stereos or radio to serve the same purpose.

Ritual Music

Despite the influence of colonialism and Christianity, Cameroon remains a country steeped in rituals. Music is an important part of these rituals, many of which serve a particular purpose. For example, in some societies, a group of people, led by important traditional religious leaders, would engage in ritual singing at the end of the year to seek forgiveness from the gods for all the evils of the previous year. In addition to using song to seek absolution for the village or community, the singers would also use their songs to request protection and good fortune for the village in the coming year. Music also features prominently in other rituals, such as the rite of passage, puberty, marriage, and death. Special instruments are often used to accompany the singers. Within some grasslands groups, women who are unable to bear children may request special songs to be sung to the gods to restore their fertility and enhance their chances of becoming mothers. Parents who are sending a son or daughter out of the country for further studies may request a song to be sung to the gods so that the gods can look over their child. Certain individuals are known to be quite adept at singing to the spirits and successfully getting them to intervene on behalf of people. Hence, individuals who need intervention may consult these "spirit singers" and request that they sing songs to the gods on their behalf.

Festival Music

Songs are used to praise the gods, give thanks for past blessings, and ensure future prosperity. In addition, songs can be used to show an affirmation in ancestors and other spiritual beings, make social commentary, express joy and happiness, indicate fear, and show grief and sadness. In Cameroon, music is also used as a way for the masses to comment on political and social issues. Some people consider music the poor man's "op-ed" page, giving him the opportunity to critically evaluate governance and the political system. In fact, the various festivals that the country holds each year allow participants to use music to speak their minds and comment on issues that affect their lives or that are important to them.

Traditional songs often mock various people in society—those who cheated their way to the top; those who are without honor, are dishonest, morally bankrupt, and have strayed from the traditions and customs of their ancestors; those who have taken on the "white man's ways" and no longer consider tradition important; women who are no longer virgins; men who frequent prostitutes and have abandoned their families; those who are rich and believe they no longer need their kinfolk; and so on. Such criticisms can be problematic, especially in small communities where people know their neighbors well and can easily determine from the songs who is being mocked.

Songs are useful for political commentary in societies where such commentary is not permitted or the avenues for it are closed by the authorities. Commentators, of course, try to make their songs as contemporary as possible, usually dealing only with current events. During the presidency of Ahmadou Ahidjo, there were two types of commentaries by song: (1) songs designed to massage the egos of Ahidjo and other high-ranking members of the Cameroon National Union (the only legal political party in the country) and garner for the singer(s) or those represented by the singer significant benefits (which included appointments to highly lucrative public positions) and (2) songs that criticized the incumbent government's authoritarian nature and its blatant abuse of human rights. Of course, songs praising Ahidjo and members of his ruling coalition dominated the airwaves and were played at virtually all public festivals. In addition, the lyrics of these songs were more direct, poured a lot of praise on the president, and portrayed him as the country's "savior," "father," "messiah," and "liberator." Songs that criticized his rule and considered him a traitor to the country's post-independence aspirations were not so direct; they often used metaphors and other indirect ways to make their points. These songs were never played on public radio or performed at government sponsored public festivals. These were likely to be performed at privately funded events.

Some groups use festivals to present to the public new musical talent that has developed since the last event. Hence, new artists work hard to develop new songs, which they can present at the festival to introduce themselves to the public. Some songs may be written specifically for a particular festival; other musicians may attend to simply allow the public to sample their music.

Recreational Music

Recreation is an important activity in Cameroon. Throughout the years, music has been developed to meet the needs of virtually all recreation activities. Dancing, which is an important form of recreation, has its own music. In the urban areas, most dancing is done in nightclubs and, to a lesser extent, at parties in people's homes. During these parties, live bands or a record player operated by a DJ may provide the music for dancing. Drinking beer and locally produced palm wine usually accompanies dancing. In the rural areas, people engage primarily in traditional dancing, which is usually associated with festivals. However, some rural inhabitants, especially those who consider themselves more progressive, enjoy modern dances. Many rural areas in Cameroon have bands that play popular music and are available for rent to individuals or groups interested in organizing an activity that requires dance music.

MODERN MUSIC

Modern music primarily serves the same functions as traditional music. Of course, modern music, as produced in Cameroon, continues to be influenced by traditional music. Most modern music, however, is geared primarily toward entertainment and the selling of products or ideas. Politicians use music to campaign for public office—they come up with catchy lyrics for songs played on television and radio to help voters remember them. Businesses use music to launch new products or remind consumers that an existing or old product has been revamped and improved. Policymakers use songs to promote important public programs (e.g., vaccination against communicable diseases such as cholera; HIV/AIDS education; universal education, especially for girls). Many songs have been composed and sung to introduce and sustain important public programs. Village leaders use songs to reinforce important customs, taboos, and traditions. Cameroon musicians have used their craft effectively to advocate social, political, and economic change. Since the colonial period, musicians have been important in using song to push for institutional change. In the late 1980s, when Cameroonians were engaged in concerted efforts to force the Biya government to democratize the political system, musicians were helpful in providing the music that sustained the movement. Today, Cameroonian musicians continue to use their music to criticize national political leadership and force it to respect human rights, as well as to institute reforms to improve the welfare of all citizens.

Christian Music

Christian music, brought to Cameroon by missionaries beginning in the mid-1800s, remains an important part of the country's musical tradition. Christian songs are an integral part of the worship ceremony of all churches. It energizes worshipers and helps recruit new ones. Although most churches have choirs, which are supposed to have more expertise in singing the songs than other members of the congregation, singing at church usually involves all in attendance. Depending on the type of church, individuals may clap their hands, shout, dance, and jump up and down, as they sing Christian songs in church.

During the early years, many of the Christian denominations required their worshipers to follow strict rules regarding singing in church—although clapping was allowed, dancing and other forms of movement were not permitted. In fact, church members were not expected to show any emotions while they participated in the worship ceremony. However, in recent years, especially with the arrival of the "born-again" movement, worship ceremonies at Christian churches have acquired most of the characteristics of traditional ceremonies and festivals. Dancing, shouting, and clapping and waving hands, as well as the expression of various emotions, have become important parts of the worship services of many Christian churches.

During the early days, the leading missionary groups were hostile to traditional Cameroon religions and the music and instruments associated with them. In fact, the early converts to Christianity were required to rid themselves of all traditional musical instruments and stop performing ritual songs in order to enjoy full membership in the new religion. However, as many of these Christian churches began to replace indigenous priests with European ones, there was pressure on the new European priests to enhance the quality of worship ceremonies by incorporating traditional practices. For example, some critics argued that the use of local languages would enhance understanding, make sermons more interesting and lively, and bring more people to church. Some Christian priests began to incorporate into their services clapping, dancing, spontaneous praying, and other activities that were utilized in traditional worship ceremonies. It is not unusual to find dancing and merry making in many Christian churches today.

Classical Music

Christian churches and Western education have brought the appreciation of classical music to Cameroon. Cameroonians returning from studies abroad also have made classical music quite popular in the country. Christian churches often use this kind of music in their worship ceremonies, and the national radio in the 1970s had a popular program called "music of the masters" which played classical music. The music of such Western composers as Ludwig von Beethoven and George Frederick Handel is popular. During the Christmas season, Handel's "Messiah" is quite popular. In addition to the national radio, Cameroonians can satisfy their appetite for this kind of music by tuning to foreign radio broadcasts (e.g., the BBC).

Despite the popularity of classical music among the educated urban elite and the Christian churches, this type of music is not yet considered a serious subject for study at the local universities. In addition, few Cameroonians return from abroad with graduate degrees in the subject. Although some of the country's musicians have studied music at Western universities or conservatories, no serious indigenous composers have yet emerged, and local composers have not yet established a neoclassical tradition to develop compositions that can rival those of the European masters.

Makossa

Shortly after World War II, a form of dance music, called *highlife,* which had started in Ghana and was popular in neighboring Nigeria, moved to Cameroon and became a staple in the nightclubs of the port city of Douala. Played with a variety of instruments, including the bugle, various military brass instruments, accordion, guitar, harmonica, two-finger guitar, and gongs made by local artists, Nigeria's brand of highlife soon spread to the interior of Cameroon. Congolese rumba and imported tunes from Cuba complemented highlife music in Douala's bars and nightclubs.

On the streets of the city, which were populated by the poor and newly arrived migrants from the rural areas, music was dominated by a spirited folk sound called *ambasse bey.* Played with relatively simple instruments (primarily a guitar and stick-and-bottle percussion), the street sound was extremely popular among young people. During the 1950s and early 1960s, various improvements were made to this sound, and, in the mid-1960s, Eboa Lotin, working with a harmonica and a guitar, brought the various elements of this uniquely Cameroonian sound together and produced what was later named *makossa*.

Makossa artists were unable to develop the sound any further because of poor recording facilities. However, after pioneer artist, Ekambi Brillant, moved to Paris and gained access to a modern studio, work on improving the sound accelerated, and, by the early 1980s, many more makossa artists had joined Brillant in Paris. These artists, guitarists, and singers, continued to improve on the unique sound—producing a sweet, fizzy intoxicating sound that characterized the heyday of makossa in Paris. Contributing to the development of this rich musical culture were guitarist Toto Guillaume, bassist Aladji Touré, singers Dina Bell, Guy Lobé, Ben Decca, Manulo Donleur, and Pièrre de Moussy. The Duala language was the main vehicle for delivering the makossa sound.

Later makossa artists, notably Lapiro de Mbanga, who blends both makossa and *soukous* (Congolese) sounds, have preferred pidgin English, a language understood by more Cameroonians than Duala. In addition to singing in pidgin English, Lapiro has also used his brand of makossa to engage in political satire, further creating a significant level of interest in his work, especially among the disenfranchised masses. The Paris scene also produced several new makossa artists, including Charlotte Mbango, Prince Eyango, and Grace Decca. Pioneers of the Paris scene, Toto and Aladji, went on to make more innovations, blending makossa with *zouk,* a highly popular party style from the French Antilles. The blended sound has gained global attention and ranks high on international dance charts. The *makozouk* sound has proven to be a very successful formula for singers Guy Lobé and Petit Pays.

In recent years, especially with the migration of many Cameroonians to the United States in the late 1980s and early 1990s, makossa veterans have taken their music to North America and other parts of Western Europe. Many of them have worked out of Washington, D.C. Paris-based Cameroonian session players have contributed significantly to the works of jazz violinist Jean-Luc Ponty's Tchokola project, as well as in Paul Simon's Rhythm of the Saints band, which featured Cameroon's enormously successful guitarist, Vincent Nguini.[3]

One of Cameroon's best-known musicians is Manu Dibango. He showed an interest in music quite early in life, and, at 15 years of age, he left his homeland for Paris. His parents, both of whom were quite religious, did not support his decision to pursue a musical career. In France, Dibango studied classical piano and the saxophone, eventually securing a job with fellow Cameroonian exile, musicologist, writer, and performer, Francis Bebey. Dibango eventually left Paris for Brussels, where he benefited significantly from the city's vibrant jazz scene. Then, in 1961, he returned to Africa and settled in Kinshasa just as the Congolese rumba revolution (which would eventually lead to the creation of the slick and sweet Congolese sound now known as *soukous*) was under-way. He lived in Kinshasa for two years and during this time recorded 100 singles with the legendary Africa Jazz of Joseph Kabesele. He then moved to Douala, although he visited Paris regularly. At this time, he decided to explore Cameroon's emerging makossa sound along with his new love for American soul music. Soon, he merged the two sounds together to create a tune called "Soul Makossa" that burst into the scene in 1973 and captured the interest of listeners worldwide. "Soul Makossa" was a surprise hit single in Europe and North America and went on to sell more copies than any African single before it. With the international acclaim, Dibango took his band, Makossa Gang, to various studios in New York, Lagos, Abidjan, Paris, and Kingston, Jamaica, where he recorded several tunes. In Jamaica, he worked with reggae's top rhythm section, Sly and Robbie. In the 1980s, fresh from his world tour, Dibango returned to jazz and brought together several African musicians to record "Tam Tam pour l'Ethiopie," to raise funds to fight hunger and famine in Ethiopia. In the 1990s, Dibango embraced hip-hop and rap and released Wakafrika, which spotlighted a wide variety of African singers and provided listeners with new interpretations of the continent's pop classics.[4]

Bikutsi

In the days before makossa developed into a national sound, many musical groups, many of which were located in the rural areas and sang primarily in traditional languages, worked the various towns and entertained people with folkloric music. Some of the more popular types of folk music included *assiko, mangambe,* and *bikutsi.* Bikutsi—which dates back to the 1940s when it was first recorded by veteran singer Anne-Marie Nzie and has its roots in the music of the Beti people who inhabit the areas around Yaoundé—eventually developed into an electric urban sound that is now challenging makossa for the position of the country's national sound.

In the 1960s and 1970s, Messi me Nkonda Martin and his band Los Camaroes transformed the traditional bikutsi, using electric keyboards and guitars to produce dance music that became popular in the urban centers. The pioneering electric bikutsi brought sexually suggestive dancing back to the urban nightclub scene. Another group called Les Vétérans also contributed significantly to the development and popularization of the electric bikutsi. However, the bikutsi was introduced to the rest of the world when preco-cious advertising student Jean-Marie Ahanda launched the musical group,

Têtes Brûlées in 1987. She developed a unique image for them—colorfully painted bodies, torn clothing, and partially shaved heads—and combined the group's carefully cultivated spiky, bucking rhythms with space-age innovations to produce a sound that was both titillating and sensual. Although the Têtes Brûlées remain the main force in the global bikutsi revolution, they face significant competition, especially in Cameroon, from groups led by such singers as Mbarga Soukous and Jimmy Mvondo Mvelé.[5]

Highlife

Highlife music was born in Ghana during the colonial period and traveled to Nigeria and Cameroon in the 1930s and 1940s. It became popular in the coastal urban areas and, by the late 1950s, had penetrated the interior of the country. The music, which was played with a variety of instruments, including the bugle, various military brass instruments, accordion, guitar, harmonica, two-finger guitar, and locally produced gongs, represented a fusion of African traditional sounds and Western music. The name "highlife" is believed to have originated from the genre's popularity with urban high culture. By the 1960s, highlife had become so popular that it dominated the dance and bar scenes in most of West Africa's urban centers. Despite its spread throughout the region, Ghanaian and Nigerian bands remained the dominant force in its production.

Cultural and artistic developments in British Cameroons were influenced significantly by what was happening in major metropolitan areas in Nigeria, especially Enugu. Most of Nigeria's guitar highlife bands grew out of older acoustic "Ibo blues" and so-called palm wine music. By the 1950s, Enugu had become an important center for Nigeria's unique and Ibo-dominated brand of highlife, which was brought to Southern Cameroons and became popular in coastal towns such as Victoria (now Limbe) and Tiko, as well as Douala in French Cameroons. Despite the fact that Cameroonians enjoyed the highlife sound, due to various constraints, including the absence of effective recording studios, a local highlife sound never really emerged, because the population continued to dance to Nigerian-based bands and their recordings. However, in 1976, following the end of the civil war in Nigeria, a Cameroonian living in Nigeria named Prince Nico and his band the Rocofil Jazz produced the highlife hit called "Sweet Mother," which is the best-selling African record ever. The hit, which successfully fused highlife with Congolese jazz, has sold over 13 million copies.

Pop Music

Cameroonians enjoy both domestic and imported music. In addition to music from other parts of Africa (notably Congolese, Nigerian, and Egyptian

—which is quite popular among northern Muslims—South African—especially liberation music of the apartheid era as played by such luminaries as Hugh Masikela and Miriam Makeba—Ghanaian, and Kenyan), Cameroonians also enjoy imports from Western Europe (French artists are popular, and ABBA is popular, especially among the youth) and the Caribbean (Bob Marley and Jimmy Cliff are the most popular, especially among young people). Afro-Cuban, Haitian meringue, Trinidadian calypso, and, of course, Jamaican reggae are the most popular Caribbean imports in Cameroon. Reggae is so popular among the college crowd that its most important disciples, Jimmy Cliff and Bob Marley, have been raised to the level of gods. Indian music is popular among northern Muslims.

The United States has provided Cameroonians with contemporary blues, jazz, spirituals, gospel, pop music, hip-hop, rock-'n'-roll, country, and rap. Many Cameroonian artists have adopted the instruments and rhythms of various American performers. Despite the changing times and the introduction of new music forms from the United States, some seasoned American performers remain popular. James Brown, Aretha Franklin, Elvis Presley, and Tina Turner are still idolized by many. Among the older crowd, country music is popular, and such entertainers as Jim Reeves, the Everly Brothers, Patsy Cline, George Jones, Loretta Lynn, and Tammy Wynette are popular.

When local artists imitate foreign music genres, the main audience seems to be urban youth, most of whom—as a result of foreign broadcasts, the Internet, and technological innovations (e.g., the compact disk) in the delivery of music—are already quite familiar with global developments in music. In fact, before Cameroonian artists started imitating American rap and trying to produce their own unique rap sound, young people had already been dancing to American rap music purchased at record stores in the urban centers, downloaded from the Internet, or heard on the radio. Local artists incorporate foreign instruments or rhythms into traditional music such as makossa and bikutsi and invent new sounds. Many of Cameroon's musicians have taken part in this tradition of fusing local traditions with foreign rhythms to produce unique sounds that have gained global popularity. Of course, Manu Dibango's "Soul Makossa" is one of the most famous Cameroon exports. Prince Nico's "Sweet Mother," which fuses highlife with Congolese and other sounds, remains Africa's most important pop music tune of the last century.

MUSICAL INSTRUMENTS AND SINGING STYLES

Music is produced in Cameroon with an array of instruments, ranging from drums, gongs, bells, and flutes to stringed and keyboard devices. Instruments can be blown (the trumpet), shaken (*sekere*), scraped (sticks), struck (drums or xylophone), or plucked (stringed instruments). The most pervasive and beloved of all musical instruments is the drum. Cameroonian music and performers rely heavily on the drum. As well, various stringed instruments, flutes, trumpets, bells, rattles, and wooden sticks are all used to produce the rhythm that enhances the music.

Musical instruments can be divided into four groups. First is the aerophone group, which represents all wind instruments. Most of them are made from bamboo, shells, animal horns, gourds, wood, and metal. Sound is produced by making the instrument produce vibrations from its air columns. Second are chordophones—tension strings with sound boxes that serve as resonators. Third are membranophones, which include a variety of drums. Finally, there are idiophones, which include the hand piano, xylophone, rattles, and calabash drums.

Some of the instruments, such as the drum, serve other purposes besides producing music. The drum is used by various groups in Cameroon for communication purposes. In the villages, drums can be used to inform people of a death, alert people of an emergency, seek help in case of an emergency, rally troops for war, and call children for dinner or school. The trumpet is used in many grasslands kingdoms to announce the arrival of the sovereign; the beginning and end of an important event or ceremony, including war; a major disaster (e.g., flood, fire, epidemic); and the arrival of an important visitor to the community.

Some of Cameroon's traditional musical instruments are gradually becoming extremely rare, primarily because the people capable of playing them have not passed on those skills to the younger generation. One such instrument is the transversal flute called the *oding*, which is reserved exclusively for women. The player usually combines vocal with blown instrumental sounds. This instrument is common in southern Cameroon, although the plant from which it is made is not indigenous to the region, implying that the instrument was originally from a different area.

Portable xylophones are very important in the musical traditions of groups in the area that stretches from south-central Cameroon to Congo, Gabon, and other parts of the Great Lakes area. The type popular in Cameroon has a rail that allows the player to hold the instrument away from his or her body. It also contains gourd resonators, which are equipped with mirliton buzzers and is believed to have come from the south, most likely from present Republic of Congo (Congo-Brazzaville). Comparable instruments were seen in the old kingdom of Kongo by European missionaries in the seventeenth century. According to oral tradition among Cameroon's southern peoples, when a king decided to make a trip to visit neighboring kingdoms, he sent his xylophone band ahead. The band, which consisted of four musicians, played processional music and cleared the way for the king's entourage to follow. Hence, this type of xylophone was designed to be specifically portable. The possession of a band that played portable xylophones came to represent a symbol of authority and power among many of the chieftaincies in the southern part of the country.[6]

Although the drum is usually considered one of the most versatile and typical of African musical instruments, in areas of the continent where trees are sparse (in the north), wooden drums are absent. In Cameroon, as in other parts of Africa, the types of musical instruments that dominate performances in a given region are those that are made from local materials. In addition, instruments that are produced by skilled blacksmiths are found only in those areas where such skills have been developed.

Musical instruments are used to enhance the singer. The song, however, holds together the various instruments played in an ensemble to produce rhythms that are pleasing to the audience. A song can be a poem, ballad, incantation, or a long piece of prose. The prose may be made up of one or more stanzas. Good songwriters are also masters of language who manipulate words and music to elicit the appropriate emotions. Hence, a songwriter commissioned to produce a piece to be used in the enthronement of a new sovereign would compose a song that would bring out joy, jubilation, excitement, humility, pride, and all the other emotions associated with this important occasion. The singer is also as important as the songwriter—the singer is expected to use voice and body to produce the rhythms and sounds that help elicit the right emotions in the audience. As an interpreter, the singer is allowed to take liberties with the words. During the performance, a singer may frown, smile, and make other facial expressions as needed to enhance the delivery of the song's message.

DANCE

In Cameroon, most singing is accompanied by dancing. Of course, there are occasions in which singing and dancing do not go together: funeral processions, removal of the skulls of ancestors and their preparation for transport to another location, and burial of the dead. Most Cameroonians generally associate music with dance or at least with some form of physical response from the audience or listeners. Music and dance are part of Cameroonians' daily activities. Both reflect their experiences with life, leisure, tragedy, success, failure, and death. Music and dance are integral parts of the various festivities and celebrations that mark the life of a Cameroonian. Through music and dance, people are brought together; dance transcends age, class, and gender, as people come together either to dance or watch others perform. Among the grasslands sovereigns, however, certain important dignitaries (including the sovereign himself) may not participate in dances involving subjects. In addition, the sovereign's wives, as well as his daughters may dance only under strictly regulated conditions and usually only at the palace.

Among most groups in Cameroon, participants in traditional dances are usually segregated by sex—women and men occupy separate parts of the dance hall or field. In another variation, the dancers are placed in concentric circles with the women in the innermost circle, separated from the men by a circle of young girls. The boys form the outermost circle. Where dancers react to rhythmic beats (e.g., from a drum and other instruments), movement can be rigorous and intense, requiring only those who are physically fit to participate. Choreographed dancing, where participants move in specified ways, is common, even in traditional performances. It is rare in traditional dances to find women and men in performances that allow them to touch each other. In modern forms of dancing (e.g., nightclub dancing), men and women do dance together, either as couples or as part of a crowd.

Although modern dancing (especially the type that takes place in nightclubs and discos) does not differentiate between male and female dancing, traditional dance usually distinguishes between dances reserved for males and those expressly for females. Both sexes are also costumed accordingly—in fact, among the grasslands kingdoms, masks for female dancers are quite different from those for their male counterparts. In addition, dancers may be differentiated by occupations (e.g., dances performed only by court jesters or hunters). From the Muslim-dominated north to the coastal areas of the south, highly trained professionals perform various dances, all of which are associated with certain traditional rites and ceremonies. As a result of colonialism, many of these rites have become extinct, and there has also been a decline in professional dance. The revival of many grasslands courts since the late 1970s has brought back the tradition of professional dancing. Many of these dancers, however, must secure other jobs because they cannot earn a living by dancing. Recognition by the post-colonial government of traditional dance as part of the country's heritage may eventually make the profession respectable again and enhance its economic viability. Already in various urban areas such as Douala and Yaoundé, professional dancers participate in important events (e.g., National Day celebrations) and perform for tourists. Many of these urban-based groups have commercialized their performances to appeal to tourists, especially those from Western Europe and North America.

Dancing is associated with virtually all religious groups in Cameroon—Christian, Muslim, and traditional. These groups all use dance in their various rituals. Traditional dances are used to deal with all sorts of issues, ranging from pleasing the spirits of ancestors to seeking intervention for a sick relative or an infertile wife. Ritualistic dance is usually performed by a group. In the case where an individual wants to perform a dance to seek the intervention of an ancestor for a sick child or an infertile wife, a diviner may be engaged to perform the dance. In many villages one can find individuals who specialize in dances to appease the spirits. Such dancers also perform other services, including serving as an intermediary between the dead and the living.

When musicians give a public performance, it is usually judged as good if it leads to spontaneous dancing. Quite often, musicians invite members of the audience to join them. Many dances do not require any special costumes, although dancers may carry and use special instruments (e.g., masks, leather fans) to enhance their movements. The dancer may move his or her body in many ways to enhance the performance—the dancer may clap his hands, slap his buttocks with his hands, raise his hands, bend at the waist, and stamp his feet. Many female dancers use a piece of cloth the size of a bandana to enhance their dancing.

An important difference between Cameroon (and, to a certain extent, sub-Saharan African) and European dance cultures is movement. In European dance, the body is moved as a single block, whereas in Cameroon dance (and African American dance), movement is split into several independent body areas. In dance and music, there usually is more than one motional center. In addition to producing sounds with the instrument, the musician also rhythmically moves the various parts of his body (hands, fingers, legs, head, and shoulders) in a highly coordinated manner during the entire production. Usually, these movements are improvised—an important part of the musical traditions of most groups in Cameroon.

The Functions of Dance

Dance has many practical applications in Cameroon, ranging from its use to appease ancestors to activities designed to celebrate birth. Special dances are associated with multiple births. As children grow up, dance is used to help them socialize and integrate into the community. In various villages, there may be dance groups for children and youth. These dance groups help children learn important lessons about culture and tradition of their ancestors, as well as provide them with the opportunity to socialize. In recent years, especially with the arrival of Western education and culture, some youth have formed dance groups whose performances criticize certain traditional practices that they consider anachronistic or oppressive. In addition, some of these groups have also used dance to criticize the authoritarian practices of the post-colonial government. In fact, during the Ahidjo years, when most forms of political protest were forbidden to the people, dance was often used effectively to criticize the government. Today, many young people use dance to show support for the various political parties that they favor. Politicians recruit dancers and use them to perform dances that generate support for them and criticize their opponents. Dances are also used to generally criticize and condemn people who break the laws and customs of society (e.g., prostitutes, wife beaters, and parents who abuse their children).

Young people usually continue to dance with the transition to adulthood and marriage. The transition process itself may involve various dances, which may include an initiation dance, a wedding dance, and a dance to welcome the new adult. This may be followed by joining an adult dance or singing group. A person will have dances performed for him or her throughout life and also will perform many dances either individually or as a member of a group. The birth of a child and its christening/naming will be accompanied by dancing; circumcision for boys will be accompanied by dancing, and so will many other activities during the child's life and transition to adulthood. On dying, dance will be used to send a person on his or her journey to meet ancestors.

Dance, of course, is a critical part of religious practice. In traditional religions, certain performers dance themselves into a trance in which they are able to communicate with spirits—in such a state, they can bring messages from ancestors to the living and vice versa. Dance is also used to transmit culture and customs from one generation to another. Today, Cameroonians use dances to commemorate important milestones in their individual and collective history and events that have shaped their communities and societies such as independence from colonialism and other important political transitions (e.g., reunification).

Modern technology, specifically improved recording systems, has allowed for the preservation of the musical and dance traditions of many groups in Cameroon. During the colonial period, Christian churches and the colonial government condemned and banned many forms of traditional music and dance, claiming that they were heathen and uncivilized. However, since independence, the government and many nongovernmental organizations have taken an interest in traditional music and dance and provided significant support for their revival. As a result, both domestic and foreign groups have recorded their music and dance. Such recordings can be purchased in the major metropolitan areas in North America and Western Europe. Although the motivation behind making the recordings is to make money, their work is helping preserve an important part of the country's heritage.

Christianity and European colonialism brought to Cameroon such European dances as the waltz, Latin American tango, quickstep, and foxtrot. Many Cameroonians, especially the well-to-do and highly educated urbanites, embraced these dances, and various local bands formed to provide the music for them. Some of the residential secondary schools taught some of these dances as part of physical education. In urban areas, learning to perform these dances came to be associated with modernization and acceptance of European culture. Hence, Western-educated elites attempted to differentiate themselves from the rest of society by forming exclusive clubs at which these dances were common fare.

NOTES

1. Harold D. Nelson, M. Dobert, G. C. McDonald, J. McLaughlin, B. Marvin, and P. W. Moeller, *Area Handbook for the United Republic of Cameroon* (Washington, DC: U.S. Government Printing Office, 1974), p. 129.

2. Nelson, et al. (1974), p. 129.

3. Afropop Worldwide, "Makossa," http://www.afropop.org/explore/style_info/ID/9/Makossa/.

4. Afropop Worldwide, "Manu Dibango," http://www.afropop.org.

5. Afropop Worldwide, "Bikutsi," http://www.afropop.org.

6. J. Murray, ed., *Cultural Atlas of Africa* (New York: Checkmark Books, 1998), p. 95.

Glossary

abele. dance imported from Nigeria into Cameroon in about the 1920s

agbada. flowing gown

a ka u ku mfe mfe. form of writing introduced among the people of the Bamoun Kingdom by King Njoya at the end of the nineteenth century

Alhaja. title for Muslim women who have performed the pilgrimage to Mecca

Alhaji. title for Muslim men who have performed the pilgrimage to Mecca

ambasse bey. spirited folk music common in coastal cities in Cameroon in the 1950s

angaangang. Nso' diviners—usually expected to attack the misdeeds of witches and those misusing their sem

angaashiv. Nso' healers/medicine-men

anyuy. Nso' divinities and divinized ancestors

ashiko. dance imported into Cameroon from Nigeria in about 1925

ataanto'. individuals charged with carrying and caring for objects used in cu, an Nso' ritual designed to worship Nyuy (God)

azabaa'en. plural of azabaajo

azabaajo. free woman in Fulbe society; a woman who is between husbands, has "experienced" men but is currently not married

bikutsi. electric urban pop sound with its roots in the music of the Beti of Cameroon

boubou. ample cotton garment that is comfortable even in the high desert heat of the north; it is a poncho sewn at the sides

buba. traditional blouse

cu. Nso' ritual used to worship Nyuy (God); this word is now used in modern Nso' vocabulary to refer to the mass of the Catholic Church

danshiki. traditional variation of the poncho; usually covers the body from the shoulders to the waist

debbo. in Fulbe society, a fertile woman who is ready to produce children for her husband

faay-woo-ku 'un-ne. Nso' threshold of the main lineage house where ntanri sacrifices are made

fon. western grasslands king or sovereign

fufu. carbohydrate food

gari (garri). powder made of cassava

gay. basic organizational social unit of the Matakam, one of the largest ethnic groups that inhabit the hills of northern Cameroon

Gbaso. Gbaya word for genies or spirits that inhabit the forests around Gbaya territories; also designates God or the Great Spirit among the Gbaya. So has replaced Gbaso as the Supreme Being. Gbaso is now considered an evil being

gbia koo. Gbaya divorce in which the wife leaves her husband; one of three types of Gbaya divorces

gourouna. annual festival of the people of the flood plains in which the men gorge on milk

imam. Muslim prayer leader

jihad. holy war (Muslim)

juju. popular music

kibam ke won. "bag of the country," special container used to carry the camwood (bii) used in the Nso' ritual called cu

kofe. "brideservice," a process that requires young Gbaya boys (or men) courting a girl (or woman) to perform various services for their future wives

kossa. children's hand-clapping game in Cameroon; it is from this game that the now world famous Cameroonian sound called makossa got its name

lamibé. plural of lamido, head of the lamidat; traditional Fulani rulers

lamidats. Fulani territories

lamido. head of a lamidat (Fulani territory)

makossa. uniquely Cameroonian musical sound that developed in the coastal city of Douala in the late 1950s and early 1960s and was made world famous by such artists as Ekambi Brillant and Manu Dibango

makozouk. musical blend of makossa and zouk

malam. Muslim neighborhood teacher; usually helps children learn the Qur'an (Koran)

mangambe. folk music found in many rural areas of central Cameroon in the 1940s and 1950s

marabouts. Islamic religious teachers

mbansie. most important regulatory society in King Njoya's court

mboo-zu. "molding one's head; submission," a condition in Gbaya marriage in which there is harmony in the family—the husband and wife are both patient, kind, generous, and bring peace and harmony to the home

mbusiri. standard Fulani dish that consists of a mixture of milk and either maize (corn) or millet

nda koo. Gbaya divorce in which the husband sends or chases away his wife; one of three types of divorces among the Gbaya

Ndzeendzev. Nso' installer and most senior counselor at the court of the sovereign

ngaa-cu. Catholic priest in modern Nso' language

nggay. assembly hall of the dynastic group (Nso')

ngoyou. famous dynastic Kom sculptures produced by King Fon Yu (1865–1912); they depict a ruler, his first wife, and the queen mother

ngu. chamber in the palace at Foumban that housed the royal ancestral skulls and relics

nkap. special type of Bamiléké marriage that does not involve the transfer of bridewealth

ntanri. Nso' ritual used to honor ancestors and seek their intervention on issues important to individuals and the community

ntanri-menwer. second of three rituals used to honor ancestors among the Nso'—usually used to honor the remotest ancestor that can be identified or traced

nuet nkuete. "pursue to attain," text of the new doctrine of salvation introduced to the Bamoun people by King Njoya

nyiiri. important Fulbe dish that is made primarily of thick porridge

Nyuy. Nso' Supreme Being (God)

Nyuy shon wan. "children stolen by God" (Nso')

nzum. evil spirit (singular) among the Bamoun

nzuom. Bamoun term for prayer; also covers an oath (e.g., one used in the installation of a new counselor for the kingdom; the nzuom was recited at various occasions, including the burial of the dead, investiture of an heir, installation of the sovereign, and swearing in of new judges

oding. transversal flute reserved exclusively for women; common in southern Cameroon

ouankoulou. Toubouri (Tupuri) ruler

pagne. rectangular piece of cloth that is wrapped around the body from the breast to the ankles and makes up part of the three-piece costume of northern married women

pagüm. evil spirits (plural) among the Bamoun

penyinyi. Bamoun ancestors and diviners

poncho. variety of traditional dresses such as the boubou

puldebbo. postmenopausal Fulbe woman

Ramadan. 30-day fasting period among Muslims (also known as *fête du Ramadan*)

saay anyuy. first of three forms of sacrifices used to honor ancestors among the Nso'

Sabon Gari. also referred to as "Hausa Quarters," it is a community of migrants who live in separate neighborhoods

samarooka. Fulbe man who cooks for himself instead of letting a woman do so; carries negative connotations

Saré. group of Fulani houses belonging to members of one family; a Fulani compound

sem. part of the Nso' belief system; refers to a psychic power that is said to be possessed by some people within Nso' society and can be used for either good or evil

Sharia. Islamic legal system

shiv. medicine (Nso')

shuu-san. Nso' year

So. Also So-e-wi; in Gbaya it means "God-place-man," or the Great God who created the universe and everything in it; highest ranking of all Gbaya gods; proper noun

so-daa. (common noun), lesser Gbaya gods or spirits who fall below so-kao

so-kao. (common noun), lesser Gbaya gods who are superior to so-daa

soukous. popular Congolese music genre

sov-kidiv. third of three sacrifices used to honor ancestors among the Nso'

sultan. king or sovereign, especially of a Muslim state

Taawon. sacrificial deputy (male) of the Nso' sovereign

tiehead. traditional headdress for women

ve kpu. individuals who officiate at Nso' rural burials (also see vibay ve duy)

vibay ve duy. individuals who officiate at Nso' rural burials

vire ve anyuy. Nso' ritual sites

wi-kofe. Gbaya bridegroom-to-be who is performing required services for his future in-laws

Yeewon. sacrificial deputy (female) of the Nso' sovereign

yua-koo. "fleeing one's wife," Gbaya divorce in which the husband abandons his sick or terminally ill wife; one of three types of divorce in Gbaya

zouk. highly popular party music style from the French Antilles

Selected Bibliography

Ahidjo, A. *The Political Philosophy of Ahmadou Ahidjo*. Yaoundé: Imprimerie Nationale, 1967.

Aletum, M. T. *Political Conflicts within the Traditional and Modern Institutions of the Bafut, Cameroon*. Louvain: Vauder, 1975.

Aletum, M. T., and C. F. Fisiy. *Socio-political Integration and the Nso' Institutions*. Yaoundé: SOPECAM, 1989.

Ardener, E. W. *Historical Notes on the Scheduled Monuments of West Cameroon*. Buea: Government Printer, 1965.

Ardener, S. G. *Eye-witnesses to the Annexation of Cameroon, 1883–1887*. Buea: Government Printer, 1968.

Ardener, S., E. W. Ardener, and W. A. Warmington. *Plantation and Village Life in the Cameroons: Some Economic and Social Studies*. London: Oxford University Press, 1960.

Austen, R. A. "Duala versus Germans in Cameroon: Economic Dimensions of a Political Conflict." *Revue Française d'Histoire d'Outre-Mer* 64 (4) (1977): 477–497.

Azarya, V. *Dominance and Change in North Cameroon: The Fulbe Aristocracy*. New York: Sage, 1976.

Bayart, J.-F. *L'état au Cameroun*. Paris: Presses de la Fondation Nationale des Sciences Politique, 1979.

Bederman, S. H. *The Cameroons Development Corporation: Partner in National Growth*. Bota, West Cameroon: CDC, 1968.

Berrill, K. *The Economy of the Southern Cameroons under United Kingdom Trusteeship*. Cambridge, England: Cambridge University Press, 1960.

Biya, P. *Communal Liberalism*. London: Macmillan, 1987.

Bjornson, R. *The African Quest for Freedom and Identity: Cameroonian Writing and the National Experience*. Bloomington: Indiana University Press, 1991.

Blier, S. P. *The Royal Arts of Africa: The Majesty of Form.* New York: Harry M. Abrams, 1998.

Brain, R. *Bangwa Kinship and Marriage.* Cambridge, England: Cambridge University Press, 1972.

Burnham, P. *Opportunity and Constraints in a Savanna Society: The Gbaya of Meiganga, Cameroon.* New York: Academic Press, 1981.

Chiver, E. M. *Zintgraff's Explorations in Bamenda, Adamawa and the Benue lands 1889–1892.* Buea: Government Printer, 1966.

Chiver, E. M., and P. M. Kaberry. "From Tribute to Tax in a Tikar Chiefdom." *Africa* 30 (1) (1960): 1–19.

Chiver, E. M., and P. M. Kaberry. "Sources of Nineteenth-century Slave Trade: The Cameroons Highlands." *Journal of African History* 6 (1) (1965): 117–120.

Chiver, E. M., and P. M. Kaberry. *Traditional Bamenda: The Pre-colonial History and Ethnography of the Bamenda Grassfields.* Buea: Government Printer, 1968.

Clignet, R., and F. M. Stark. "Modernization and Football in Cameroon." *Journal of Modern African Studies* 12 (3) (1974): 409–421.

Commonwealth Secretariat. *The Parliamentary Elections in Cameroon, May 17, 1997: The Report of the Commonwealth Observers' Group.* London: Commonwealth Secretariat, 1997.

Courade, G. *Organisations Paysannes, Sociétés Rurales, État et Developpement au Cameroun, 1960–1980.* Leiden: African Studies Center, 1988.

Davis, L. "Opening Political Space in Cameroon: The Ambiguous Response of the Mboro." *Review of African Political Economy* 22 (64) (1995): 213–228.

Ebune, J. B. *The Growth of Political Parties in Southern Cameroons 1916–1960.* Yaoundé: CEPER, 1992.

Enonchong, H. N. A. *Cameroon Constitutional Law: Federalism in a Mixed Common-law and Civil Law Society.* Yaoundé: CEPMAL, 1967.

Epale, S. J. "The Mobilization of Capital in a Rural Milieu: The Example of the Bakweri of the South West Province of Cameroon." *Rural Africana* (Fall 1978): 69–88.

Eyoh, D. "Conflicting Narratives of Anglophone Protest and the Politics of Identity in Cameroon." *Journal of Contemporary African Studies* 16 (2) (1998): 249–276.

Eyoh, D. "Through the Prism of a Local Tragedy: Political Liberalization, Regionalism and Elite Struggles for Power in Cameroon." *Africa* 68 (33) (1998): 338–359.

Eyongetah, T., and R. Brain. *A History of Cameroon.* London: Longman, 1974.

Fardon, R. O. *Raiders and Refugees: Trends in Chamba Political Development, 1750–1950.* Washington, DC: Smithsonian Institution Press, 1988.

Feldman-Savelsberg, P. *Plundered Kitchens, Empty Wombs: Threatened Reproduction and Identity in the Cameroon Grassfields.* Ann Arbor: University of Michigan Press, 1999.

Fombad, C. M. "Cameroon and the Dilemma of Media Pluralism." *Communication* 24 (1) (1998): 21–31.

Fombad, C. M. "The Constitutional Protection of Freedom of Expression in Cameroon: A Comparative Appraisal. *S. A. Public Law* 14 (1) (1999): 25–45.

Fombad, C. M. "An Experiment in Legal Pluralism: The Cameroonian Bijural/Unijural Imbroglio." *University of Tasmania Law Review* 16 (2) (1997): 209–234.

Fombad, C. M. "The New Cameroonian Constitutional Council in a Comparative Perspective: Progress or Retrogression?" *Journal of African Law* 42 (2) (1998): 172–186.

Fowler, I., and D. Zeitlyn, eds. *African Crossroads: Intersections between History and Anthropology in Cameroon.* Providence, RI: Berghahn Books, 1996.

Gardinier, D. E. *Cameroon: United Nations Challenge to French Policy.* Oxford: Oxford University Press, 1963.

Geary, C. M. "Bamum Two-figure Thrones: Additional Evidence." *African Arts* 16 (4) (1983): 46–53.

Geary, C. M. *Images from Bamum: German Colonial Photography at the Court of King Njoya, Cameroon, West Africa, 1902–1915.* Washington, DC: National Museum of African Art, 1988.

Geary, C. M. *Things of the Palace: A Catalog of the Bamum Palace Museum at Foumban (Cameroon).* Translated by K. M. Holman. Wiesbaden: Steiner-Verlag, 1983.

Geary, C. M. *The Voyage of King Njoya's Gift: A Beaded Sculpture from the Bamum Kingdom in the National Museum of African Art.* Washington, DC: National Museum of African Art, 1994.

Geschiere, P. "The Articulation of Different Modes of Production: Old and New Inequalities in Maka (South East Cameroon)." *African Perspectives* (Leiden) 2 (1978): 45–68.

Geschiere, P. *Village Communities and the State: Changing Relations among the Maka of South East Cameroon since the Colonial Conquest.* London: Kegan Paul, 1982.

Gillard, P. *Ahmadou Ahidjo: Patriote et Despote, Batisseur de l'État Camerounais 1922–1989.* Paris: Groupe Jeune Afrique, 1994.

Goheen, M. *Men Own the Fields, Women Own the Crops: Gender and Power on the Cameroon Grassfields.* Madison: University of Wisconsin Press, 1996.

Guyer, J. I. "The Food Economy and French Colonial Rule in Central Cameroon." *Journal of African History* 19 (4) (1978): 577–598.

Guyer, J. I. *Women's Work in the Food Economy of the Cocoa Belt: A Comparison.* Boston: African Studies Center, Boston University, 1978.

Gwellem, J. F. *Fru Ndi and the SDF Revolution.* Bamenda, Cameroon: Unique Printers, 1996.

Harter, P. *Arts Anciens du Cameroun (Arts d'Afrique Noire supp. T.40).* Arnouville: Arts d'Afrique Noire, 1986.

Hata, N. "The Village Community of the Domon Society in Nord Cameroun." *Kyoto University African Studies* 10 (1976): 273–293.

Historical Section of the Foreign Office (United Kingdom). *German African Possessions (late).* London: Her Majesty's Stationery Office, 1920.

Hurault, J. *La Structure Sociale des Bamiléké.* Paris: Mouton, 1962.

Jeffreys, M.D.W. "Some Notes on the Customs of the Grassfields Bali of Northwestern Cameroon." *Afrika und Übersee* 46 (3) (1962): 161–168.

Jeffreys, M.D.W. "Traditional Sources Prior to 1890 for the Grassfields Bali of Northwestern Cameroon." *Afrika und Übersee* 46 (3) (1962): 168–199 and 46 (4) (1962): 296–313.

Johnson, W. R. *The Cameroon Federation: Political Integration in a Fragmented Society.* Princeton, NJ: Princeton University Press, 1970.

Joseph, R. A., ed. *Gaullist Africa: Cameroun under Ahmadu Ahidjo.* Enugu, Nigeria: Fourth Dimension, 1978.

Joseph, R. A. *Radical Nationalism in Cameroun: Social Origins of the U.P.C. Rebellion.* London: Oxford University Press, 1977.

Joseph, R. A. "Ruben Um Nyobé and the "Kamerun Rebellion." *African Affairs* 73 (293) (1974): 428–444.

Jua, N. *The Petty Bourgeoisie and the Politics of Social Justice in Cameroon.* Leiden: African Studies Center, 1988.

Kaberry, P. M. "Nsaw Political Conceptions." *Man* 59 (1959): 138–149.

Kaberry, P. M. *Women of the Grassfields.* London: Her Majesty's Stationery Office, 1952.

Kaberry, P. M., and E. M. Chiver. "An Outline of the Traditional Political System of the Bali-Nyonga, Southern Cameroons." *Africa* 31 (4) (1961): 355–371.

Kale, P. M. *Political Evolution in the Cameroons.* Buea, West Cameroon: Government Printer, 1967.

Keller, W. *The History of the Presbyterian Church in West Cameroon.* Victoria (Limbe), West Cameroon: Presbook, 1969.

Kling, G. W., M. L. Tuttle, and W. C. Evans. "The Evolution of Thermal Structure and Water Chemistry in Lake Nyos." *Journal of Volcanology and Geothermal Research* 39 (1989): 151–165.

Kofele-Kale, N., ed. *The Bilingual Cameroon Republic since Reunification.* Boulder, CO: Westview Press, 1980.

Kofele-Kale, N. *Tribesmen and Patriots: Political Culture in a Polyethnic African State.* Washington, DC: University Press of America, 1981.

Konings, P. "Privatization of Agro-industrial Parastatals and Anglophone Opposition in Cameroon." *Journal of Commonwealth and Comparative Politics* 34 (3) (1996): 199–217.

Konings, P. Le "Probléme Anglophone" au Cameroun dans les Années 1990." *Politique Africaine* 62 (1996): 25–34.

Kuban, S. P., and R. Ngwa-Nyamboli. *Paul Biya and the Quest for Democracy in Cameroon.* Yaoundé: Editions CLE, 1985.

Kwast, L. E. *The Disciplining of West Cameroon: A Study of Baptist Growth.* Grand Rapids, MI: Erdmans, 1971.

LeVine, V. T. *The Cameroons: From Mandate to Independence.* Berkeley: University of California Press, 1964.

Lockwood, J. P., and M. Rubin. "Origin and Age of the Lake Nyos Maar, Cameroon." *Journal of Volcanology and Geothermal Research* 39 (1989): 117–124.

Mbaku, J. M. "Cameroon's Stalled Transition to Democratic Governance: Lessons for Africa's New Democrats." *African and Asian Studies* 1 (3) (2002): 125–163.

Mbaku, J. M., and J. Takougang, eds. *The Leadership Challenge in Africa: Cameroon under Paul Biya*. Trenton, NJ: Africa World Press, 2004.

Mbiba, R. Y. *Nso' and Her Neighbors: A Study in Intergroup Relations in the Nineteenth and Twentieth Centuries*. Master's Thesis, University of Yaoundé, Yaoundé (Cameroon), 1991.

Mbu, A.N.T. *Civil Disobedience in Cameroon*. Douala: Imprimerie Georges Freres, 1993.

Mbuagbaw, T. E., R. Brain, and P. Palmer. *A History of Cameroon*. London: Longman, 1987.

Mbunwe-Samba, P., P. Mzeka, M. Niba, and C. Wirmum, eds. *Rites of Passage and Incorporation in the Western Grassfields of Cameroon,* Vol. 1. Bamenda, Cameroon: Kaberry Research Center, 1993.

McCulloch, M., M. Littlewood, and I. Dugast. *Peoples of the Central Cameroons*. London: International African Institute, 1954.

Mohammadou, E. *Traditions Historiques des Peuples du Cameroun Central, Vol. 1: Mbéré, Mboum, Tikar*. Tokyo: ILCAA, 1991.

Mope Simo, J. A. "Customary Land Tenure Regimes in North Western Cameroon." In *The Dynamics of Resource Tenure in West Africa,* eds. C. Toulmin, P. L. Delville, and S. Traoré. London: James Currey, 2002.

Mukong, A. *The Case for the Southern Cameroons*. Uwani-Enugu, Nigeria: Chuka Publishing Company, 1990.

Mullendorf, P. "The Development of German West Africa (Kamerun)." *Journal of the Royal African Society* 2 (5) (1902): 70–92.

Murray, J., ed. *Cultural Atlas of Africa,* revised edition. New York: Checkmark Books, 1998.

Mveng, E. *Histoire du Cameroun*. Paris: Présence Africaine, 1963.

Mzeka, P. N. *The Core Culture of Nso'*. Agawam, MA: Paul Radin, 1980.

Mzeka, P. N. *Four Fons of Nso'*. Bamenda: Spider Press, 1990.

Ndikum, T. *Government and Opposition in Cameroon in the Multiparty Era*. Bamenda, Cameroon: Nooremac Press, 1991.

Nelson, H. D., M. Dobert, G. C. McDonald, J. McLaughlin, B. Marvin, and P. W. Moeller. *Area Handbook for the United Republic of Cameroon*. Washington, DC: U.S. Government Printing Office, 1974.

Ngoh, V. J. *Cameroon 1884–1985: A Hundred Years of History*. Limbe, Cameroon: Navi-Group Publications, 1988.

Ngoh, V. J. *Southern Cameroons, 1922–1961: A Constitutional History*. Aldershot, England: Ashgate, 2001.

Ngwa, J. A. *A New Geography of Cameroon*. London: Longman, 1979.

Njeuma, M., ed. *Introduction to the History of Cameroon in the Nineteenth and Twentieth Centuries*. New York: St. Martin's Press, 1989.

Njiassé-Njoya, A. *Naissance et Evolution de l'Islam en Pays Bamum (Cameroun)*. Thèse pour le doctorat du 3me cycle, Université I, Paris, 1981.

Njoya, A. N. *Njoya, Reformateur du Royaume Bamoum.* Paris and Dakar: ABC & NEA, 1978.

Njoya, Sultan de Foumban. *Histoire et Coutumes des Bamum (Redigée sous la Direction du Sultan Njoya.* Traduction du Pasteur Henri Martin. Douala: Institut Français de l'Afrique Noire, 1952.

Nkwi, P. N. *Traditional Government and Social Change: A Study of the Political Institutions among the Kour of the Cameroon Grassfields.* Fribourg: Fribourg University Press, 1976.

Northern, T. *The Art of Cameroon.* Washington, DC: Smithsonian Institution Press, 1984.

Northern, T. *Royal Art of Cameroon: The Art of Bamenda-Tikar.* Hanover: University of New Hampshire Press, 1973.

Noss, P. A., ed. *Grafting Old Rootstock: Studies in Culture and Religion of the Chamba, Duru, Fula, and Gbaya of Cameroon.* Dallas, TX: International Museum of Cultures, 1982.

Nyamndi, N. B. *The Bali Chamba of Cameroon: A Political History.* Paris: Editions Cape, 1988.

Nyamnjoh, F. B. "Cameroon: A Country United by Ethnic Ambition and Difference." *African Affairs* 98 (390) (1999): 101–118.

Nyamnjoh, F. B. *The Cameroon GCE Crisis: A Test of Anglophone Solidarity.* Limbe, Cameroon: Nooremac, 1996.

Nyamnjoh, F. B. *Mass Media and Democratization in Cameroon.* Yaoundé: Friedrich-Ebert Stiftung, 1996.

Nyamnjoh, F. B., and M. Rowlands. "Elite Associations and the Politics of Belonging in Cameroon." *Africa* 68 (3) (1998): 320–337.

Nzouankeu, J. M. *La Pensée Politique d'Ahmadou Ahidjo.* Monte Carlo: Paul Bory, 1968.

Okafor, G. M. *Christians and Muslims in Cameroon.* Würzberg, Germany: OrosVerlag, 1994.

O'Neil, R. *A History of Moghamo, 1865–1940: Authority and Change in a Cameroon Grassfields Culture.* Ph.D. dissertation, Columbia University, New York, 1987.

O'Neil, R. *Mission to the British Cameroons.* London: Mill Hill Mission Press, 1991.

Price, D. "Descent, Clans and Territorial Organization in the Tikar Chiefdom of Ngambe, Cameroon." *Zeitschrift für Ethnologie* 112 (1) (1987): 85–103.

Price, D. "The Palace and Its Institutions in the Chiefdom of Ngambe." *Paideuma* 31 (1985): 85–103.

Quinn, F. "Beti Society in the Nineteenth Century." *Africa* 50 (3) (1980): 293–304.

Quinn, F. "Charles Atangana of Yaoundé." *Journal of African History* 21 (4) (1980): 485–495.

Regis, H. A. *Fulbe Voices: Marriage, Islam, and Medicine in Northern Cameroon.* Boulder, CO: Westview Press, 2003.

Rubin, N. *Cameroun: An African Federation.* New York: Praeger, 1971.

Rudin, H. R. *Germans in the Cameroons, 1884–1914: A Case Study in Modern Imperialism.* New Haven, CT: Yale University Press, 1938.

Savary, C. "Situation et Histoire des Bamum (II)." *Bulletin Annuel de la Musée d'Ethnographie, Geneve* 22 (1979): 21–22, 121–161.

Schatzberg, M. G. and I. W. Zartman, eds. *The Political Economy of Cameroon.* New York: Praeger, 1986.

Sigvaldason, G. E. "International Conference on Lake Nyos disaster, Yaoundé, Cameroon, 16–20 March, 1987: Conclusions and Recommendations." *Journal of Volcanology and Geothermal Research* 39 (1989): 97–107.

Smith, W. D. *The German Colonial Empire.* Chapel Hill: University of North Carolina Press, 1978.

Sopca, A. *Démocratisation et Autochtonie au Cameroun: Trajectoire Regionales Divergentes.* Leiden: Université de Leyde, 2002.

Tabapssi, F. T. *La Modéle Migratoire Bamiléké (Cameroun) et sa Crise Actuelle: Perspectives Économiques et Culturelles,* Ph.D. dissertation, University of Leiden, Leiden, 1999.

Takougang, J. "Cameroon at the Democratic Crossroads: The Struggle for Power and Authority in an African State." *Asian and African Studies* (Haifa) 27 (1993): 241–262.

Takougang, J., and M. Krieger. *African State and Society in the 1990s: Cameroon's Political Crossroads.* Boulder, CO: Westview Press, 1998.

Tardits, C. *Contribution de la Recherche Ethnologique à l'Histoire des Civilisations du Cameroun.* Paris: CNRS, 1981.

Tardits, C. "L'organisation Politique Traditionelle du Royaume Bamoum (Cameroun)." *Paideuma* (Wiesbaden) 25 (1979): 73–87.

Tardits, C. *Le Royaume Bamoum.* Paris: Librarie Armand Colin, 1980.

Thorbecke, F. *Im Hochland von Mittel-Kamerun,* 4 vols. Hamburg: L. Freiderichsen, 1914–1924.

Van Slageren, J. *Les Origins de l'Église Évangelique au Cameroun.* Yaoundé: Editions CLE, 1972.

Vaughan, J. H. Jr. "Culture, History and Grassroots Politics in a Northern Cameroons Kingdom." *American Anthropologist* 66 (5) (1964): 1078–1095.

Vernon-Jackson, H.O.H. *Language, Schools and Government in Cameroon.* New York: Teachers College, Columbia University Press, 1967.

Visonà, M. B., Robin Poynor, Herbert M. Cole, and M. D. Harris. *A History of Art in Africa.* New York: Harry N. Abrams, 2001.

Walker, S. S. "From Cattle Camp to City: Changing Roles of Fulbe Women in Northern Cameroon." *Journal of African Studies* (Spring 1980): 54–63.

Warnier, J.-P. *Échanges, Développement et Hierarchies dans le Bamenda Pré-colonial (Cameroun).* Stuttgart: Franz Steiner-Verlag, 1985.

Warnier, J.-P. *L'ésprit d'Enterprise au Cameroun.* Paris: Karthala, 1993.

World Bank. *African Development Indicators, 2002.* Washington, DC: World Bank, 2002.

Zintgraff, E. *Nord-Kamerun.* Berlin: Paetel, 1895.

WEBSITES

Official Cameroon homepage
  http://www.camnet.cm
Country profile on the situation of youth: Cameroon (by Youth at the United Nations)
  http://esa.un.org/socdev/unyin/countrya.asp?countrycode = cm
News and resources about Africa, including Cameroon
  http://www.africaonline.com
Information from the African Studies Center at the University of Pennsylvania
  http://www.sas.upenn.edu/African_Studies/Country_Specific/Cameroon.html
U.S. State Department's Consular Information Sheet: Cameroon
  http://travel.state.gov/cameroon.html
Cameroon Football Federation
  http://www.cameroon.fifa.com/cda/cda_container/0,1503,countryCode%3
  Dcmr_localeID%3D104_siteCategoryID%3D2044_siteID%3D1001,00.
  html
Travel Guide (Columbus Guides)
  http://www.travel-guide.com/data/cmr/cmr.asp
Information from the publishers of *Africa South of the Sahara*
  http://www-sul.stanford.edu/depts/ssrg/africa/camer.html
United States Embassy in Cameroon
  http://usembassy.state.gov/yaounde/
Embassy of the Republic of Cameroon in the United States
  http://www.embassy.org/embassies/cm.html
Mount Cameroon (West Africa's highest mountain)
  http://web.ukonline.co.uk/mountains/cam.htm
Cameroon Chamber of Commerce
  http://www.g77tin.org/ccimhp.html
Information from the African Studies Center at Columbia University
  http://www.columbia.edu/cu/lweb/indiv/africa/cuvl/Cameroon.html
U.S. State Department Annual Report on Human Rights in Cameroon
  http://www.state.gov/www/global/human_rights/1999_hrp_report/
  cameroon.html
Cameroon/Chad Development Project (also known as the Cameroon/Chad Oil Pipeline)
  http://www2.exxonmobil.com/Chad/Library/News/Chad_NW_mediabis_
  011098.asp

Index

About the Author

JOHN MUKUM MBAKU is Professor of Economics at Weber State University.